Essential Test Tips Video from Trivium Test Prep

Dear Customer,

Thank you for purchasing from Trivium Test Prep! Whether you're looking to join the military, get into college, or advance your career, we're honored to be a part of your journey.

To show our appreciation (and to help you relieve a little of that test-prep stress), we're offering a **FREE *LSAT Essential Test Tips* Video** by Trivium Test Prep. Our video includes 35 test preparation strategies that will help keep you calm and collected before and during your big exam. All we ask is that you email us your feedback and describe your experience with our product. Amazing, awful, or just so-so: we want to hear what you have to say!

To receive your **FREE *LSAT Essential Test Tips* Video**, please email us at 5star@triviumtestprep.com. Include "Free 5 Star" in the subject line and the following information in your email:

1. The title of the product you purchased.

2. Your rating from 1 – 5 (with 5 being the best).

3. Your feedback about the product, including how our materials helped you meet your goals and ways in which we can improve our products.

4. Your full name and shipping address so we can send your **FREE *LSAT Essential Test Tips* Video**.

If you have any questions or concerns please feel free to contact us directly at 5star@triviumtestprep.com.

Thank you, and good luck with your studies!

LSAT Prep 2025-2026

2 Practice Exams and Study Book for the Law School Admission Test [3rd Edition]

B. Hettinger

Copyright ©2024 Trivium Test Prep

ISBN-13: 9781637985205

ALL RIGHTS RESERVED. By purchase of this book, you have been licensed on copy for personal use only. No part of this work may be reproduced, redistributed, or used in any form or by any means without prior written permission of the publisher and copyright owner. Trivium Test Prep; Accepted, Inc.; Cirrus Test Prep; and Ascencia Test Prep are all imprints of Trivium Test Prep, LLC.

Table of Contents

Introduction 1
   What is the LSAT? 1
   What is on the LSAT? 1
   How Is the LSAT Administered? 2
   Fees 3
   How to Use This Book 3
   Preparing for the LSAT: Materials 4
   Test-Taking Tips 4

Chapter 1 - Fundamental Logical Concepts 6
   How Arguments Work 6
   LSAT Logic Vocabulary 12
   Patterns of Reasoning 14
   Formal Logic (Deductive Reasoning) 15
   Informal Logic (Inductive Reasoning) 32
   Principles and Applications 37

Answer Key 40

Chapter 2 – Flawed Patterns of Reasoning 42
   Common Fallacies on the LSAT 42
   Fallacies of Relevance 44
   Fallacies of Strength 50
   Fallacies of Presumption 53
   Fallacies of Ambiguity 58
   Fallacies of Formal Logic (Deductive Reasoning) 61

TRIVIUM
— TEST PREP —

Answer Key 71

Chapter 3 – Logical Reasoning: Questions 76
Question Types: An Overview 76
Strategies for Solving Logical Reasoning Questions 77
Passage-Based Questions 81
Hypothetical Questions 92
Critical Reasoning Questions 99
Parallel Reasoning Questions 104

Answer Key 109

Chapter 4 – Reading Comprehension 115
The Passage 115
The Questions 115
Five Tips for Effective Reading 116
Question Types 118
Time Management 121

Answer Key 128

Chapter 5 – Argumentative Writing Sample 131
What Is the LSAT Argumentative Writing Sample? 131
Tips for the Writing Sample 131
Practice Writing Sample 132

LSAT Practice Test #1 134
Section I – Reading Comprehension 134
Section II – Logical Reasoning 143
Section III – Logical Reasoning 151
Section IV – Logical Reasoning (Unscored Section) 158

Answer Key #1 167
Section I – Reading Comprehension 167
Section II – Logical Reasoning 172

Section III – Logical Reasoning 176

Section IV – Logical Reasoning (Unscored Section) 180

LSAT Practice Test #2 185

Section I – Reading Comprehension 185

Section II – Logical Reasoning 194

Section III – Logical Reasoning 202

Section IV – Reading Comprehension (Unscored Section) 210

Answer Key #2 220

Section I – Reading Comprehension 220

Section II Answer Key – Logical Reasoning 224

Section III Answer Key – Logical Reasoning 228

Section IV Answer Key – Reading Comprehension (Unscored) 232

Scoring Worksheets and Raw Score Conversion Chart 236

Introduction

Congratulations on your decision to study law—few other professions are so rewarding! By purchasing this book, you've already taken the first step toward succeeding in your career. The next step is to do well on the Law School Admission Test (LSAT), which will require you to demonstrate abilities in logical reasoning and reading comprehension.

This book will walk you through the important concepts in each of these subjects and provide you with inside information on test strategies and tactics. Even if it has been years since you last opened a textbook, don't worry; this book contains everything you'll need for the LSAT.

What is the LSAT?

The Law School Admission Test (LSAT) is administered by the Law School Admission Council (LSAC) to candidates for law school admission. Law schools in the United States, Canada, and countries around the world use the LSAT as part of their admissions processes to gauge the skills and potential of applicants.

Specifically, the LSAT evaluates reading comprehension and logical reasoning. There is also an "Argumentative Writing Sample" portion, which must be completed in order for LSAC to release your scores to the schools to which you are applying.

The LSAT is offered throughout the year. As of August 2023, candidates may now take the LSAT up to five times over the course of the current reportable score period, which is five years. Candidates are allowed to sit for the exam no more than seven times over the course of their lifetimes.

What is on the LSAT?

The LSAT evaluates the test taker's abilities on three main skills: logical reasoning, reading comprehension, and the ability to write a convincing argument in favor (or against) a stated issue. All questions (except for the writing sample portion) are multiple-choice, with five answer options.

Candidates may choose to sit for the Argumentative Writing Sample portion the day of the exam or eight days prior to sitting for the exam. LSAT scores will not be released until the Argumentative Writing Sample portion is completed. (Test takers who have already taken the LSAT and completed the writing portion of the exam at that time do not need to submit a second writing sample unless they desire to do so.)

There are four sections with multiple-choice questions: two Logical Reasoning sections, one Reading Comprehension section, and one unscored section. The unscored section is considered experimental and allows the LSAC to test new questions for future use. Since you will not know which section is unscored, it is critical that you make sure to answer all of the questions. The experimental section will concern either Logical Reasoning or Reading Comprehension.

For examinees who take the Argumentative Writing Sample portion the same day, the test takes about three hours (excluding breaks). Examinees receive a short, ten-minute break after the second section.

Section Type and Amount	Number of Sections	Number of Questions	Time Allowed
Logical Reasoning	2	24 – 26 multiple-choice (*per section*)	35 minutes (*per section*)
Reading Comprehension	1	≈27 multiple-choice (4 sets, each with 5 – 8 questions)	35 minutes
Unscored Section (*either* Logical Reasoning or Reading Comprehension)	1	Logical Reasoning: 24 – 26 multiple-choice (*per section*) OR Reading Comprehension: ≈27 multiple-choice (4 sets, each with 5 – 8 questions)	35 minutes
Argumentative Writing Sample	1	≈27 multiple-choice (4 sets, each with 5 – 8 questions)	50 minutes

The Argumentative Writing Sample

If you have already taken the LSAT and completed a writing sample at that time, you have the option of submitting a second writing sample when you sit for the exam on subsequent occasions. After registering for the exam, candidates may access and complete the Argumentative Writing Sample eight days before sitting for the exam; access will be available through candidates' LSAC JD online accounts.

Please refer to https://www.lsac.org/lsat-writing for the most up-to-date information about this portion of the exam.

Scoring

The number of questions answered correctly comprises the raw score. That number is then converted to a scaled score ranging from 120 to 180. The highest possible score is 180.

How Is the LSAT Administered?

The LSAT is administered digitally. There are no paper answer sheets; test takers tap the screen to select the answer option of their choosing.

Test takers have the option of taking the exam remotely or in person at a testing site. Regardless of whether you choose the remote option or in-person option, the multiple-choice sections will be proctored by Prometric. The Writing Sample portion will be administered by ProctorU.

Registration for the LSAT is handled by the LSAC. Visit https://www.lsac.org/lsat/register-lsat to learn more and register for the exam.

There are numerous checklist items for test takers, and they differ depending on whether you will take the exam remotely or at a test center. Please consult https://www.lsac.org/lsat/taking-lsat so that you know exactly what is needed on test day.

Fees

Taking the LSAT (including the Argumentative Writing Sample portion) costs $238. Please note that additional fees are required to send your scores to law schools. For details and additional pricing packages, visit https://www.lsac.org/lsat/register-lsat/lsat-cas-fees.

You will need to sign up for LSAC's Credential Assembly Service to submit your transcripts and letters of recommendation. This is an additional fee of $207.

How to Use This Book

While working your way through this book, the following should be among your goals:

1. Learn how the test works:

- Make sure you know what to expect on test day. You will not know what they are going to ask you, but you should be well prepared for how they are going to ask it.
- Learn how the test works, what kind of questions you will be asked, and how to use reason to find the answers to those questions.
- NOTE: On test day, the LawHub platform may present the sections (Logical Reasoning and Reading Comprehension) in an order which differs from practice exams, including LawHub's own practice exams.

2. Read and work through different types of questions:

- Do a few practice questions for each question type. This will give you a feel for the difficulty and structure of LSAT questions.

3. Master the logical concepts in the Fundamentals section:

- This book is concise, but this means that a lot of information is packed into a few sentences. Reread these sections until you are so comfortable with the concepts that you could teach them to someone else.

4. Take a practice test:

- Once you have learned some of the fundamentals, take a practice test or a thirty-five-minute section of a test. If you find the time limit difficult, you should take more untimed practice tests until you have confidently learned the material.

5. Diagnose and review:

- As you work through practice questions, spend time reviewing your work. This reinforces what you are doing correctly and clarifies errors.

6. Target your weaknesses and improve:

- As you review your completed tests, take note of the types of questions you are missing, and use this book to hone your skills in those areas.
- Draft sample LSAT questions.
- Explain the concepts to a friend.
- Create arguments out of real-life scenarios, and ask every LSAT question you can think of about each of these arguments:
    - Is it sound?
    - How would you strengthen it? Weaken it? Justify it?
- Identify the types of questions you are missing, and then work through the respective sections in this book.

Preparing for the LSAT: Materials

Copies of actual, officially administered LSAT tests are available for the public to purchase. Candidates may wish to complete several full practice tests under timed conditions before taking the official LSAT.

Preparation Materials from 2007 and Earlier

The tests from 2007 to present, for example, include the new Comparative Reading passage in the Reading Comprehension section; older tests do not. The LSAT has undergone a few other minor changes:

- Recent Logical Reasoning sections have included more Sufficient Assumption questions than in the past.
- Recent Reading Comprehension passages are often viewed as more difficult.
- Recent tests tend to have less ambiguous wording.
- The thirty-five-minute, unscored Writing Sample portion may be taken separately (up to eight days earlier) from the rest of the exam.

Test-Taking Tips

Trust Yourself

The LSAT is simply a test of your ability to think logically and methodically. There is no one best way to solve the questions on the LSAT.

On the LSAT, you will have to put aside your own notions of right and wrong and focus on evaluating whether the arguments presented are logically sound; **whether they are factually true in real life is irrelevant**.

An answer is never wrong because "it is too easy." If your confidence is faltering on test day, resolve to go with your gut instinct instead of second-guessing yourself.

Focus on the Big Picture

It is easy to get lost in the details, both on the LSAT and in law school. LSAT questions will reference unfamiliar people, situations, or terms. These details are not important; solving the question is what matters.

- In Logical Reasoning, worry about the big picture only:
    - Separate the facts from the conclusion(s) in each argument and focus on answering the question at hand.
- In Reading Comprehension, develop a grasp of what the author is trying to prove to the reader.

Manage Your Time

Logical Reasoning

You will have an average of **one minute and twenty-four seconds (1:24) per question**. Pace yourself. On a Logical Reasoning section, the most difficult questions tend to fall between questions 11 and 21. Aim to complete the first ten questions in ten minutes; by doing this, you will have ample time for the remaining questions. Remember that all questions have equal worth, so skip (or guess on) a question that poses a risk of consuming too much time.

Reading Comprehension

Allocate approximately **eight minutes and forty-five seconds per passage**. This includes reading the passage and answering the questions.

Chapter 1 - Fundamental Logical Concepts

This section is a general review of how arguments work and the various patterns of reasoning on the LSAT. While these fundamentals primarily apply to the Logical Reasoning sections of the LSAT, they are also relevant to the Reading Comprehension section.

Be sure to distinguish these types of arguments and argumentative techniques from the actual questions you will be asked on the LSAT.

These patterns of reasoning densely populate the LSAT Logical Reasoning sections. For any given argument, you may be asked many possible questions. Understanding the pattern of reasoning in each argument will help you determine what might be missing from an argument.

These patterns of reasoning also appear in the Reading Comprehension section. Many authors incorporate analogies or examples that often advocate a suggestion or predict an outcome.

How Arguments Work

Premises, Conclusions, and Assumptions in Arguments

How do arguments work? Let's begin by examining a simple argument:

> **Premise:** Laura drives a blue Ford Focus.
>
> **Premise:** Laura gets twenty-five miles per gallon.
>
> **Conclusion:** Therefore, if Jordan buys a blue Ford Focus, Jordan will also get at least twenty-five miles per gallon.

This is an argument. The components of an argument are premises and conclusions. Premises are based on facts; opinions are conclusions. Arguments are made by people daily: based on facts (premises), people give opinions (conclusions) that they want someone else to believe.

In any argument, there is at least one premise and at least one conclusion. The **conclusion** is whatever is trying to be proven. **Premises** are the facts, evidence, or other supports that are provided to back up the conclusion.

Certain words and phrases signal a conclusion:

- therefore
- so
- thus
- accordingly
- consequently

- as a result
- hence

Other words signal a premise:

- because
- since
- for
- seeing as
- in light of the fact that

Note that the conclusion is not necessarily the last sentence of an argument. For example, the example argument above would be logically identical if it said, "Jordan will get at least twenty-five miles per gallon if he buys a blue Ford Focus, because Laura drives a blue Ford Focus, and Laura gets twenty-five miles per gallon."

The order of sentences within an argument does not matter on the LSAT. That said, it may help to first read the premises, and then say to yourself, "Therefore," followed by the conclusion. Untangle arguments in this way as you encounter them. Isolate the conclusion from the facts, and see whether the facts provided support the conclusion offered.

Argument Versus Explanation

Note the difference between the following two passages:

1. The meteor that landed in Mexico 63 million years ago killed the dinosaurs. It caused earthquakes and tidal waves, and it kicked up clouds of dust that gave the dinosaurs fatal respiratory diseases.

2. The meteor that landed in Mexico 63 million years ago must have killed the dinosaurs because it caused earthquakes, tidal waves, and lingering dust clouds just before the dinosaurs went extinct, and there are no other known events that could have killed all of the dinosaurs.

Note that there does not need to be an actual debate or disagreement in order to have an argument. Argument does not mean "debate" in the logical sense; rather, an **argument** is a set of one or more premises offered in support of one or more conclusions.

The first passage in the example above is simply an explanation. There is no argument here because the passage simply presents two facts. It does not tell us that one of the statements is true because the other statement is true.

The second passage in the example above is an argument. The first clause ("The meteor . . . must have killed the dinosaurs") is the conclusion. The word *because* indicates that what follows are the premises. This is an argument because the passage tells us that the first clause follows logically from the second.

In Logical Reasoning sections, most passages are arguments; however, there are some question types that are occasionally accompanied by bare fact sets, not by arguments. Specifically, the passages that accompany Inference questions and Resolve the Paradox questions may sometimes be fact sets rather than actual arguments.

For all question types, be sure to distinguish the author's premises from the conclusions.

Strong and Weak Arguments

An argument is **strong** if the conclusion is very likely to follow from the premises. An argument is **weak** if there is great uncertainty as to whether the conclusion will follow from the premises. Keep in mind that **strength has nothing to do with truth**.

For example, the following argument is very strong:

> Almost everyone who wears blue tends to score above 170 on the LSAT. Almost everyone who scores above 170 on the LSAT wears blue. Therefore, a large group of LSAT takers who wear green is likely to have a lower average LSAT score than a large group of LSAT takers who wear blue.

This argument may be ridiculous, but so are many of the arguments you will encounter on the LSAT. Based on the premises (everything before the word *therefore*), the conclusion follows logically.

Going back to the Ford Focus argument earlier, which is moderately strong, consider these facts:

- Laura drives a blue Ford Focus, and she gets twenty-five miles per gallon.
    - That does not guarantee that Jordan will also get the same gas mileage if he buys a blue Ford Focus.

For example, we do not know anything about Laura and Jordan's driving habits; maybe Laura drives entirely on rural highways, whereas Jordan drives in urban traffic. If this were true, then our conclusion (that Jordan will get twenty-five miles per gallon) would be less likely, because Jordan's driving habits are less fuel efficient. Consider the following premises (weakeners) that would weaken this argument:

- Laura's car is new, but Jordan's car is older and less fuel efficient.
- Jordan tows more weight than Laura.
- Jordan uses more air-conditioning than Laura.
- Laura optimizes her fuel efficiency with regular maintenance, whereas Jordan does not.

As you add each of these additional premises to your original argument, the argument becomes weaker and weaker:

Premises: Laura drives a blue Ford Focus and gets twenty-five miles per gallon. Jordan also buys a blue Ford Focus, but he buys an older one, tows more weight, drives more in the city, uses more air-conditioning, and foregoes regular maintenance.

Conclusion: But Jordan will still get at least twenty-five miles per gallon.

This is an example of a weak argument: all the additional evidence indicates a poorly supported conclusion.

Now, what if we wanted to make the argument stronger by using strengtheners? There are three ways to do this:

1. Add in a new premise that rules out a potential weakener.

2. Add in a new premise that makes the conclusion more likely. (This may overlap with number 1, but it goes beyond merely ruling out the potential weakener.)

3. Add in a new premise that makes the conclusion 100 percent certain. Table 1.1 contains examples of these strengtheners.

Table 1.1. Weakeners and Strengtheners	
Weakeners	<ul><li>Laura's car is new, but Jordan's car is older and less fuel efficient.</li><li>Jordan tows more weight than Laura.</li><li>Jordan uses more air-conditioning than Laura.</li><li>Laura optimizes her fuel efficiency with regular maintenance, whereas Jordan does not.</li></ul>
Strengtheners	<ul><li>Jordan's car is at least as new as Laura's.</li><li>Jordan does not tow more weight than Laura.</li><li>Jordan does not use more air-conditioning than Laura.</li><li>Jordan performs the same fuel-efficiency-optimizing maintenance Laura performs.</li></ul> *These strengtheners operate by ruling out potential weakeners.* <ul><li>Jordan's Focus has a smaller, more fuel-efficient engine than Laura's</li><li>Jordan drives entirely on country roads, where he maximizes his fuel efficiency.</li></ul> *These operate by making the conclusion more likely.* <ul><li>The only factor that affects fuel efficiency is the model of the car.</li><li>All cars of the same color get the same mileage per gallon.</li></ul> *These not only strengthen the argument, but also fully justify it.*

Let's detail those three different ways of strengthening the argument:

1. Ruling Out Potential Weakeners

All of the strengtheners in the first set negate premises that would weaken the argument. These strengtheners are also necessary assumptions; that is, in making the argument that Jordan will get twenty-five miles per gallon, the author must necessarily assume that Jordan's car will be at least as new as Laura's and that Jordan will not tow more weight, use more air-conditioning, or perform poorer maintenance than Laura. If the author does not assume these things, there would be no way for the author to conclude that Jordan will get the same gas mileage as Laura. These statements are called **assumptions** because the author has not actually stated them in the argument, so they are unstated premises. If we add these sentences to the argument as stated premises that we know are true, then the conclusion would become more likely.

2. Adding Anything That Makes the Conclusion More Likely

The strengtheners in the second group go beyond merely negating potential weakeners. The first statement does not merely say that Jordan's car is as fuel efficient as Laura's, but rather that it is *more* fuel efficient than Laura's. This absolutely does rule out a potential weakener (it rules out "Laura's car is more fuel efficient than Jordan's"), but it goes further. By telling us that Jordan's car is more fuel efficient, the likelihood that Jordan will receive twenty-five or more miles per gallon is even higher.

3. Adding a Premise to Prove the Conclusion with 100 Percent Certainty

The strengtheners in the third group qualify not only as strengtheners, but as sufficient assumptions. **Sufficient assumptions** are statements that would turn an otherwise mediocre argument into a certain one. Adding either one of the premises listed would make our conclusion 100 percent inescapable.

Take the first one, for example:

Premise (added): The only factor that affects fuel efficiency is the model of the car.

Premise (original): Laura drives a blue Ford Focus.

Premise (original): Laura gets twenty-five miles per gallon.

Conclusion: Therefore, if Jordan buys a blue Ford Focus, Jordan will also get at least twenty-five miles per gallon.

Now that we have added in a strengthener, there is no way out of the conclusion; Jordan is buying the same model car as Laura, so Jordan will get the same fuel efficiency as Laura. These kinds of strengtheners are called **sufficient assumptions** because if the statement is assumed to be true, it is enough to make the conclusion certain. Sufficient assumptions are discussed in detail in the next section.

If we were worried about analyzing the factual correctness of our argument, we would be correct to object to the following statement: "The only factor that affects fuel efficiency is the model of the car." Factually speaking, this statement is false in real life.

However, logical validity is a separate inquiry from factual correctness. The LSAT tests your ability to use logic and reason. Thus, you might need to add in an unlikely premise (like "All cars of the same color get the same mileage per gallon") to make an argument stronger. Consider the following argument, which is absurd but logically valid:

Premise: All spiders have wings.

Premise: Anything with wings can fly.

Conclusion: Therefore, all spiders can fly.

Necessary and Sufficient Assumptions

The following is a common point of confusion among even the most adept LSAT candidates, so read carefully.

Necessary assumptions are unstated premises that the author must believe in order to make an argument. If the author is not assuming these premises, she will not be able to make the argument and believe that the conclusion is plausible.

When LSAT questions ask you to **identify a necessary assumption**, they are asking you to **identify something that must be true based on the information stated in the argument**—something that the conclusion requires in order to stand.

If a necessary assumption is false, it will destroy the argument. Similarly, if a necessary assumption is negated, the author ends up with a factor that severely weakens or destroys the argument.

On the other hand, the author does not necessarily believe sufficient assumptions. **Sufficient assumptions** are statements that fully justify the argument and render its conclusion valid if the reader assumes them to be true.

In Logical Reasoning questions, you will be asked to justify conclusions. This requires making an argument perfectly strong by adding in a sufficient assumption. Usually, you can craft a statement that is both necessary and sufficient for an argument to work. Take this argument, for example:

Premise: You're bleeding!

Conclusion: So, you must need a bandage.

This is an ordinary argument that someone might make. The argument they are actually making is:

Premise: You're bleeding!

Unstated premise (assumption): People who are bleeding need bandages.

Conclusion: So, you must need a bandage

Of course, you would never say to someone, "Oh, you're bleeding! And people who are bleeding need bandages. So, you must need a bandage." Nevertheless, you have an unstated premise that people who are bleeding need bandages. If you did not believe that, then you would not be able to argue your conclusion. Furthermore, because our stated premise is "You're bleeding," adding in this unstated premise is sufficient to prove our conclusion ("You must need a bandage").

Consider this argument:

Property taxes are evil because they infringe on citizens' natural rights.

Premise: Property taxes infringe on citizens' natural rights.

Conclusion: Therefore, property taxes are evil.

The following would be an assumption that is both necessary and sufficient:

- Things that infringe on citizens' natural rights are evil.

The following would be an assumption that is necessary but not sufficient to prove the conclusion:

- Not all things that infringe on citizens' rights are good.

The following would be an assumption that is sufficient but not necessary to prove the conclusion:

- Anything that infringes on anyone's rights is evil.

> **Helpful Hint:**
>
> Create your own arguments and practice identifying assumptions that are necessary, sufficient, and both necessary and sufficient. This will help strengthen your Logical Reasoning and Reading Comprehension skills.

Table 1.2. summarizes necessary and sufficient assumptions.

Table 1.2. Necessary and Sufficient Assumptions	
NECESSARY ASSUMPTIONS	**SUFFICIENT ASSUMPTIONS**
If the argument's conclusion is true, then the assumption must be true.	If the assumption is true, then the argument's conclusion must be true.
The *author* is making the assumption.	The *reader* is making the assumption to prove that the author is correct.

Chapter 1 - Fundamental Logical Concepts

Table 1.2. Necessary and Sufficient Assumptions	
NECESSARY ASSUMPTIONS	**SUFFICIENT ASSUMPTIONS**
The assumption must be true (it is required; hence "necessary" assumption).	The assumption might be totally implausible. However, if the assumption were true, it would make the argument airtight.
If you add in this assumption, there might still be holes in the argument.	If you add in this assumption, there will be absolutely no holes in the argument.
If you negate this assumption, the argument will be severely weakened or fall apart entirely.	You can negate this assumption, and the argument may still follow logically.

LSAT Logic Vocabulary

There are no magic LSAT words. Every word on the LSAT is used according to a normal dictionary definition; however, if you have not had experience in analyzing arguments in the past, you might not know at first glance the differences between an analogy, an example, and an illustration. The terms and phrases on the following pages appear frequently in both Reading Comprehension and Logical Reasoning questions, so be sure you are familiar with them and can tell them apart.

> **Did You Know?**
>
> Imply vs. Infer: To **imply** is to present propositions which, if true, result in some other proposition being true. To **infer** is to draw a conclusion from given premises. Statements imply; readers infer.

Verbs

The following verbs frequently appear in Logical Reasoning (Method of Reasoning questions) and in Reading Comprehension (Author's Purpose questions):

- *state, set out, set forth, say, present*
- *overlook, ignore, fail to consider*
- *compare*
- *illustrate, demonstrate, exemplify*
- *show, prove, demonstrate*
- *dismiss, discredit, discount, disregard (to exclude or eliminate a proposition)*
- *cause, influence, foster, promote, induce, encourage, facilitate, lead to, produce*
- *assume, presuppose, take for granted*
- *appeal to, use, rely on*
- *justify, establish, allow the conclusion to be properly drawn*
- *strengthen, support, bolster, further, advance*
- *refute, disprove, deny, negate*
- *weaken, undermine, call into question, make vulnerable to criticism, cast doubt on*

Nouns

- **alternatives:** different options or ways of achieving a result
- **analogy:** an argument that uses the underlying reasoning in a similar situation and applies that reasoning to the situation in the primary argument
- **application:** a statement that draws a conclusion about an actual, specific case on the basis of a general principle
- **assumption:** an unstated premise
- **cause:** a factor whose occurrence results in the occurrence of some effect
- **claim (conclusion):** what the author is trying to prove as a logical consequence of the premises
- **conclusion (claim):** what the author is trying to prove as a logical consequence of the premises
- **condition:** a circumstance that affects the occurrence of another event (necessary conditions are required for the other event to occur; sufficient conditions ensure that the other event will occur)
- **consequence:** a result
- **contrapositive:** a conditional statement of the form $\sim B \to \sim A$, logically equivalent to $A \to B$
- **correlation:** a relationship between two variables where the frequency of one variable is tied to the frequency of the other variable (either directly or inversely)
- **counterexample:** an illustration presented to refute a proposition
- **effect:** a phenomenon whose occurrence is the result of some other factor
- **event (phenomenon):** any observable behavior or occurrence
- **example:** an illustration of a proposition
- **fact (support/premise/reason):** evidence offered to prove a conclusion
- **general principle:** a broad statement that could apply to many cases and from which is drawn a conclusion about a specific case
- **historical fact:** any historical evidence from the past that is offered to prove a conclusion
- **hypothesis:** a theoretical belief that has not yet been proven true
- **illustration:** a statement that applies a general principle to a specific, actual situation
- **main idea/main point:** the conclusion (if an argument has only one conclusion) or the ultimate conclusion that is supported by all other conclusions (if an argument has more than one conclusion)
- **phenomenon (event):** any observable behavior or occurrence
- **premise (reason/fact/support):** evidence offered to prove a conclusion
- **problem:** a conflict or situation that needs a solution
- **proposal (suggestion/recommendation):** a course of action that someone is supporting
- **proposition:** a sentence (in arguments, a premise or conclusion)
- **reason (fact/support/premise):** evidence offered to prove a conclusion

- **recommendation (proposal/suggestion):** a course of action that someone is supporting
- **solution:** an answer to a problem
- **suggestion (recommendation/proposal):** a course of action that someone is supporting
- **support (premise/reason/fact):** evidence offered to prove a conclusion

Patterns of Reasoning

Patterns of reasoning can also be thought of as types of arguments. Most arguments made in life are not absolutely, conclusively valid. For example, one might argue as follows:

Premise: Mike is ten minutes late to the meeting.

Premise: He has never been late to meetings that he knows about.

Conclusion: So, I bet he did not know about the meeting.

The conclusion is that Mike did not know about the meeting. This conclusion may very well be true; after all, Mike is never late, and now he is ten minutes late. But is this certain? No. Why not? Because today might be the first time Mike is late to a meeting that he knows about.

If we knew more about the situation, we might be able to say with greater certainty whether the conclusion of this argument ("Mike did not know about the meeting") is likely or unlikely; as it stands, the argument is not conclusive.

This is an example of inductive reasoning (also called informal logic). In this sort of argument, you can potentially bring in new, or additional, information to prove or disprove the conclusion. It is called **inductive logic** because you can induce, or bring in, more premises to evaluate the conclusion.

The Ford Focus argument is an inductive argument, and we practiced adding in additional premises to strengthen or weaken it. We do not technically refer to inductive arguments as valid or invalid; instead, we refer to them as strong or weak. The LSAT will ask you to strengthen or weaken inductive arguments in the Logical Reasoning sections.

Deductive reasoning, on the other hand, exists where your conclusion follows directly and conclusively from your premises, with 100 percent certainty. For example:

Premise: If Mike had remembered the meeting, he would have been here early.

Premise: But he is late.

Conclusion: So, Mike must not have remembered the meeting.

Given the premises, the conclusion is certain. This argument is a deductive argument. It is called deductive logic because one can deduce, or figure out, the conclusion directly from the premises without looking elsewhere. There is no way to strengthen or weaken the argument. When an argument is this strong, it is called **valid**. Arguments that attempt to be valid deductive arguments but use faulty reasoning (explained below) are called **invalid**.

Now, you might be thinking, "But what if Mike had car trouble? Or what if he just decided to sleep in? Just because he is late, how can you say it is certain that Mike did not remember the meeting?" The reason this argument is still perfectly valid is that our premise states, "If Mike had remembered the meeting, he would have been here early." Based on this premise, we know with certainty that Mike would have been early if he had remembered the meeting.

Maybe you disagree with this premise, but your disagreement is a factual challenge to the argument, not a logical challenge. On the LSAT, your task is never to dispute the facts (premises) presented; your task is only to evaluate the logical soundness of the conclusions that are supposed to follow from those facts. Even if the LSAT states, "The moon is made of green cheese" as a premise in an argument, your thought should not be, "No, it is not." Just worry about the logic in the argument.

Diagramming

Table 1.3. defines some common symbols in diagramming logical arguments.

Table 1.3. Symbols Used in Diagramming Logical Arguments		
SYMBOL	MEANING	EXAMPLE
→	If...then	A → B (If A is true, then B is true.)
~	not	~A (A is not true/A is false.)
∴	therefore	∴A (Therefore, A is true.)

As you work through LSAT problems, you may find it useful to diagram some of the logical arguments in the passages, especially conditional statements ("if . . . then" statements).

For example, take the statement "If life as we know it exists, then there must be water." You might denote this simply as follows:

$$L \rightarrow W$$

Here, *L* stands for "Life as we know it exists," and *W* stands for "There is water." The arrow (→) denotes the "if . . . then" relationship: "If *L* is true, then *W* must also be true."

Students often diagram the sentence "If life as we know it exists, then there must be water" as "*L* = *W*." But this is incorrect. The statement "*L* = *W*" could easily be confused with "*W* = *L*."

Our conditional statement, however, only goes in one direction ("if life, then water"); it does not mean "If there is water, then there is life." That is why we use a one-directional arrow to convey conditions: "*L* → *W*" just means if there is life, then there is water. It is not the same as "*W* → *L*."

The LSAT will test your ability to understand and apply conditional statements correctly. If you find yourself facing several conditional statements in a complex argument, diagramming the argument in the margin can be a useful tool to help you understand what the author is trying to convey. Using shorthand is useful for saving time as you do this—and for focusing on the structure of the argument rather than the details of what is being said.

Formal Logic (Deductive Reasoning)

Mixed Hypothetical Arguments

Here we have provided two common valid patterns of reasoning, as well as two common invalid patterns of reasoning. These are called **mixed hypothetical arguments** because they all take a hypothetical ("if . . . then") statement and apply it to an actual situation.

> **Helpful Hint**:
> Do not use an equal sign (=) to represent a conditional statement.

Table 1.4. Mixed Hypothetical Arguments

VALID (POSITIVE) ARGUMENT		VALID (CONTRAPOSITIVE) ARGUMENT	
Pattern: If A is true, then B is true. A is true. Therefore, B is true.	**Shorthand:** A → B A ∴ B	**Pattern:** If A is true, then B is true. B is false. Therefore, A is false.	**Shorthand:** A → B ~B ∴ ~A
Example: If the car is running, then it has gasoline. This car is running. Therefore, this car has gasoline. (This is a perfectly valid deductive argument.)		**Example:** If the car is running, then it has gasoline. This car is out of gas. Therefore, this car is not running. (This is a perfectly valid deductive argument.)	
Invalid (Mistaken Reversal)		Invalid (Mistaken Negation)	
Pattern: If A is true, then B is true. B is true. Therefore, A is true.	**Shorthand:** A → B B ∴ A	**Pattern:** If A is true, then B is true. A is false. Therefore, B is false.	**Shorthand:** A → B ~A ∴ ~B
Example: If the car is running, then it has gasoline. This car has gasoline. Therefore, this car is running. This argument is fatally flawed. Gasoline is necessary for the car to run. However, just because the car has gasoline does not ensure that the car *will* run. For example, the car might have a faulty battery. This argument assumes that "If the car is running, then it has gas" is the same as "If the car has gas, then it is running." This is always flawed logic. In abstract (pattern) terms, this argument wrongly assumes that "If A then B" is the same as "If B then A." This is always flawed logic. See the mistaken reversal discussion for more information.		**Example:** If the car is running, then it has gasoline. This car is not running. Therefore, this car is out of gas. This argument is fatally flawed. If the car is running, this is sufficient to ensure that the car has gasoline. However, the fact that the car is not running does not necessitate that it is out of gas. Perhaps it has a faulty battery or a missing engine. This argument assumes that "If the car is running, then it has gas" is the same as "If the car is not running, then it is out of gas." This is always flawed logic. In abstract (pattern) terms, this argument wrongly assumes that "If A then B" is the same as "If no A, then no B." This is always flawed logic. See the mistaken negation discussion for more information.	

The LSAT tests your ability to recognize these and other common patterns of reasoning. In some cases, you will be given two of an argument's three components, and your task will be to come up with an answer that provides the third component in such a way as to complete a valid argument.

The valid, positive argument form in Table 1.4. is very common. Consider the following examples:

Premise: If you work hard, you will succeed. W → S

Premise: Bob works hard. W

Conclusion: Therefore, Bob will succeed. ∴ S

Premise: You cannot travel to Mexico if you do not have a passport.

~P → ~T

Premise: Jerry does not have a passport. ~P

Conclusion: Therefore, Jerry cannot travel to Mexico. ∴ ~T

Note that the "if . . . then" statement in premise 1 here is essentially "If no passport, then no travel." Pay careful attention to where the "if" falls in conditional statements. Also note that premise 1 is still a conditional statement, even though it does not explicitly use "if . . . then." The conditional relationship is "If good grades, then study." According to this statement, without studying, it is impossible to get good grades; thus, this is a perfectly valid argument.

Note that these are not circular arguments. The first premise of each argument is a purely hypothetical statement that tells us what would happen if some condition were to come true. Then, the second premise tells us about an actual situation where that condition actually does come true. Based on those premises, we are able to draw our conclusion about this actual situation.

The valid, contrapositive argument form is also very common. Consider these examples:

Premise: To get good grades, you must study. G → S

Premise: Carol refuses to study. ~S

Conclusion: Therefore, Carol will not get good grades. ∴ ~G

Premise: If you are eligible to vote, you must be eighteen or older. E → 18

Premise: Jonathan is seventeen. ~18

Conclusion: Therefore, Jonathan is not eligible to vote. ∴ ~E

If you are wondering what all this diagramming is about, realize that every argument you have ever made follows some pattern of reasoning.

Even our example "Oh, you are bleeding . . . you must need a bandage" follows the valid, positive form of argumentation:

Premise: If you're bleeding, you need a bandage.

Premise: You're bleeding.

Conclusion: So, you must need a bandage.

As previously noted, you would probably never say the unstated "if . . . then" premise, but you are still using this pattern of reasoning. The LSAT tests your ability to recognize and make convincing arguments, skills that you will need both in law school and in your future as an advocate.

Disjunctive Argument (Either-Or)

While the preceding mixed hypothetical arguments are the most common patterns of deductive reasoning on the LSAT, Tables 1.5. through 1.7. show a few other patterns that you are likely to encounter. (Note: The disjunctive argument is a valid argument; do not confuse it with the invalid either-or fallacy.)

Table 1.5. Disjunctive Arguments (Either-Or)

PATTERN	SHORTHAND	EXAMPLE
Either A is true or B is true.	A or B	Everyone must take either Spanish or French.
A is false.	~A	Cheryl is not taking Spanish.
Therefore, B is true.	∴ B	Therefore, Cheryl is taking French.

Table 1.6. Pure Hypothetical Argument

PATTERN	SHORTHAND	EXAMPLE
If A is true, then B is true.	A → B	If it is a dog, then it is a mammal.
If B is true, then C is true.	B → C	If it is a mammal, then it has hair.
So, If A is true, then C is true.	∴ A → C	So, if it is a dog, then it has hair.

Table 1.7. Constructive Dilemma

PATTERN	SHORTHAND	EXAMPLE
If A is true, then B is true.	A → B	If I go to law school, then I will be a lawyer.
If C is true, then D is true.	C → D	If I go to medical school, then I will be a doctor.
Either A is true or C is true.	A or C	I am going to either law school or medical school.
So, either B is true or D is true.	∴ B or D	So, I will be either a lawyer or a doctor.

The variations in Table 1.8. are all mixed hypothetical patterns of reasoning, but they involve more premises than the simple positive and contrapositive forms. In theory, no limit exists for the number of premises that you can have in an argument, although LSAT Logical Reasoning passages do not usually support conclusions with more than five premises.

As noted earlier, the LSAT frequently tests your ability to fill in missing links in order to turn partial arguments into complete arguments that follow patterns.

Table 1.8. Mixed Hypothetical Patterns of Reasoning

PATTERN	SHORTHAND	EXAMPLE
If A is true, then B is true.	A → B	If it is a dog, then it is a mammal.
If B is true, then C is true.	B → C	If it is a mammal, then it has hair.
A is true.	A	Fido is a dog.
Therefore, C is true.	∴C	Therefore, Fido has hair.
If A is true, then B is true.	A → B	If you are a lawyer, you went to law school.
If B is true, then C is true.	B → C	If you went to law school, you took the LSAT.
C is not true.	~C	Ashley never took the LSAT.
Therefore, A is not true.	∴~A	Therefore, Ashley is not a lawyer.
If A is true, then B is true.	A → B	If you are a lawyer, you went to law school.
If B is true, then C is true.	B → C	If you went to law school, you did well on the LSAT.
If D is not true, then C is not true.	~D → ~C, or C → D	If you did not know how to tell apart patterns of reasoning, you would not have done well on the LSAT.
A is true.	A	Ashley is a lawyer.
Therefore, D is true. As discussed later, ~D → ~C is the same as C → D	∴D	Therefore, Ashley knows how to tell apart patterns of reasoning.

Conditional Statements

So far, we have dealt with conditional statements mostly in their "if . . . then" forms. On the LSAT, you will see conditional statements in a variety of forms. For example, consider the following statements:

1. If it is an animal, then it is mortal.

2. If it is not mortal, then it is not an animal.

3. Only if it is mortal is it an animal.

4. It is not an animal unless it is mortal.

   5. It must be mortal or else it is not an animal.

   6. Either it is mortal or it is not an animal.

   7. It is mortal if it is an animal.

   8. Only mortals are animals.

   9. It is an animal only if it is mortal.

   10. All animals are mortals.

Recognize that no matter the values of A and B in your conditional statement, you can rearrange the sentence into any of these thirteen forms without changing the meaning of the statement. **Just be careful not to confuse any form of "If A, then B" with any form of "If B, then A."**

   1. No animals fail to be mortal.

   2. Being an animal is sufficient for being a mortal.

   3. Being a mortal is necessary for being an animal.

Hopefully, as you read these statements, you noticed that all thirteen sentences express the exact same condition with absolutely zero variation in meaning. You should note that none of these statements says "If it is mortal, then it is an animal" or any variation on that sentence, which would be a mistaken reversal. Here is another conditional statement expressed all thirteen ways:

   1. If you get a 170 or higher on the LSAT, then you studied hard.

   2. If you do not study hard, then you will not get a 170 or higher on the LSAT.

   3. Only if you study hard will you get a 170 or higher on the LSAT.

   4. You will not get a 170 or higher on the LSAT unless you study hard.

   5. You must study hard or else you will not get a 170 or higher on the LSAT.

   6. Either you study hard or you do not get a 170 or higher on the LSAT.

   7. You studied hard if you got a 170 or higher on the LSAT.

   8. Only those who study hard get 170 or higher on the LSAT.

   9. You get a 170 or higher on the LSAT only if you study hard.

   10. All 170+ scorers studied hard.

   11. No 170+ scorer fails to study hard.

   12. Scoring 170 or higher on the LSAT is sufficient to assert that you studied hard.

   13. Studying hard is necessary for scoring 170 or higher on the LSAT.

In shorthand, here are the same thirteen forms. All of these mean "A → B" and its equivalent "~B → ~A."

   1. If A is true, then B is true.

   2. If B is false, then A is false.

   3. Only if B is true is A true.

   4. A cannot be true unless B is true.

   5. B must be true or else A is false.

6. Either B is true or A is false.

7. B is true if A is true. (Again, notice where the "if" is. This is not saying "If B then A.")

8. Only B is A.

9. A only if B.

10. All A is B.

11. No A fails to be B.

12. A is sufficient for B. (Or, A ensures B.)

13. B is necessary for A. (Or, A requires B.)

If A, Then B

"If A, then B" is usually the easiest form for working with conditional statements. The phrase, "If A, then B" is clearer than "A only if B" or "No A unless B," even though all of these forms have the same meaning.

As you spot conditional statements (on any section of the LSAT), process the statement and articulate it to yourself in "If A then B" form; therefore, on test day this statement is diagrammed as "A → B."

Also, when you see "if" in the middle of a sentence, you should start reading the sentence from "if":

- The lawn will get wet *if* it rains.
- Read this sentence as: "*If* it rains, the lawn will get wet."

> **Helpful Hint:**
> Recognize that no matter the values of A and B in your conditional statement, you can rearrange the sentence into any of these thirteen forms without changing the meaning of the statement. Just be careful not to confuse any form of "If A, then B" with any form of "If B, then A."

Just be careful not to read the sentence as "If the lawn gets wet, then it rained." Doing so would change the meaning of the sentence entirely.

Only If

"Only if" is not the same as "if." Consider the difference between the following two sentences:

- The dog barks if there is an intruder.
- The dog barks only if there is an intruder.

We could read sentence 1 as "If there is an intruder, then the dog barks." (This is the conditional statement that we learned immediately prior: I → B.)

Sentence 2, however, says that the *only* time the dog barks is when there is an intruder: "If the dog barks, there is an intruder." On test day, this conditional statement would be diagrammed as "B → I."

In sentence 1, knowing that there is an intruder guarantees that the dog is barking; however, other things might also make the dog bark. In fact, this dog may always be barking.

In sentence 2, knowing that the dog is barking guarantees that there is an intruder; however, just because there is an intruder does not mean this dog will bark. In fact, this dog may never bark, even if there are intruders present.

Chapter 1 - Fundamental Logical Concepts

Be sure to understand the difference: Sentence 1 says that the presence of an intruder is <u>sufficient</u> for the dog to bark. Sentence 2 says that the presence of an intruder is <u>necessary</u> for the dog to bark. Changing the "if" to "only if" changes the subsequent condition from a sufficient condition to a necessary condition.

As you read sentences in the form "A is true only if B is true," you should mentally reword them as "If A is true, then B is true."

If and Only If

A speaker may want to express the idea that the dog barks when there is an intruder, and that when the dog barks, we know there is an intruder. That is where a sentence like this comes in: "The dog barks if, and only if, there is an intruder."

This is really just a combination of sentences 1 and 2 above. When you encounter "if and only if" (or "if but only if") statements on the LSAT, you should treat them accordingly. "If A is true, then B is true" and "If B is true, then A is true." On test day, this statement is diagrammed as "A ←→ B." That said, these sorts of statements appear rather infrequently on the LSAT. A common source of confusion is how we use conditional statements in real life.

Often, when someone says, "My dog only barks if there is an intruder," they mean two things:

1. My dog will not bark if there is not an intruder. (I.e., My dog barks only if there is an intruder.)

2. My dog barks if there is an intruder. (I.e., If there is an intruder, my dog barks.)

Rarely will someone actually take the time to say in real life, "My dog barks if, and only if, there is an intruder." Be aware of how you use conditional statements in your own life. If you use "if" statements to mean "if and only if," then consider changing your ways. Think about the confusion that might arise from these examples:

1. Father to son: "You can have dessert if you clean your room."

In this example, even if the son does not clean his room, he might still be able to have dessert. The father should not say this if he wants to require his son to clean his room in order to have dessert. Instead, he could say, "You can have dessert if, and only if, you clean your room." As written in sentence 1, all the father has done is guaranteed that the son can have dessert if he cleans his room; he has not said what happens if the son does not clean his room.

2. Academic policy: "Students graduate if they complete 120 credit hours."

In this example, the school guarantees students that completing 120 credit hours results in graduation. However, what if the school has other requirements, such as a minimum GPA? The way this sentence is written, there are no other requirements for graduation; all we know is that attaining 120 credit hours ensures graduation. If the school wanted 120 credit hours to be a requirement (while allowing for the possibility of other requirements), the policy should say, "Students graduate only if they complete 120 credit hours."

3. Postal employee: "The letter will arrive tomorrow if you use express mail."

In this example, the postal employee says that using express mail will guarantee delivery tomorrow; however, this does not exclude the possibility that other forms of mail will also result in delivery tomorrow. If the postal employee wanted to convey that there is no other way for the letter to arrive tomorrow, he should have said, "The letter will arrive tomorrow if, and only if, you use express mail."

Unless

Consider the examples:

- You cannot drive unless you have a driver's license.
- You cannot vote unless you are eighteen or older.
- You will succeed in life unless you become selfish. These would be expressed in "if...then" form as follows:

There are two lessons here: First, any conditional form in the phrase, "A is not true unless B is true" is identical to "If A is true, then B is true." Similarly, the phrase, "A is true unless B is true" is identical to "If A is not true, then B is true." Second, the word *unless* essentially means "if not"; therefore, sentence 3 could be rephrased as follows:

- You will succeed in life unless you become selfish. (original)
- You will succeed in life if you do not become selfish. (rephrased)
- If you do not become selfish, you will succeed in life. (rephrased, and starting with "if")

Table 1.9. Recap of Diagrams

CONDITIONAL STATEMENT	EXAMPLE	DIAGRAM ON TEST DAY	NOTES
if A, then B	If Jake eats a slice of key lime pie, he will be full.	P → F	Remember, eating a slice of key lime pie is *sufficient but not necessary* for Jake to be full. Hypothetically, Jake could also be full by eating a brownie or ice cream sundae.
only if	Only if Jake eats a slice of key lime pie will he be full.	F → P	Now, eating a slice of key lime pie is the only way that Jake can be full. Thus, eating a slice of key lime pie is a *necessary condition* for Jake to be full.
if and only if	If and only if Jake eats a slice of key lime pie will he be full.	P ⟷ F	Now, If Jake eats a slice of key lime pie, he will be full, *and* only if Jake eats a slice of key lime pie will he be full. Now, eating a slice of key lime pie is both a *necessary* and a *sufficient condition* for Jake's fullness.

Disproving Conditional Statements

To disprove the statement, "If A is true, then B is true," it is not good enough to show that A is false. Take, for example, "If the moon were made of green cheese, then it would smell bad." You cannot disprove this statement by proving that the moon is not made of green cheese. To disprove the statement, you would need to show that (1) the moon is made of green cheese, and (2) it does not smell bad. **This is a fundamental principle of logic: to disprove "If A is true, then B is true," you must show "A is true. (And) B is false."**

Chapter 1 - Fundamental Logical Concepts

Sufficient Conditions and Necessary Conditions

We have already mentioned sufficient conditions and necessary conditions. These are important terms that the LSAT will use in Logical Reasoning answer options, and you should master the relationship between a sufficient condition and a necessary condition.

By definition, when we say, "If A, then B," we are designating A as a sufficient condition for B, and B as a necessary condition for A. Remember that the following are equivalent forms:

1. If A is true, then B is true.
2. A is sufficient for B.
3. A ensures B.
4. A requires B.
5. B is necessary for A.

> **Did You Know?**
>
> *Unless* is a word that even highly educated individuals misuse on a regular basis. Consider the following statement: "We will not hire another employee unless we double our sales." You might think this means that if we double our sales, we will hire another employee, but that is a mistaken reversal. All we know is that if we do not double our sales, we will not hire another employee.

This is true for any "if . . . then" statement. For example, "If you are making pancakes, then you have flour." Using these five variations, we could say the following:

1. If you are making pancakes, then you have flour.
2. That you are making pancakes is sufficient to assert that you have flour.
3. That you are making pancakes ensures that you have flour.
4. Making pancakes requires flour.
5. Flour is necessary for making pancakes.

Observe the relationship here. "Making pancakes" is the sufficient condition, and "flour" is the necessary condition.

Again, watch out for mistaken reversals and mistaken negations. These fallacies occur when someone wrongly assumes that a necessary condition is really a sufficient condition. The following is a mistaken reversal:

Premise: If you are making pancakes, then you have flour.

Premise: Jim has flour.

Conclusion: So, Jim must be making pancakes.

This wrongly assumes that flour (a necessary condition for making pancakes, according to our first premise) is a sufficient condition for making pancakes. In factual terms, we would say that just because Jim has flour, it does not mean he is making pancakes.

Finally, consider the examples in Table 1.10. in terms of sufficient and necessary conditions.

Table 1.10. Sufficient and Necessary Conditions		
CONDITIONAL STATEMENT	**SUFFICIENT CONDITION**	**NECESSARY CONDITION**
You cannot drive unless you have a license.	driving	driver's license
You cannot vote unless you are eighteen or older.	voting	being eighteen or older
You will succeed unless you become selfish.	not succeeding	becoming selfish
My dog barks only if there is an intruder.	dog barking	intruder
My dog barks if there is an intruder.	intruder	dog barking

Categorical Formal Logic

"All," "Some," and "None" Statements

So far, we have looked at deductive arguments that primarily use conditional statements ("if," "only if," "unless," etc.); however, not all deductive arguments use conditional statements. Some use statements with the terms *all*, *some*, or *none*. For example:

>**Premise:** All plants are green.
>
>**Premise:** Some plants are decorative objects.
>
>**Conclusion:** Therefore, some decorative objects are green.

This is a valid argument, and it follows this pattern:

>**Premise:** All A is B.
>
>**Premise:** Some A is C.
>
>**Conclusion:** Therefore, some C is B.
>
>(Note: "Some B is C" would be equivalent here.)

Sometimes, it is useful to visualize all/some/none statements. We can see that this argument is valid by drawing out the premises. Figure 1.1 shows how you might visualize the first premise. ("All plants are green."):

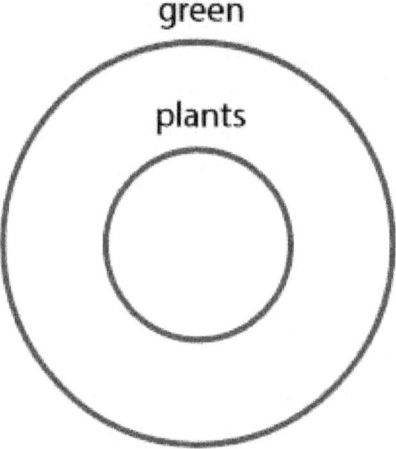

Figure 1.1. "All plants are green."

It becomes clear from the diagram that every plant is contained within the set of things that are green.

Figure 1.2 draws in the second premise. ("Some plants are decorative objects."):

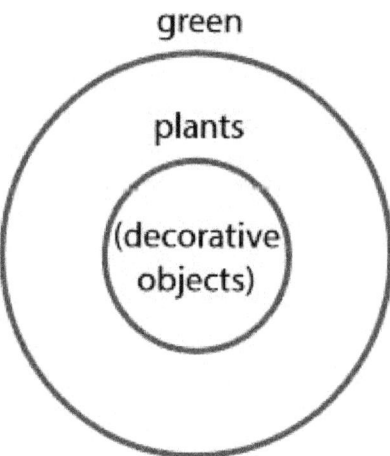

Figure 1.2. "Some Plants Are Decorative Objects"

Note that you should not diagram the conclusion; you should only diagram the premises of the argument presented, and then look at the diagram to see if the premises provided are sufficient to prove the conclusion. If the argument is valid, you should be able to draw just the premises, and the conclusion should be apparent from your drawing, as a logical consequence of the premises.

In the case of "Some plants are decorative objects," our conclusion is that some decorative objects are green. Looking at Figure 1.2, it is apparent that some decorative objects must indeed be green, thus proving that this is a valid pattern of reasoning.

An important note: In Figure 1.2., notice how "decorative objects" is written in parentheses. This is because our sentence is that *some* plants are decorative objects. We are not saying that *all* decorative objects are plants. If we wanted to say that, we would write "decorative objects" inside of another circle that is entirely within "plants." Instead, writing "(decorative objects)" indicates that there are some decorative objects that are plants, without ruling out the possibility that there are also decorative objects that are not plants. To denote "Some A is B," write A inside of B in a different way than you would write to denote "All A is B."

"All" Statements and "If" Statements

Note that using a visual diagram, such as the circles, is helpful for diagramming arguments that contain "some" statements; after all, you cannot effectively use the arrow (→) to represent a sentence like "Some plants are decorative objects."

However, if your argument just contains "all" statements, consider how these statements are similar to "if . . . then" statements. For example, the following two arguments are essentially the same:

Premise: All humans are mortal.   **Premise:** If human, then mortal.

Premise: This man is human.   **Premise:** This man is human.

Conclusion: So, this man is mortal.   **Conclusion:** So, this man is mortal.

You could diagram both of these arguments in one of two ways:

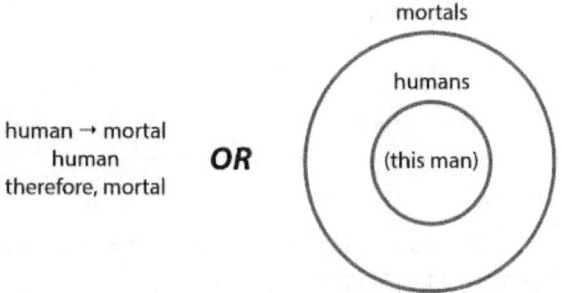

Figure 1.3. "All" and "If" Statements

Diagramming "if . . . then" statements tends to be easier than diagramming a bunch of concentric circles in complex passages. When you see an "all" statement, it might be helpful to turn it into an "if . . . then" statement so that you can look for possible patterns of reasoning that follow conditional reasoning patterns. However, if your argument has "some" statements, you are probably better off visualizing the argument with either a diagram (e.g., the circles above or a Venn diagram), depending on your preference.

"No"/"None" Statements

Examine the following statement:

No advanced society fails to take care of its elderly.

Some readers will interpret this statement as, "If you are not an advanced society, then you fail to take care of your elderly." This, however, is wrong. This statement is really saying "All advanced societies do take care of their elderly." Rewriting this statement in "if . . . then" terms results in "If a society is advanced, then it takes care of its elderly," not "If a society is not advanced, then it does not take care of its elderly." The latter is a **mistaken negation**.

The following steps describe the transformation process for reading a "no" statement more directly:

- Start with "No advanced society fails to take care of its elderly."
- Process the "no":
  - "Advanced societies do not fail to take care of their elderly."
- Remove the double negative:
  - "Advanced societies take care of their elderly."

Some additional examples (equivalent forms) appear in Table 1.11.

Table 1.11. Equivalent Forms		
NO/NONE STATEMENT	**ALL STATEMENT**	**"IF…THEN" STATEMENT**
No apes can talk.	All apes are incapable of talking.	If it is an ape, then it cannot talk.
None of the chairs are blue.	All of the chairs are not blue.	If it is a chair, then it is not blue.
No fried foods are healthy.	All fried foods are unhealthy.	If it is a fried food, then it is unhealthy.
None of the candidates has any experience.	All of the candidates lack experience.	If a candidate, then no experience.

Numbers

Many people get confused by the LSAT's use of words like *some*, *few*, *many*, and *most*. These words seem vague, but they do have consistent definitions.

Some means "one or more"—not "more than one." If you say, "Some of the books on the shelf are green," you are saying, "There are one or more green books on the shelf." Even though you say, "some green books," using the plural form of books, you are not actually saying that there are two or more green books. Consider what you have to do to disprove someone who makes a "some" statement:

Person 1: "Some of the books on the shelf are green."

You: "That's not true. There are no green books on the shelf."

Here, your counterargument is effective. But consider this:

Person 1: "Some of the books on the shelf are green."

You: "That's not true. There is one green book on the shelf."

Here, your counterargument is not effective. You have not disproved person 1, because you have not shown that there are no green books on the shelf.

Also note that saying "Some of the books on the shelf are green" does not imply that some of the books on the shelf are not green. It may be the case that all of the books on the shelf are green. Even so, it would still be true that some books on the shelf are green.

The term *most* means "more than half." If you have one hundred students, "most students" would be fifty-one or more. If you have ten students, "most" would be at least six students. Consider the following argument:

Premise: Most French majors are familiar with Latin.

Premise: Most French majors are well versed in poetry.

Conclusion: Therefore, some people who are familiar with Latin are well-versed in poetry.

This is a valid argument. If we pretend that there are one hundred French majors, then there must be at least fifty-one who are familiar with Latin, and fifty-one who are well-versed in poetry. Even if we try to minimize the amount of overlap between those who are familiar with Latin and those who are well-versed in poetry, there will still be some overlap, so the conclusion follows with 100 percent certainty that some people who are familiar with Latin are well-versed in poetry.

The words *few* and *many* are relative to each other. *Few* means "less than many." *Many* means "more than a few."

You may think those are ridiculous definitions, but consider how we use the term *many*. If we are talking about grains of rice, is ten enough to qualify as "many"? Probably not. One hundred would probably not count as "many." But if we are talking about elephants, three elephants could be many elephants. *Many* is a relative term, depending on the object it modifies. It is fair to assume that the word *many* means "at least two"; however, be careful with the phrase "too many." As you well know, sometimes even one of a thing can be too many—it all depends upon context.

Few is also a relative term. A "few" blood cells could mean "hundreds" of blood cells, while a "few" skyscrapers may mean "one or two." When you see the term *few*, it is best to treat it like the term *some* and note that it is simply "smaller than many."

The term *all* and the phrase "not all" are opposites. The argument "All plants are green" could be disproved by the simple statement "Not all plants are green." "Not all" does not mean that no plants are green, so the counterargument is valid. This makes extreme statements like "All plants are green" very difficult to support; the burden of proof for defeating such arguments is very low. On the contrary, the burden of proof for defeating statements like "Some plants are green" is much higher, since you would have to show that every single plant in existence is not green.

Extreme Language in LSAT Arguments

A fundamental principle of logic is that the conclusion cannot be stronger than the premises supporting it. For example, consider the following flawed argument:

Premise: Larry and Ted smoke two packs of cigarettes a day and stay in excellent health.

Conclusion: So, most people could smoke two packs of cigarettes a day and stay in excellent health.

The problem with this argument is that it uses a premise about two people to support a broad conclusion about most people. Just because something is true of two people does not mean that it will apply generally. For LSAT questions asking what must be true, choose answers whose truth is 100 percent certain based on the given information.

Table 1.12 lists common modifiers, organized from extreme to modest.

Table 1.12. Common Modifiers

EXTREME	MODERATE	MODEST
every/everyone	most	some
any	all	few
all	-	not all
none	-	-
only	-	-
always	often	sometimes
never	seldom, rarely	-
will	tends to/generally	may
must	probably	can
-	likely	could
should/ought to	-	-

Remember, your premise should be at least as strong as your conclusion. It is okay if your premise is stronger than your conclusion, but you cannot make a sound argument if your conclusion is more extreme than your premise.

Practice Questions

Each statement means either "B → I" or "I → B." None of the statements are ambiguous. None of the statements mean more than one of these two conditional expressions.

1. For each of the conditional statements below,
   - Diagram the statement as "B → I" if it is equivalent in meaning to "If the dog is barking, then there is an intruder."
   - Diagram the statement as "I → B" if it is equivalent in meaning to "If there is an intruder, then the dog is barking."

Conditional Statement	Your Diagram
A) The dog does not fail to bark when there is an intruder.	
B) Either there is an intruder or the dog is not barking.	
C) There cannot be an intruder unless the dog barks.	
D) There must be an intruder in order for the dog to bark.	

E) The dog cannot bark unless there is an intruder.	
F) Either the dog is barking or there is no intruder.	
G) The presence of an intruder requires that the dog barks.	
H) If the dog is not barking, then there is no intruder.	
I) There is an intruder only if the dog barks.	
J) The dog barks only if there is an intruder.	
K) If there is no intruder, then the dog is not barking.	
L) If the dog barks, then there is an intruder.	
M) The presence of an intruder ensures that the dog barks.	
N) The dog's barking ensures that there is an intruder.	
O) The dog's barking is sufficient to assert that there is an intruder.	
P) There is an intruder if the dog barks.	
Q) The dog's barking requires that there be an intruder.	
R) The dog must bark for there to be an intruder.	
S) The dog barks if there is an intruder.	
T) Only if there is an intruder does the dog bark.	
U) Only if the dog is barking is there an intruder.	
V) The presence of an intruder is sufficient to assert that the dog barks.	
W) The dog must be barking or else there would not be an intruder.	

2. Rewrite the following conditional statements in "if . . . then" form.
    A) Completing law school requires lots of reading.
    B) Mark will not become a Supreme Court clerk unless he develops better interviewing skills.
    C) In order to be elected, Griswold must change his rhetoric.
    D) The tide must have come in, or else she would be selling seashells on the seashore.
    E) Whales are mammals.
    F) Only mammals are whales.

Chapter 1 - Fundamental Logical Concepts

> G) Slovakia will only refrain from invading Poland in the event of rapid economic improvement.
> H) Meteors could not have killed the dinosaurs unless debris is fatal.
> I) Only ham and cheese sandwiches are available for five dollars from Jimmy John's.
> J) My cell phone will ring only if I forget to turn it on silent.
> K) Lindsey must have eaten too many hot peppers, or she would not be suffering from acid reflux.

Informal Logic (Inductive Reasoning)

As mentioned earlier, informal logic (inductive reasoning) is used in any argument that can be strengthened or weakened by bringing in additional premises. In the sections that follow, the patterns of reasoning discussed will generally occur in inductive arguments.

For a thorough analysis of an inductive argument, please review the Ford Focus example.

You should recognize that you can turn an inductive argument into a deductive argument by adding a sufficient assumption that guarantees the argument's conclusion. Once you have guaranteed the argument's conclusion with 100 percent certainty, there is nothing you can do to make the conclusion any stronger or weaker. This, by definition, would be a deductive argument.

At first glance, these logical concepts may seem foreign. Consider, though, that you already use inductive and deductive reasoning on a regular basis. You simply did not know that the way in which you argued was called "inductive." Take charge of the language and logic that you use on a daily basis; become so fluent in the concepts laid out here that you can easily explain them to a peer.

You will find that improving on the LSAT is a matter of practice, experience, and familiarity. This is not a test for which you can cram a lot of information and hope to do well. Rather, you improve on the LSAT by confronting your mistakes one at a time, examining your thought process, and recalibrating your logical processes so that you will not make the same mistakes in the future. Improving on the LSAT is a lot like learning a language: memorizing flash cards is nearly useless, while actually learning how the grammar and structure of the language works (through immersion or textbook learning) is far more effective.

Condition, Correlation, and Causation

Do not confuse correlation with causation. This trap is all over the LSAT, and you should learn to watch out for it. Consider the following situation:

> **Proposition 1:** Jordan drinks coffee on Mondays.
>
> **Proposition 2:** Jordan gets headaches on Mondays.

Here, we have an example of a correlation between two things: coffee and Jordan's headaches. We say these two things are correlated because they happen together; the incidence of Jordan's headaches is related to the incidence of Jordan's coffee drinking. Other examples of correlations include "Crime tends to be higher in low-income neighborhoods" (here, crime and poverty are correlated), or "Rugby players generally weigh more than average" (here, weight and playing rugby are correlated).

Just because two things are correlated, however, does not mean that one of those things causes the other. For example:

> **Premise:** Jordan drinks coffee on Mondays.
>
> **Premise:** Jordan gets headaches on Mondays.
>
> **Conclusion:** Therefore, coffee causes Jordan's headaches.

You will see arguments like this over and over again on the LSAT. They are all flawed. Based on the correlation between coffee and Jordan's headaches, there are several possibilities:

1. Coffee causes Jordan's headaches.

2. Headaches cause Jordan to drink coffee.

3. A third factor causes Jordan to get headaches and to drink coffee.

4. It is coincidental that Jordan drinks coffee and gets headaches on the same day (i.e., some factor causes Jordan to drink coffee and some other, unrelated, factor causes Jordan's headaches).

On the LSAT, it is common to immediately assume that the first possibility is true without first stopping to rule out other possibilities. This is a problem, because if all we have to go on is the correlation, we really do not know that coffee causes Jordan's headaches. Perhaps Jordan gets headaches every Monday and then drinks coffee to cure them. Or, perhaps Jordan stays out late on Sunday nights, resulting in a headache and the need to drink coffee the next morning. These are all possibilities. Of course, it is also possible that one factor causes Jordan to drink coffee, and a different factor causes Jordan to get headaches. This would be an example of **coincidence**.

Here's how you would argue causation based on a correlation:

Premise: Jordan drinks coffee on Mondays.

Premise: Jordan gets headaches on Mondays.

Premise: Nothing else other than coffee could plausibly cause Jordan's headaches.

Conclusion: Therefore, coffee causes Jordan's headaches.

Thus, given a correlation between two factors X and Y, these are the possibilities:

1. X causes Y.

2. Y causes X.

3. There is a common cause of both X and Y.

4. One factor (A) causes X, and another factor (B) causes Y (coincidence).

If the first possibility is your conclusion, you would strengthen this conclusion by ruling out possibilities 2 – 4. "Nothing else could cause Y" is a broad statement and does well. Similarly, you would weaken this conclusion by adding in any one of possibilities 2 – 4. In an argument flaw question, you would point out that an argument concluding any one of these possibilities "fails to consider the possibility that" one of the others is true. Keep this in mind as you complete Logical Reasoning sections: cause-and-effect arguments should be a red flag that makes you look for correlation-causation confusion.

Note that correlation and causation are both distinct from condition. A conditional statement would be "If Jordan has a headache, then he has drunk coffee." This is different from causation, because this statement does not tell us whether headaches cause Jordan to drink coffee or vice versa. As we discussed earlier, all this sentence tells us is that Jordan's headache is a sufficient condition to assert that Jordan has drunk coffee, and that drinking coffee is a necessary condition for asserting that Jordan has a headache. Do not assume from a conditional statement like "If A, then B" that A causes B.

The following are independent concepts:

- If there was a flood, then it rained a lot. ≠ The flood caused it to rain a lot.

- If the dog barked, then there was an intruder. ≠ The dog's bark caused there to be an intruder.

The following set of examples illustrates the difference between correlation, condition, and causation:

Correlation: Competitive parents tend to have more aggressive children than collaborative parents.

Condition: If parents are competitive, then their children will be aggressive.

Causation: Competitive parents influence their children to become aggressive.

Argument by Analogy, Example, or Illustration

An **argument by analogy** exists when you attempt to prove your conclusion by appealing to logic in a similar argument. Let's say you are trying to get a parking ticket dismissed:

Premise: I got a parking ticket in front of my own house in broad daylight.

Premise: I know I was blocking the driveway, but it was my driveway.

Premise: Last week, Mr. Smith got a ticket for blocking the driveway in front of his own house, and he got his ticket dismissed.

Conclusion: I should get my ticket dismissed also.

Here, you are arguing that the same reasoning that applied to Mr. Smith should apply to you as well. This style of reasoning will be one of the major components of your law school written work, so it is to your benefit to understand analogies.

Note that this is an **inductive argument**, which means that the conclusion does not follow with 100 percent certainty from the premises. It is certainly possible to add additional premises to the argument that would either strengthen or weaken the conclusion. For example, what if Mr. Smith were only blocking six inches of his driveway, while the author here blocked his entire driveway? Or what if Mr. Smith lived by himself, while the author here lived with others and prevented them from using the driveway? If these distinctions were true, then the argument would become weaker.

Examples and illustrations are different from analogies. An **example** or **illustration** is a specific instance of a broad or general statement. For example:

Premise: It is unfair to prevent people from using their own property according to their wishes.

Example: For example, it would be unfair to prevent someone from destroying artwork that they own entirely.

Conclusion: Therefore, we should be lenient when drafting our state's property laws to allow people to use and destroy property according to their wishes.

Advocacy

Many LSAT arguments advocate a recommendation: they conclude with a statement about what someone *should* do in a given situation. These "should" statements are also called **normative statements**. A fundamental principle of logic is that, in order to prove a normative conclusion, you must have a normative premise. Consider the following argument:

Premise: Antonio, the bus driver, was going thirty-five miles per hour over the speed limit.

Premise: Antonio was also talking on his phone and trying to eat a cheeseburger.

Premise: Clearly, Antonio caused the accident.

Conclusion: Therefore, the bus company should sanction Antonio.

Now, you might be saying to yourself, "Sounds fine to me." It is true; this is not a bad argument. The problem is that we cannot conclude that the bus company should sanction Antonio without some kind of premise that defines when sanctions are appropriate. We need another premise—something like "The bus company should sanction drivers who recklessly cause accidents."

If we add this as a premise and then read our other premises (telling us that Antonio was a driver who recklessly caused an accident), then we can draw our conclusion with certainty. Again, consider this argument:

Premise: Proposition 24 would cut texting while driving in half by raising the fine to $1,000.

Premise: If we cut the incidence of texting while driving in half, there would likely be five hundred fewer accidents each year.

Conclusion: Therefore, we should support Proposition 24.

What is missing here is a statement like "We should support propositions that are likely to reduce the number of accidents." If we add this "should" statement to our premises, then our conclusion is logical.

If a course of action is possible, does that mean you should do it? Even if the action has good consequences, does that necessarily mean you have an obligation to take it? Eating broccoli, creating jobs for unemployed individuals, and providing subsidized education to the poor may all be courses of action that are possible and good, but just because you could do something does not automatically mean that you should.

In your day-to-day life, you have various normative principles that tell you which courses of action you personally should do. Sometimes, a possible course of action might have significant costs or disadvantages. For example, what if Proposition 24 (discussed earlier) costs $100 million to implement and enforce. Is it still worth it? Whether it is or not is a subjective value judgment, and that is why we need to have a "should" premise in any argument in which we are trying to justify a "should" conclusion.

Arguments that Rule Out Alternatives

Frequently, LSAT arguments operate by eliminating alternatives. For example, if there are three possible courses of action, an author might provide evidence that refutes two of the courses of action in order to conclude that the third is advisable. For example:

> The only ways we can maintain our market share are to develop a new product, to create a new marketing campaign, or to lower our prices. Unfortunately, lowering our prices is unrealistic because we cannot remain profitable. Furthermore, the costs involved in developing a new product are prohibitive, given our current lack of cash flow. Accordingly, we should start a new marketing campaign immediately.

This argument advocates one of three possible solutions, and it arrives at its conclusion by ruling out the other two alternatives. Keep this pattern of reasoning in mind on Method of Reasoning questions.

Predictions

Many LSAT arguments operate by making a **prediction**:

> Speeding tickets in Mason County are now so costly that no one saves enough money by speeding to justify paying the fine. Therefore, since people prefer to save money when they can, drivers will no longer speed in Mason County.

Notice the difference between this prediction and the earlier advocacy examples. There are no normative statements here, nothing about whether someone should or should not speed. This is an

objective prediction about what is likely to happen, given the premises about the cost of speeding. When you see a prediction like this, you should consider whether the prediction is likely to come true, based on the premises. If the prediction is likely to come true based only on the premises stated, then the argument is strong; if the prediction is unlikely, then the argument is weak.

Usually, these kinds of arguments do not address every possible factor that may bear on the predicted outcome. That is, there are unknowns that impact whether the conclusion is likely or unlikely. The author making the argument must assume that these unknowns are in the author's favor. You can strengthen a prediction by showing that these unknown factors are true, or weaken a prediction by showing that these unknown factors are false. For example, the following is a weakened question, based on the preceding argument:

> *A study conducted in a small town found that the installation of surveillance cameras in public areas resulted in a 25 percent decrease in crime rates over the course of a year; therefore, the town council concluded that installing more surveillance cameras would continue to reduce crime rates in the future.*

Which of the following answers would WEAKEN the argument above?
- A) The crime rates in neighboring towns without surveillance cameras also decreased by a similar amount in the same period.
- B) The surveillance cameras were installed in areas that already had low crime rates.
- C) The presence of surveillance cameras shifted some criminal activities to areas not covered by cameras.
- D) The town also increased the number of police patrols and community outreach programs during the same period.
- E) The surveillance cameras are subject to frequent malfunctions and require constant maintenance.

The best answer option is D:

The premises support a correlation between surveillance cameras and decreased crime rates. The conclusion argues that surveillance cameras reduce the incidence of crime; however, as we saw earlier, there are alternative possibilities that this argument has failed to eliminate. What are all of these possibilities?

> 1. It is possible that surveillance cameras really do reduce crime rates.
>
> 2. It is possible that other factors influenced the crime rate in the small town.
>
> 3. It is possible that the decrease in crime was purely coincidental.

Since the author's hypothesis depends upon the truth of the first possibility, we can weaken his argument by having one of the other possibilities be true instead. Let's find an answer:

Option A is incorrect. While this option suggests a correlation between reduced crime rates and alternative factors, it does not provide a direct cause-and-effect relationship that weakens the town council's conclusion about the effectiveness of their own cameras.

Option B is incorrect. While this option states that the cameras were placed in less critical areas, it does not directly weaken the conclusion that more cameras will continue to reduce crime.

Option C is incorrect. This option suggests that the crime was displaced by the cameras, which would only weaken the argument if it were not the case that the overall crime rate decreased.

Option D states that the town implemented other measures in an effort to reduce crime; namely, it increased police patrols and community outreach programs. Either of these efforts may be responsible for the decrease in crime rates. Bearing this in mind, it is entirely possible that the cameras had no impact, and that it was these other factors that drove the change.

Option E is incorrect. Although it would be a burden to continually maintain the cameras, and malfunctions may make them less efficacious in recording crime, it does not challenge the idea that the presence of the cameras was enough to have an impact on the crime rate.

Likelihood

Note that the word *probably* means "likely." Consider this argument:

> "The Tigers have the best players and the best coach, so they are probably going to win the series."

However, consider the difference between likelihood and certainty:

> "The Bears are the most likely team to win the playoffs. Thus, the Bears are almost certain to win."

What if there were nineteen teams in the playoffs? The Bears might have a 10 percent chance of winning, and each of the other teams might have a 5 percent chance of winning. The Bears would be the most likely to win, but with a 10 percent chance of winning, this does not support the conclusion that they will almost certainly win. Such a conclusion would require a much greater likelihood of winning than 10 percent.

> **Helpful Hint**:
>
> Remember to read these principles as "if . . . then" statements:
>
> 1. If there is intended benefit and actual benefit, then the act is good.
>
> 2. If the act is wrong, then it harmed another.
>
> 3. If the act destroys another's property and was done without permission, then it is wrong.

Practice Question

3. A recent study found that intermittent fasting leads to a 91 percent higher risk of dying from heart disease. On the basis of this evidence, the author hypothesized that intermittent fasting is a significant cause of heart disease.

Which one of the following, if true, casts the MOST doubt on the author's hypothesis?
A) The individuals in the study who practiced intermittent fasting were also more likely to be sedentary and to smoke, and the study did not take these factors into account.
B) The study was funded by an organization that promotes a competing dietary approach.
C) Intermittent fasting is associated with other health benefits, such as improved insulin sensitivity and weight loss.
D) The study was conducted over a short period, making it difficult to establish long-term health effects.
E) The study participants who did not practice intermittent fasting experienced other health issues unrelated to cardiovascular disease.

Principles and Applications

What is a principle? A **principle** is a general rule that could apply to more than one situation. We use principles to guide our decisions, and we apply principles to situations in order to make judgments about those situations. The following describe some categories of principles, with examples of each kind.

Moral Principles

- An act is good if it is intended to benefit another individual and succeeds in benefiting that individual. (IB + SB → G)
- An act is wrong only if it harms another individual. (W → H)
- It is wrong to destroy another individual's property without permission. (WP → WD)

Duties and Obligations (not necessarily moral in nature)

- Lawyers have a duty to put their clients' interests above their own.
- People in positions of power should not exploit their influence.
- Everyone who earns income must pay taxes.

General Tendencies

- Rugby players tend to weigh more than baseball players.
- On average, organic tomatoes are half the size of common tomatoes.
- Slightly overweight people are generally healthier than very underweight people.

Applications

So how are principles actually used? Well, let's take our set of moral principles (above) and apply them to this scenario:

Marcia wanted to do a favor for her neighbor, David, so she shoveled the snow off of his driveway.

Based on our first principle and this scenario, what can we conclude? Marcia intended to benefit David, and Marcia succeeded in benefiting David; therefore, Marcia's act was good.

What if we had this scenario:

Allison intentionally stepped on Christopher's foot, harming him severely.

Based on our principles and this scenario, what can we conclude? If you answered, "Nothing," then you are exactly right.

Our first principle provides that if there is intended benefit and actual benefit, then the act is good. Here, we do not have intended or actual benefit, so the principle cannot be used to prove anything. We therefore move on.

Our second principle says that if an act is wrong, it must harm another individual. Another way of saying this is if an act does not harm another individual, then it is not wrong. Note that this principle can never be used to argue that an act is wrong. If we know that someone did not harm another, then we know that an act is not wrong, but we have no basis whatsoever for concluding that an act is wrong. Just because an act harms another individual does not mean it is wrong; that would invoke a mistaken reversal. The only valid arguments you can make using the second principle are as follows:

- An act is wrong only if it harms another individual. (W → H)
- Ben's act was wrong. (W)
- Therefore, Ben's act harmed someone else. (W → H)

or

- An act is wrong only if it harms another individual. Ben's act did not harm anyone else.

- Therefore, Ben's act was not wrong.

In shorthand, our principle is "wrong → harm." The only things this principle can prove are "harm" (given the premise "wrong"), or "~wrong" (given the premise "~harm").

If you wanted to prove that an act was wrong, you would need a principle that you could write out as "[set of conditions] → wrong." For example, you might create the principle "It is wrong to injure another individual's body parts intentionally." Then, given our scenario with Allison, we would be able to logically conclude that Allison's act of intentionally stepping on Christopher's foot was wrong.

Logical Reasoning Tip

On many Logical Reasoning questions, you will be asked to add principles into arguments to "justify" the conclusion (i.e., to make the conclusion 100 percent certain based on the premises and your new principle). Look carefully at the conclusion. If the conclusion says, "We should save the bald eagle," what do you need to look for? You need to look for a premise that tells you what you *should* save, not a premise that tells you what you should not save. Try adding in a principle to justify the following argument:

Our borders are vulnerable to enemy attack, so we should deploy additional troops. (V → D)

You do not want an answer that says, "When borders are secure, we should not deploy additional troops." You want an answer that says, "When borders are not secure, we should deploy additional troops" (NS → D). That is the sort of principle that will justify the conclusion in the argument.

Practice Question

4. Speeding tickets in Mason County are now so costly that no one saves enough money by speeding to justify paying the fine. Therefore, since people prefer to save money when they can, drivers will no longer speed in Mason County.

Which of the following answers would WEAKEN the argument above?
 A) People care about long-term savings as much as they care about short-term savings.
 B) People abide by the law only when it makes sense for them to do so.
 C) People generally underestimate the risk of being stopped for speeding.
 D) People treat speeding tickets as day-to-day expenses.
 E) People derive pleasure from speeding when police are not present.

ANSWER KEY

1. These statements are variants of "If B, then I (B → I)": B, D, E, K, L, M, O, P, Q, R, and U.

These statements are variants of "If I, then B (I → B)": A, C, F, G, H, J, N, S, T, V, W, and X.

2. A) If you complete law school, then you have read a lot.

B) If Mark became a Supreme Court clerk, then he developed better interviewing skills.

C) If Griswold was elected, then he must have changed his rhetoric.

D) If the tide has not come in, then she sells seashells on the seashore.

E) If it is a whale, then it is a mammal.

F) If it is a whale, then it is a mammal.

G) If Slovakia refrains from invading Poland, then there was rapid economic improvement.

H) If meteors killed the dinosaurs, then debris is fatal.

I) If it is available for five dollars from Jimmy John's, then it is a ham and cheese sandwich. (Note: "If it is a five-dollar sandwich from Jimmy John's, then it is ham and cheese" is incorrect. This would allow other food items besides sandwiches to be available for five dollars, which is inconsistent with the condition expressed.)

J) If my cell phone rings, then I forgot to turn it on silent.

K) If Lindsey suffers from acid reflux, then she has eaten too many hot peppers.

3. A: Notice the leap from the premises to the conclusion. The premises support a correlation between intermittent fasting and increased incidence of cardiovascular disease. The conclusion argues that intermittent fasting causes cardiovascular disease; however, as we saw earlier, there are alternative possibilities that this argument has failed to eliminate. What are all of the possibilities?

1. It is possible that intermittent fasting really does cause cardiovascular disease.

2. It is possible that the study ignores other lifestyle factors that might be contributing to cardiovascular disease.

3. Alternatively, it is possible that those who choose to practice intermittent fasting are likely to have common traits that are factors in the development of cardiovascular disease.

4. Finally, the apparent link between intermittent fasting and cardiovascular disease might be coincidental.

Since the author's hypothesis depends upon the truth of the first possibility, we can weaken his argument by having one of the other possibilities be true instead:

Option A tells us that the participants were more likely to be sedentary and smokers; both of these factors are known to contribute to cardiovascular disease. If it is true that the study did not take this into account, then it is likely that intermittent fasting had nothing to do with the increased cardiovascular risk in participants. This is a great weakener because it provides an alternative explanation for the higher incidence of cardiovascular disease in participants who engaged in intermittent fasting.

Option B is incorrect. Although this option reveals a bias in the company that conducted the study, it does not provide a direct reason that intermittent fasting might not cause cardiovascular disease. It questions the study's credibility, but not the causal link revealed therein.

Option C is incorrect. Although this option discusses potential health benefits of intermittent fasting, it does not address the specific issue of cardiovascular disease and does not weaken the causal link found by the study.

Option D is incorrect. This option questions the validity of the study due to its length, but it does not address the causal link found by the study. It introduces a concern, but is not as impactful as option A.

Option E is incorrect. This option asserts that participants who did not practice intermittent fasting also had negative health outcomes, even if they were not cardiovascular in nature. Even if this is true, it does not weaken the link between intermittent fasting and cardiovascular disease.

4. C: Option C weakens the argument by telling us that people do not know when they stand to be pulled over. Thus, even though speeding tickets cost more than people will save by speeding, people may continue to speed because they think they will get away with it.

Answer option D is a distractor. The passage tells us that people prefer to save money when they can, so it does not matter how people account for their speeding tickets. Whether they are day-to-day expenses or special expenses, people still want to avoid them when it is worthwhile to do so.

Chapter 2 – Flawed Patterns of Reasoning

Common Fallacies on the LSAT

Now that we have seen some of the ways in which arguments work, let's run through some of the common ways in which arguments can go wrong.

The LSAT evaluates your ability to analyze the logical soundness of an argument. In Logical Reasoning, and occasionally in Reading Comprehension questions, the LSAT will ask readers to identify what is wrong with an argument. Before reviewing the answer options, you must be able to spot logical errors (fallacies or flaws) to understand why an argument is flawed.

The LSAT commonly tests twenty-four fallacies. Nineteen are fallacies of inductive reasoning, as shown in Table 2.1.

Table 2.1. The Nineteen Fallacies of Inductive Reasoning: Informal Logic	
Fallacies of relevance	<ul><li>appeal to emotion (*ad populum*)</li><li>argument against the person (*ad hominem*)</li><li>false analogy</li><li>red herring</li><li>straw man</li><li>absolute properties versus relative properties; numbers and proportions</li><li>missing the point (non sequitur)</li></ul>
Fallacies of strength	<ul><li>argument from ignorance</li><li>appeal to inappropriate authority</li><li>false cause</li><li>hasty generalization</li><li>accident; "can" versus "will"</li><li>unjustified assumption</li><li>circular reasoning</li><li>false dilemma</li><li>starting point fallacy</li></ul>

Table 2.1. The Nineteen Fallacies of Inductive Reasoning: Informal Logic	
Fallacies of ambiguity	• equivocation • composition • division

The other five fallacies are those of deductive reasoning (formal logic):

1. mistaken reversal
2. mistaken negation
3. either-or fallacy
4. undistributed middle
5. contradiction

A solid understanding of these twenty-four fallacies is needed in order to spot fallacies quickly and precisely. Some courses and materials contain a seemingly endless list of fallacies (as many as one hundred). Resist the urge to create new categories; the fallacies that you will encounter on the LSAT will fall into the categories given in Table 2.1. (inductive reasoning) and listed above (deductive reasoning).

When you see a fallacy that appears to be a new type, stop and consider the twenty-four fallacies and where the new type of fallacy belongs within those twenty-four. If you cannot place the fallacy as a variation on one of the twenty-four, at least place it in one of the five broad categories:

1. relevance
2. strength
3. presumption
4. ambiguity
5. formal logic

As you work through Argument Flaw Logical Reasoning questions, spend time reviewing those that you miss to make sure you understand exactly which fallacy the argument is committing.

Learning twenty-four fallacies is a manageable task, especially if you learn them in groups and develop working definitions and examples of each type. Each of the following twenty-four entries contains the following:

- the common name of the fallacy
- an explanation of the fallacy
- the definition of the fallacy, worded to reflect the wording of the answer options you will see on Argument Flaw Logical Reasoning questions
- a real-life example of the fallacy
- an example of the fallacy from an actual LSAT Logical Reasoning question

Expect to encounter these fallacies in almost every type of Logical Reasoning question on the test as well as in some Reading Comprehension passages. Be careful not to commit these fallacies yourself; you may find yourself attracted to incorrect answer options.

Fallacies of Relevance

In **fallacies of relevance**, an author either uses an irrelevant premise in an argument or makes the wrong conclusion altogether. The following are fallacies of relevance that use **irrelevant premises**:

- **appeal to emotion (*ad populum*):** persuasion by emotional rather than by intellectual means
- **argument against the person (*ad hominem*):** arguing against another's argument by attacking that person's character or conduct
- **false analogy:** supporting a conclusion by means of an apparent analogy without justifying the proposition that the two arguments are actually worthy of comparison
- **red herring** (a broad category that includes appeal to emotion, argument against the person, and false analogy): offering a deliberately misleading premise

The following are fallacies of relevance using **mistaken conclusions**:

- **straw man:** distorting an opponent's argument to make it easier to defeat
- **absolute properties versus relative properties** (numbers and proportions): using a relative property (or percentage) as a premise and an absolute property (or number) as a conclusion
- **missing the point** (non sequitur; a broad category that includes straw man and numbers and propositions): drawing an irrelevant, mistaken, or overbroad conclusion; jumping to conclusions

Appeal to Emotion

Ordinarily, arguments work by appealing to reason. Given a set of facts, the reader's reasoning leads the reader to agree with the author's conclusion. Sometimes, however, authors will appeal to the reader's emotions (conscience, fear, or sense of pity) in order to get the reader to agree with a point. **Appeals to emotion** may include emotionally charged language. Sample LSAT answer options that reflect this fallacy include the following types of statements:

- those that seek to persuade by emotional rather than by intellectual means
- those in which the author appeals to conscience rather than reason
- those that use emotive language in labeling the proposals
- those that use hyperbolic, inflammatory language that obscures the issue at hand
- those that appeal to a person's emotions rather than to that person's reason

Example: Advertisements and patriotism are common sources of emotional appeals:

1. Everyone in the know reads the *Wall Street Journal*. Subscribe today!

2. Ronald fought tooth and nail for our country's independence. He poured his sweat and blood out for our freedom. How could any worthy citizen now turn his back on such a gallant candidate for office as Ronald?

This example appeals to the conscience of the reader by making the reader feel left out; however, no rational basis is provided for subscribing. This is also called the **bandwagon effect**.

This use of patriotism appeals to the audience's emotions; no rational basis is provided to support Ronald's candidacy for office.

Argument Against the Person (*ad hominem*)

If your argument is directed against your opponents' conclusion, it is a fallacy to use a premise that attacks your opponents themselves. That is, **you should always argue against the opposing argument, not against the source of the opposing argument**.

It is an attack against the person to use a premise about a person's character or conduct to support a conclusion about that person's argument. This is a fallacy because the person's character is usually unrelated to the person's argument. A premise that concerns the person's character is irrelevant to your conclusion.

Sample LSAT answer options that reflect this fallacy include the following:

- those that avoid the issue by focusing on supporters of the proposal
- those that attack the opponents' motives instead of their argument
- those that question the motives of one side rather than offering reasons for the conclusion defended
- those that reject the conclusion of an argument on the basis of a claim about the motives of those advancing the argument
- those that call into question the truthfulness of the opponent rather than addressing the point at issue
- those that dismiss the proposals because of their source rather than because of their substance
- those that draw conclusions about the merit of a position and about the content of that position from evidence about the position's source

> **Helpful Hint**:
> The following would NOT be an attack on the person: "Dr. Ziegler is not organized and fails to keep complete records on his patient. Therefore, Dr. Ziegler is not a responsible physician." This is not a fallacy because the conclusion is about the doctor. Some LSAT questions trap you into identifying an argument like this as an *ad hominem* argument; however, when the argument's premises AND conclusion are about a person, even where the argument overtly attacks that person, it is not a fallacy. The fallacy occurs when the conclusion is about the person's argument (or book, or position), and the premise is about the person himself. Facts about a person are irrelevant to a conclusion about a person's argument.

Example: Imagine Tom wrote a book, and someone comes along and says, "Don't read that book. It can't be any good. Tom's the most selfish guy I know." This person is trying to argue that the book is not worth reading, but his premise is that the book's author is selfish. This premise is irrelevant because it attacks the book's author rather than the book itself.

False Analogy

A common pattern of reasoning is to make an argument by analogy; however, every analogy is not necessarily a good analogy. Just because two arguments are similar in one way does not mean they are similar in every other important way. A false analogy is when premises do not support a comparison between the primary argument and the analogous argument.

A sample LSAT answer option that reflects this fallacy treats two kinds of things that differ in important respects as though they do not differ.

Example:

"John was overweight. He started eating spinach and subsequently lost twenty pounds. Therefore, if Jerry, who is also overweight, starts eating spinach, he will lose twenty pounds."

John's weight loss is an analogous situation to Jerry's situation because the two were both overweight, but we do not know anything else about John and Jerry. Perhaps John was also exercising while he ate the spinach. Or perhaps Jerry has a medical condition that will prevent him from losing twenty pounds. Do not assume that whatever applies to John must also apply to Jerry. When you are being asked to identify a fallacy, you should note that the argument fails to consider the possibility that the two situations are not comparable.

Red Herring

A **red herring** is any irrelevant premise offered along the way to a conclusion. *Ad hominem* attacks and appeals to emotion fall into this category as well because they are irrelevant premises. Any deliberately misleading premise falls into this broad category; consider the red herring as a sort of catchall for irrelevant information that masquerades as support for an argument. Sample LSAT answer options that reflect this fallacy include the following:

- attempts to justify a position by appeal to an irrelevant consideration
- basing its conclusion on evidence that is almost entirely irrelevant to the point at hand
- the author citing irrelevant data

Example:

"Over the past ten years, people in Springfield have increasingly reported a belief that crime is out of control. Clearly, Springfield needs to hire more police officers."

Here, the red herring is presenting the people's belief as evidence, instead of presenting actual crime statistics. Popular opinion is different from factual evidence, so this is a deliberately misleading premise.

Example:

Labrador Bus Lines is clearly the best choice for a safe trip because it consistently files the most complete annual safety reports of any transportation provider in the country.

The bus company may file complete reports, but that does not necessarily mean that it has a record of safety. Labrador's administrative responsibility is a red herring; knowing that the company actually has a solid safety record would be a relevant premise.

Straw Man

Making a straw man argument is like putting words in somebody's mouth. In a **straw man argument**, one person makes a standard argument, and then another person distorts the first person's argument into something more extreme and easier to defeat than it actually was. The second person turns the original argument into a hollow "straw man" version, which can be easily picked apart. This is a fallacy because the second person has not actually defeated the original argument; the second person has only defeated the straw man version of the argument. Sample LSAT answer options that reflect this fallacy include the following:

- misrepresentations of the position against which it is directed
- distortions of the proposal advocated by opponents

- a distorted version of one person's proposals followed by attacks of this distorted version
- an unfair redefinition of the position being argued against in order to make it an easier target

Example:

Person 1: "Modest consumption of red wine protects against artery damage and increases the level of 'good' cholesterol in the blood; therefore, modest consumption of red wine can be good for the heart."

Person 2: "What you're saying is that I should drink more alcohol in order to be healthier. But surely that's not right! People suffer from liver disease and all kinds of negative effects because of heavy alcohol consumption."

The fallacy occurs when Person 2 says, "What you're saying is . . ." but then distorts what Person 1 is actually saying. Person 1 said that modest wine consumption *can* be good for the heart—not that it *is* good for the heart. Person 2 has distorted this statement, changing "modest wine consumption" to "more alcohol," and changing "good for the heart" to "healthier." Then, Person 2 defeats the argument that drinking more alcohol would make him healthier. This is the wrong conclusion, however, because Person 2 should have been arguing the real issue: whether modest wine consumption can be good for the heart.

Absolute Versus Relative; Numbers Versus Proportions

Explanation: Words like *healthy*, *easy*, and *wise* are absolute properties when compared with words like *healthier*, *easier*, and *wiser* (relative properties). You will encounter bad arguments where the premises contain a relative property, and the conclusion contains an absolute property. (E.g., "LSAT Reading Comprehension is less difficult than GRE verbal; therefore, the LSAT is easy.")

You will also encounter bad arguments where the premises discuss absolute numbers, but the conclusion sneakily switches the matter under discussion to a proportion, or vice versa. Sample LSAT answer options that reflect this fallacy include the following:

- The option takes no account of the relative frequency of an absolute property.
- The option bases a comparison on percentages rather than on absolute numbers.
- The argument mistakes a merely relative property for one that is absolute.

Example:

Ten percent of left-handed people play the piano, and 40 percent of right-handed people play the piano. Therefore, most piano players must be right-handed.

At first glance, this might look like a valid argument, but it makes a wrong conclusion. The problem here is that the proportions in our premises tell us what percentage of left-handed people and right-handed people play the piano, but our conclusion switches to a percentage of piano players. Based on the premises, we have no way of knowing how many piano players are left-handed and how many piano players are right-handed, so we cannot draw this conclusion.

After all, it may be the case that there are one million left-handed people and only one hundred right-handed people. In such a case, even if 40 percent of right-handed people play the piano, the argument's conclusion would be false, because most piano players would be left-handed.

Finally, remember not to bring in outside information like "most people are right-handed." That is the kind of error that will keep you from seeing the fallacy at all.

Missing the Point

Missing the point is the fallacy of jumping to conclusions. When your premises appear to lead you to a certain conclusion, but you end up concluding something else altogether (or something more extreme than would follow logically), you miss the point. Missing the point involves making an irrelevant, mistaken, or overbroad conclusion. Sample LSAT answer options that reflect this fallacy include the following:

- The option draws a conclusion that is broader in scope than is warranted by the evidence advanced.
- The option ignores available, potentially useful counterevidence.
- The option offers as an adequate defense of a practice an observation that discredits only one of several possible alternatives to that practice.
- The option fails to give any reason for the judgment it reaches.
- The option argues against a point that is not one that she was making.

Example:

A promising new restaurant has just opened on Fourth Street; however, unless it markets itself better, it will not attract much of a dinner crowd. Therefore, the restaurant's success depends on improving its marketing campaign.

The premises support the idea that the restaurant could increase its patronage with better marketing, but the conclusion goes too far, arguing that success depends on better marketing. This argument has missed the point.

Practice Questions

1. *A company wants to build a factory in a small town; the factory will bring pollution and destroy a beautiful and beloved park where children play and families gather for picnics. The company argues that the factory will provide jobs for the citizens of the town and will be good overall for the people. A local environmental group argues that the factory should not be built, citing the loss of the playground and the sadness of the children and families that used to gather there.*

Which of the following MOST accurately describes the main flaw in the environmental group's argument?
   A) It does not consider the economic benefits of the factory on the town.
   B) It fails to address the environmental impact of the factory.
   C) It appeals to sentimental feelings about the park and the town's children and families.
   D) It fails to provide evidence that the park will be rendered unusable.
   E) It does not provide an alternative location for the factory.

2. *Mary Smith has proposed a new plan for reducing traffic congestion by improving the public transportation available in her town; however, Councilman Jones argues that Mary's plan should be rejected because she has been fined multiple times for speeding violations.*

Which of the following MOST accurately describes the main flaw in Councilman Jones's argument?
- A) It assumes that Mary's plan will have no effect on traffic congestion.
- B) It attacks Mary's character rather than addressing the merits of her plan.
- C) It does not consider the potential environmental impact of implementing Mary's plan.
- D) It relies on the assumption that Mary's driving record reflects her expertise in traffic planning.
- E) It does not offer an alternative plan for reducing traffic congestion.

3. *Advocates of the new educational policy argue that, just as athletes improve their performance through rigorous repetition of a prescribed set of skill-based drills and activities, students can improve their cognitive function and grades through the implementation of a standardized and intense curriculum. They conclude that implementing a curriculum based on these ideals will guarantee improved student performance.*

Which of the following MOST accurately identifies the main flaw in the advocates' reasoning?
- A) It assumes that all students have the same capacity for academic success.
- B) It overlooks that different students have different learning styles and needs.
- C) It fails to provide evidence that a standardized curriculum is effective.
- D) It presumes that rigorous training is beneficial for all types of performance improvement.
- E) It draws an analogy between athletes and students that ignores crucial differences between physical training and academic learning.

4. *The manager of a store argues that the employees do not need raises because the store has recently won an award for great customer service.*

Which of the following MOST accurately identifies the main flaw in the manager's reasoning?
- A) It introduces an irrelevant issue about an award to distract from the wage discussion.
- B) It ignores the idea that higher wages might lead to better customer service.
- C) It assumes that the employees are content with their wages due to their award-winning performance.
- D) It fails to address the financial implications of raising the minimum wage for the store.
- E) It assumes that the award was given based on objective and relevant criteria.

5. *A politician argues against a proposed law to regulate carbon emissions, stating, "My opponent claims that we need to regulate carbon emissions to combat climate change. But his plan will shut down every factory in the country, leading to massive unemployment and economic collapse!"*

Which one of the following MOST accurately identifies the main flaw in the politician's argument?
- A) It exaggerates the extremity of his opponent's plan to combat climate change to make it easier to attack.
- B) It assumes that regulating carbon emissions will only have negative outcomes.
- C) It presumes that all factories would be affected equally by the proposed regulations.
- D) It assumes that economic collapse is a necessary effect of regulating carbon emissions.
- E) It assumes that combating climate change is not a priority compared to economic concerns.

Chapter 2 – Flawed Patterns of Reasoning

6. *The importance of weight-bearing exercise has been emphasized in recent years. As a result, 70 percent of runners and 50 percent of bicyclists have introduced strength training into their fitness routines. Thus, more runners than bicyclists have begun strength training.*

Which of the following MOST accurately identifies the main flaw in the above argument?
- A) It assumes that runners have a greater need for strength training than bicyclists do.
- B) It fails to account for the possibility that bicyclists may engage in other forms of exercise that provide similar benefits to strength training.
- C) It presumes that the percentage of individuals who have introduced strength training in recent years accurately reflects the total number of people engaged in strength training.
- D) It overlooks the fact that there may be more bicyclists than runners overall.
- E) It ignores the fact that runners and bicyclists may engage in strength training for different reasons.

7. *A student argues against comprehensive exams at the end of the academic year, stating that many students find these exams stressful and often perform poorly as a result. The student argues that schools should instead focus on continuous assessment throughout the semester.*

Which of the following MOST accurately describes the main flaw in the student's argument?
- A) It overlooks the fact that some students perform well under exam conditions and benefit from the challenge.
- B) It presumes that eliminating comprehensive exams will automatically improve student performance.
- C) It ignores the main purpose of comprehensive exams, which is to evaluate overall mastery of the subject matter of a course.
- D) It assumes that comprehensive exams are inherently more stressful than other forms of assessment.
- E) It assumes that students' performances on comprehensive exams accurately reflect their understanding of the material.

Fallacies of Strength

In **fallacies of strength**, an author might have relevant premises, but the premises are too weak to support the conclusion. The following are fallacies of strength:

- **argument from ignorance:** concluding that something is true because it has not been proven false, or vice versa
- **appeal to inappropriate authority:** citing an expert as support for an argument in a field beyond the expert's expertise
- **false cause:** confusing correlation with causation, or switching a cause and an effect
- **hasty generalization:** drawing a broad conclusion on the basis of a small or unfair sample

Argument from Ignorance

Just because something has not been proven true does not mean it is necessarily false. Likewise, just because something has not been proven false does not mean it is necessarily true. An argument that attempts to use either of these lines of reasoning is an **argument from ignorance**. To remember this

fallacy, consider the adage **"Absence of evidence is not evidence of absence."** Sample LSAT answer options that reflect this fallacy include the following:

- The option confuses an absence of evidence for a hypothesis with the existence of evidence against the hypothesis.
- The option takes the failure of a given argument to establish its conclusion as the basis for claiming that the view expressed by that conclusion is false.
- The option takes lack of evidence for the existence of a state of affairs as evidence that there can be no such state of affairs.

Both of the following example arguments are arguments from ignorance:

Example:

- You have no evidence to prove there is a God; therefore, God does not exist.
- You have no evidence to prove there is not a God; therefore God does exist.

Appeal to Inappropriate Authority

Experts are useful, but only in their fields of expertise. An **appeal to inappropriate authority** is citing an expert as support for an argument in a field beyond the expert's expertise. Many advertisements commit this fallacy when they use a celebrity to endorse a product that the celebrity may know nothing about. Sample LSAT answer options that reflect this fallacy include the following:

- options that make an illegitimate appeal to the authority of an expert
- options that make an irrelevant appeal to an authority

False Cause

A mere correlation between two events does not prove causation. **False cause**—switching cause for effect, or confusing correlation for causation—is a common fallacy on the LSAT. Any time you see "cause" in a conclusion (or any of its synonyms), look for one of these mistakes: confusing a correlation for causation, confusing a temporal relationship (A happened before B) for causation (A caused B), or confusing a cause for an effect. Sample LSAT answer options that reflect this fallacy include the following:

- those which assume a causal relationship where only a correlation has been indicated
- those which mistake the observation that one thing happens after another for proof that the second thing is the result of the first
- those that confuse the coincidence of two events with a causal relation between the two
- those that mistake an effect for a cause
- those that explain one event as being caused by another event, even though both events must have actually been caused by some third, unidentified event

Example:

"Two years ago, I started buying my parts from Vic's. Now, all my customers have left. Clearly, Vic's parts have cost me my livelihood."

Just because customers left following the author's decision to buy parts from Vic's does not mean that Vic's parts caused the customers to leave.

Hasty Generalization

Drawing a conclusion about a large group of people or events requires more than a few pieces of evidence. Drawing a broad conclusion based on one or a few instances (or an unfair sample) is a **hasty generalization**.

The term *general* as in "general principle" or "generalization" is important. If a statement applies generally, that means that the statement applies to "most" cases—that is, to more than half of potential cases. "Bob eats candy when he is very hungry" is not a general principle because it can only apply to Bob. "People tend to eat unhealthy food when they become very hungry" is a general principle because it can be applied to specific people and specific food selections. Sample LSAT answer options that reflect this fallacy include the following:

- relies on evidence drawn from a sample that there is reason to believe is unrepresentative
- generalizes from only a few instances
- a few exceptional cases as the basis for a claim about what is true in general
- generalizes on the basis of a sample consisting of atypical cases

Example:

"My friend Marty has eaten red meat three times a day for forty years, and his health is excellent, so surely there is nothing wrong with eating lots of red meat." This argument hastily generalizes from Marty to a generic statement about the merits of eating red meat. Just because Marty can eat a large quantity of red meat does not mean everyone else can.

Practice Questions

8. *A scientist argues, "We have found no evidence that life exists on other planets; therefore, we can conclude that there is no life anywhere else in the universe."*

Which of the following MOST accurately identifies the main flaw in the scientist's argument?
- A) It fails to consider that life on other planets may be different from life on earth.
- B) It assumes that the lack of evidence for life on other planets is conclusive proof that life does not exist elsewhere in the universe.
- C) It presumes that scientists have already searched the entire universe for evidence of life.
- D) It ignores the possibility that life on other planets might be undetectable with current technology.
- E) It relies on the assumption that evidence of life on other planets would be easily found if it existed.

9. *A health blogger writes, "Dr. Smith, a world-renowned heart surgeon, says that taking daily vitamin supplements is essential for good health. Everyone should therefore take daily vitamin supplements to stay healthy."*

Which of the following MOST accurately identifies the main flaw in the blogger's argument?
- A) It fails to consider that some people might have adverse reactions to certain vitamin supplements.
- B) It ignores the possibility that dietary and lifestyle changes might be more effective than supplements.
- C) It presumes that all vitamin supplements are of high quality.
- D) It overlooks the fact that Dr. Smith might have a financial interest in promoting vitamin supplements.
- E) It assumes that a heart surgeon is an expert in all areas of human health, including nutrition.

10. *A marketing analyst argues, "Since our company started using green packaging, sales have increased by 20 percent; therefore, the green packaging is responsible for the increase in sales."*

Which of the following MOST accurately identifies the main flaw in the analyst's argument?
- A) It overlooks the possibility that the company's marketing campaign, which coincided with the introduction of green packaging, contributed to the sales increase.
- B) It fails to consider whether customers actually prefer green packaging over the previous packaging.
- C) It assumes that the increase in sales is directly caused by the use of green packaging without considering other factors.
- D) It fails to consider the role of customer reviews and ratings in influencing sales.
- E) It assumes that the increase in sales would have occurred even if the company had not changed its packaging.

11. *A college student argues, "The student with the highest marks in my psychology class never seems to study. He goes to parties every weekend, and I never see him at the library; therefore, studying is irrelevant to academic performance. What really matters is your natural level of intellect."*

Which of the following identifies the main flaw in the student's argument?
- A) It focuses on the habits of one student and generalizes his behavior to draw broad conclusions.
- B) It does not account for the other courses that the student with the highest marks is taking.
- C) It assumes that the student with the highest marks never studies based on limited observation of his behavior.
- D) It fails to present evidence that natural intelligence is superior to good study habits.
- E) It does not acknowledge the benefits of studying.

Fallacies of Presumption

In **fallacies of presumption**, the author assumes that an important part of the argument is true without providing a logical basis for making such an assumption. The following are fallacies of presumption:

- **accident; "can" versus "will":** applying a general rule to an individual case without considering whether the individual may be the exception to the rule; confusing a possibility with certainty
- **unjustified assumption:** assuming a premise of an argument without justification

- **circular reasoning:** assuming the conclusion is true in order to prove the conclusion is true
- **false dilemma:** presenting two of several alternatives as though they were the only possible alternatives
- **starting point fallacy:** attempting to evaluate the effects of a change without knowing the facts as they existed before the change

Accident; "Can" Versus "Will"

Accident is the opposite of hasty generalization. Hasty generalization occurs when you use one or a few instances to justify a general conclusion. On the other hand, the fallacy of **accident** occurs when you use a general principle to justify a conclusion about a specific individual without stopping to think about why that individual might be an exception to the rule. Sample LSAT answer options that reflect this fallacy will have the following characteristics:

- They will apply a generalization to an exceptional case.
- They will attribute to every member of the population the properties of the average member of the population.

Example:

"On average, graduating law students who secure jobs will earn $129,000 per year. Maria just graduated law school and has a full-time job lined up. So, Maria will be earning $129,000 next year."

The problem here is that we have taken an average and rigidly applied it to Maria's specific situation without considering that Maria might have a higher- or lower-paying job.

Example:

"People who work fifteen or more hours a day tend to take active vacations. Marcus works sixteen hours a day, so he must prefer active vacations to lying around on the beach."

The problem here is that Marcus might be an exception to the rule.

Unjustified Assumption

An **unjustified assumption** is when an argument must establish a premise in order to arrive at a conclusion, and it assumes—rather than proves—that premise. Sample LSAT answer options that reflect this fallacy include the following:

- The option presumes that most consumers heed the warning labels on beverage containers.
- The option assumes that the fact of an error is proof of an intention to deceive.

Example:

"Getting into Harvard Law School requires nothing more than an undergraduate degree, a competitive LSAT score, excellent letters of recommendation, and a solid personal statement. Cheryl has excellent recommendation letters, a very competitive LSAT score, and a bachelor's degree in chemical engineering, so she'll get into Harvard Law School."

The argument never states that Cheryl had a solid personal statement, which makes its conclusion an unjustified assumption.

Circular Reasoning (Begging the Question)

Circular reasoning occurs when the author restates the argument's conclusion as support for the conclusion. Circular reasoning is also called begging the question. It is usually easy to spot because it repeats the conclusion, in some form, as a premise of the argument. Sample LSAT answer options that reflect this fallacy include the following:

- The reasons given in support of the conclusion presuppose the truth of that conclusion.
- The argument is a circular argument made up of an opening claim followed by a conclusion that merely paraphrases that claim.
- It assumes what it seeks to establish.
- It presupposes that which is to be proved.
- It assumes at the outset what the argument claims to establish through reasoning.

Example:

"Our cookies are healthy, and we know they're healthy because the kinds of people who buy our cookies buy healthy things. How do we know that our customers buy healthy things? Because they buy our healthy cookies."

The conclusion of the argument is "Our cookies are healthy," but this is also a premise of the argument.

Example:

In the movie *The Pearls of the Crown*, three thieves fight over seven valuable pearls. The thief in the middle gives two pearls to the thief on his right and two to the thief on his left. "I will keep three," he says. "How come you keep three?" says the man on his right. "Because I am the leader." "Oh. But why are you the leader?" "Because I have more pearls."

False Dilemma

If you set up a situation in which there appears to be only two alternatives, but in reality there may be other options, you have created a **false dilemma**. A false dilemma may also exist when an argument discusses a group of individuals but only discusses the two extremes of the group without considering the middle of the group. Sample LSAT answer options that reflect this fallacy include the following:

- It assumes without warrant that a situation allows only two possibilities.
- It sets up a dichotomy between alternatives that are not exclusive.

Example:

"If we don't market our new products better, we will cease being competitive. You have my marketing plan in front of you. So, either we act on this plan, or we'll end up losing our competitiveness."

This is a false dilemma because the author sets up the two apparent alternatives: follow his plan, or do not take any action at all. What if there are other marketing plans?

Starting Point Fallacy

This fallacy is closely related to false dilemma. Sometimes, an argument will compare two things in their present states and draw a conclusion about how a course of events has affected them, without considering what differences might have existed between the two things before the course of events began. Committing a **starting point fallacy** is basing a conclusion about two entities upon information

Chapter 2 – Flawed Patterns of Reasoning

gathered at the end of a process, without considering the differences between those entities that existed before the process. Sample LSAT questions that reflect this fallacy include those in which the conclusion of the argument is properly drawn.

> **Example:** "In a recent study of one hundred overweight individuals, fifty individuals were given only a special diet and fifty individuals were given both a special diet and a rigorous exercise regimen. At the end of the study, all of the individuals had lost weight, with no noticeable difference in weight loss between the two groups. Therefore, a rigorous exercise regimen has little or no effect on weight loss when combined with the special diet used in the study."

The problem with this argument is that we have no information about the differences between those in the first group and those in the second group before the study began. It is possible that the individuals who were diagnosed as needing an exercise regimen were placed in the group that received it, while the others were not. Do not assume that the two groups of individuals started at the same point unless the argument says so.

Practice Questions

12. *On average, students who use the new online study platform score higher on their exams than students who do not use the platform. Jacob has the highest exam score in the entire school; therefore, Jacob must be using the new online study platform.*

Note: Unlike most of the other questions in this chapter, the following question asks you to find an answer in which an argument commits the same fallacy as the argument in the preceding passage.

Which answer option contains flawed reasoning that is MOST similar to that contained in the preceding argument?
- A) The chess players on the school's A team generally have higher rankings than the players on the B team. Since Sarah is a member of the A team, she is likely ranked higher than most of the members of the B team.
- B) All of the city's fire stations built after 2000 have state-of-the-art equipment. This fire station has the most advanced equipment in the city, so it must have been built after 2000.
- C) Solar panels generally produce more energy in sunny climates than in cloudy ones. These solar panels are installed in a sunny climate, so they will likely produce a lot of energy.
- D) This painting is the most valuable one in the gallery. Since paintings by famous artists are on average more valuable than those by unknown artists, this painting must be by a famous artist.
- E) The new smartphones generally have better cameras than the old models. This smartphone has the highest-rated camera on the market, so it must be a new model.

13. *Biologists expect that, ultimately, all aspects of aging will be explainable in genetic terms. Achieving this goal requires knowledge of genes and their basic functions, how genes interact, and a delineation of the physiological processes to be explained. At present, there is a substantial amount of fundamental knowledge about the basic functions of genes, and the scope and character of such physiological processes as cell repair and immune response are well understood. Thus, as the biologists claim, aspects of aging are bound to receive explanations in genetic terms in the near future.*

Which of the following MOST accurately identifies the main flaw in the biologists' argument?
- A) The conclusion contradicts the claim of the biologists.
- B) The passage does not indicate that any gene-interaction knowledge has been achieved.
- C) The passage fails to describe exactly what is currently known about the basic functions of genes.
- D) The argument does not consider the ethical implications of genetic research on aging.
- E) The argument assumes that genetic explanations will replace all other explanations of aging.

14. *A nutritionist claims that her new diet plan is effective because it helps people lose weight. She explains that the diet plan works by helping individuals reduce their calorie intake, which leads to weight loss; therefore, the diet plan is successful in helping people shed pounds because it leads to weight reduction.*

Which of the following MOST accurately identifies the main flaw in the nutritionist's argument?
- A) The nutritionist assumes that weight loss is the only measure of a diet plan's effectiveness.
- B) The argument does not provide any scientific evidence to support the diet plan's effectiveness.
- C) The argument relies on the premise that the diet plan reduces calorie intake without explaining how this reduction is achieved.
- D) The nutritionist fails to consider that different people might respond to the diet plan differently.
- E) The argument assumes the conclusion in its premise, leading to circular reasoning.

15. *An environmentalist claims that, to address climate change effectively, we must either completely eliminate fossil fuel use immediately or resign ourselves to catastrophic environmental consequences. Since catastrophic environmental consequences are unacceptable, the environmentalist concludes that we must completely eliminate fossil fuel use immediately.*

Which of the following MOST accurately identifies the main flaw in the environmentalist's argument?
- A) The argument ignores other strategies that could help address climate change.
- B) The argument overlooks the possibility of technological advances that will help to mitigate climate change.
- C) The argument does not provide evidence that current fossil fuel use is unsustainable.
- D) The argument does not consider the economic consequences of eliminating fossil fuel use.
- E) The argument fails to acknowledge the role of individual actions in combating climate change.

16. *A business consultant claims that, since a specific management strategy led to significant improvements in a small family-owned business, the same strategy will lead to similar improvements in a large multinational corporation. The consultant concludes that the strategy should be adopted by all large corporations to enhance their performance.*

Which of the following MOST accurately identifies the main flaw in the business consultant's argument?
   A) The argument fails to consider that the management strategy might be costly to implement in large corporations.
   B) The argument assumes without evidence that the small family-owned business is representative of large multinational corporations.
   C) The argument overlooks the possibility that the small family-owned business had unique characteristics that contributed to the success of the strategy.
   D) The argument does not provide evidence that the management strategy is effective in improving business performance.
   E) The argument ignores other management strategies that could be more effective in large multinational corporations.

Fallacies of Ambiguity

Fallacies of ambiguity all involve wordplay. That is, they involve words that can have multiple meanings, either independently or depending upon the words with which they are paired. As you work through LSAT problems (especially Logical Reasoning), beware of ambiguous wording. Your ability to answer the questions correctly will often depend on your awareness of these potential ambiguities. The following are fallacies of ambiguity:

- **equivocation:** using a word twice in two different ways
- **composition:** arguing that a characteristic of the parts is also a characteristic of the whole
- **division:** arguing that a characteristic of the whole is also a characteristic of the parts

In addition to these specific fallacies of ambiguity, consider the following real-world examples of general ambiguity:

Example:

A sign downtown reads, "CAUTION Slow Resident Parking."

This should be read as "Caution! Slow! Resident parking," but it can be erroneously read as "Caution! Slow resident parking."

Example:

A teacher recently posted this Facebook status: "Sign of the times: I'm trying to persuade one of my students not to drop out of school through text messaging."

This is ambiguous because "through text messaging" could modify either the verb *persuade* or the verb phrase "drop out." That is, the sentence could be read as:

"I'm trying, through text messaging, to persuade my student not to drop out."

58   Chapter 2 – Flawed Patterns of Reasoning

OR

"My student is thinking about dropping out of school through text messaging, and I'm trying to persuade him not to."

Context is key to understand meaning.

Equivocation

Whenever a word is used multiple times, there is a chance that it will be used with more than one meaning. The **fallacy of equivocation** occurs when the meaning of a key term illicitly shifts within an argument. Sample LSAT answer options that reflect this fallacy include the following:

- The option uses a certain word or term equivocally.
- The argument relies on two different uses of a certain word or term.
- The option does not distinguish between two or more senses/meanings of a word or term.

Example:

"The media has an obligation to report on whatever is in the public interest. The public interest is clearly focused on the identity of the whistleblower. Therefore, the media has an obligation to report on the identity of the whistleblower."

The problem here is that the phrase "public interest" is used twice: first to mean "the public good" and then to mean "what the public wants to hear." This is equivocation.

Composition

The truth of the parts does not necessarily hold true for the whole. Will lightweight parts make a lightweight machine? Do short sentences make short paragraphs? Will exciting chapters make an exciting story? The **fallacy of composition** argues that a characteristic of the parts is also a characteristic of the whole. Sample LSAT answer options that reflect this fallacy include the following:

- The option makes the unwarranted assumption that what is true of each member of a group, taken separately, is also true of the group as a whole.
- The option assumes that because something is true of each of the parts of a whole, it is true of the whole itself.
- The option takes for granted that a whole story will have a given characteristic if each of its parts has that characteristic.

Example:

"Every member of this band is a superb musician. Therefore, this must be a superb band."

This argument is flawed because what is true of the parts (the members being superb) is not necessarily true of the whole (the band). Do not confuse this with a hasty generalization, which would base a conclusion about all band members on a premise about one or a few band members. Composition conclusions, however, are not about the band members but about the actual band as a whole.

Division

Just because something is true of the whole does not mean it will hold true of the parts. Does a heavy machine have to be built from heavy parts? Does a slow fleet of ships have to comprise slow ships? The

fallacy of division argues that a characteristic of the whole is also a characteristic of the parts. Sample LSAT answer options that reflect this fallacy include the following:

- The option assumes what is true of a group as a whole is necessarily true of each member of that group.
- The option assumes that what is true of a group of people taken collectively is also true of any individual within that group.

Example:

"The student body at this law school takes courses in over twenty disciplines. Margaret is a student at this law school; therefore, Margaret takes courses in over twenty disciplines."

Margaret is a part of the student body, but it is a fallacy to conclude that she individually takes courses in over twenty disciplines, which is an attribute of the whole group as a collective.

Practice Questions

17. *The only pets in the pet store were dogs, but they were small dogs. So, the only pets in the pet store were small pets.*

Note: *The following question asks you to find an answer that has an argument that commits the same fallacy as the argument in the preceding passage.*

Which one of the following exhibits faulty reasoning MOST similar to the faulty reasoning in the preceding argument?
- A) People who exercise have a lower risk of cardiovascular disease. Therefore, exercise helps to prevent cardiovascular disease.
- B) Drinking more water leads to clearer skin. Therefore, the cure for acne is to drink more water.
- C) The only buildings on the block were thrift stores and coffee shops, but they were tall thrift stores and coffee shops. Therefore, the only buildings on the block were tall buildings.
- D) Students who study in groups perform better on assignments; therefore, studying in groups leads to higher grades.
- E) All vegetables are healthy, and healthy foods lower your risk of cancer; therefore, eating a diet rich in vegetables helps to lower your risk of cancer.

18. *Parents of students participating in the school's fitness challenge have criticized the standards, stating that no one can safely perform all of the tasks required to pass the challenge in a single session. The coach who designed the test states that each individual task in the challenge has been done by students in the past during the course of their normal gym classes; therefore, students will be able to complete all of the tasks required by the challenge in a single session.*

Which of the following MOST accurately identifies the main flaw in the coach's argument?
- A) It relies on the assumption that the parents are not as familiar with their children's athletic abilities as their coach is.
- B) It calls into question the motives of the parents criticizing the coach's fitness challenge.
- C) It attempts to justify the coach's decision by citing reasons that people would only find plausible if they were already convinced the conclusion is true.
- D) It takes for granted that students can safely accomplish all of the tasks in a single session just because they were able to safely perform each task on its own.
- E) It does not consider the needs and abilities of the individual students.

19. *Jane attributes her excellent physical health to her food choices. She is careful to choose mostly foods that are dense in micronutrients, and she avoids most processed items. Jane ate chocolate cake at a coworker's birthday celebration; therefore, chocolate cake is a healthy food that is dense in micronutrients and is not processed.*

Note: *The following question asks you to find an answer that has an argument that commits the same fallacy as the argument in the preceding passage.*

Which option below exhibits faulty reasoning MOST similar to the faulty reasoning in the preceding argument?
- A) Paula is dedicated to environmental sustainability. She recycles, reuses, and does her best to reduce plastic usage. She also drives an SUV. Driving an SUV is therefore environmentally sustainable.
- B) Mark is a highly organized person who manages his time efficiently. Therefore, it is okay that he spends an hour per day on social media.
- C) Patrick is dedicated to his health and fitness. He spends an hour per day working out, and only eats healthy foods. He should therefore never take a day off from these habits.
- D) Emily is a skilled photographer and owns a collection of professional camera equipment. It is therefore considered professional photography when she takes pictures with her smartphone.
- E) Sarah is an avid reader and enjoys literature from various genres; therefore, watching movies should be considered a form of literature appreciation for Sarah.

Fallacies of Formal Logic (Deductive Reasoning)

All of these fallacies occur on the LSAT, mostly in the Logical Reasoning portions of the exam:

The following are fallacies of formal logic (deductive reasoning):

- **mistaken reversal:** acting as though a condition necessary for an event is sufficient for that event
    - If A is true then B is true; B is true.
    - Therefore, A is true.

- **mistaken negation:** acting as though the absence of a sufficient condition for an event precludes that event
    - If A is true then B is true; A is false.
    - Therefore, B is false.
- **either-or fallacy:**
    - Either A is true or B is true; A is true.
    - Therefore, B is false.
- **undistributed middle:**
    - Some A is B and some A is C; therefore, some B is C.

    OR

    - All B is A, and some C is A; therefore, some B is C.
- Contradiction
    - A is true, but A is false.

Mistaken Reversal

"If . . . then" statements are conditions, not equalities. "If Harry goes to the football game, then it is sunny out" should be drawn as "G → S." Here, the letter *G* stands for "game" in "Harry goes to the game." The letter *S* stands for "sunny" as in "it is sunny out." It is read as "If game, then sunny."

Just because it is sunny out, however, does not mean that Harry goes to the football game. That would be "S → G" ("if sunny, then game"). Confusing "G → S" with "S → G" is a **mistaken reversal**.

Sample LSAT answer options that reflect this fallacy include those that mistake something that is necessary to bring about a situation for something that in itself is enough to bring about that situation.

Example:

If there is an intruder, then the dog barks.   I → B

The dog is barking.   B

Therefore, there must be an intruder.   ∴ I

This argument, like all fallacies, is not valid. It is incorrect to conclude that there must be an intruder based on the two premises given. The dog might be barking for other reasons. This argument is flawed because it mistakes a necessary condition for a sufficient condition. When there is an intruder, it is a necessary condition that the dog is barking. That is, there cannot be an intruder when the dog is not barking; however, the mere fact that the dog is barking is not sufficient to prove that there is an intruder. This argument is flawed because it treats the fact that the dog barking as necessary for there to be an intruder as though it were sufficient to prove that there is an intruder.

The LSAT will use this "necessary and sufficient" terminology, so be sure this information is clear. You could describe the flaw in the preceding argument in one of two ways:

1. The author mistakes a condition that is necessary for an event with a condition that would be sufficient for that event.

2. The author fails to consider that the dog might bark even when there is no intruder.

Here, Sentence 1 is written in general "logic" terms, while Sentence 2 is written in specific "factual" terms. Look for both general and fact-heavy answer options.

Mistaken Negation

As stated earlier, "if . . . then" statements are conditions, not equalities:

- "If Harry goes to the football game, then it is sunny out.
    - Draw "G → S" (again, read this as "if game, then sunny").

Just because Harry does not go to the football game, however, does not mean that it is not sunny:

- "~G → ~S" ("if no game, then not sunny")
    - This is a different statement.

Confusing "G → S" with "~G → ~S" is a mistaken negation. Logically, this fallacy is wrong for the same reason as a mistaken reversal: even if it is sunny out, Harry might decide not to go to the game for some other reason. The premise says that Harry's presence at the game guarantees that it is sunny; it does not say that Harry's absence from the game guarantees that it is not sunny.

Sample LSAT answer choices that reflect this fallacy include the following:

- The option assumes without warrant that just because satisfying a given condition is enough to ensure an announcement's importance, satisfying that condition is necessary for its importance.
- The argument fails to establish that a condition under which a phenomenon is said to occur is the only condition under which that phenomenon occurs.

Example:

If there is an intruder, then the dog barks.   I → B

There is no intruder.   ~I

Therefore, the dog is not barking.   ∴ ~B

More on Mistaken Reversal and Mistaken Negation

The next few pages explore mistaken reversal and mistaken negation in greater detail. Students frequently struggle with these concepts because colloquial English uses words like *if* and *only if*, so do not worry if these fallacies are not intuitive at first.

The two statements—"The dog barks if there is an intruder" and "The dog barks only if there is an intruder"—are opposite statements. They have different meanings and are not the same sentence worded in two different ways; however, these sentences are not contradictory. Either of them, or both, may be true in a given situation.

The first statement, "The dog barks if there is an intruder," could also be worded as "If there is an intruder, then the dog barks." In rewording this statement, we are moving the "if" clause from the end of the sentence to the beginning of the sentence. What this means is that the presence of an intruder is sufficient to ensure that the dog will bark. In this situation, an intruder guarantees that the dog will bark. If the dog is not barking, there must not be any intruder. Now let's consider the other statement.

The second statement, "The dog barks only if there is an intruder," means that it is necessary for there to be an intruder in order for the dog to bark. Thus, it is equivalent to "If the dog barks, then there is an intruder." In this case, the dog barking is sufficient to ensure that there is an intruder. In this situation, the presence of an intruder is necessary and must be true in the event that the dog is barking.

Therefore, if there is no intruder, then the dog cannot be barking. This has a different meaning than the first sentence.

Neither of the two statements is necessarily true or false, and neither one is necessarily valid nor invalid. They are just statements, not arguments. The first statement could be true; it might be the case that your neighbor's dog barks every time there is an intruder, so "If there is an intruder, then the dog barks." This situation does not exclude the possibility that "If the kids are playing, then the dog barks," or "If the dog wants to go out, then the dog barks." If you wanted to convey the idea that the dog will bark every time there is an intruder, you would want to say, "The dog barks if there is an intruder," or one of its equivalents.

The second statement also could be true; it might be the case that your other neighbor's dog has been trained to bark only if there is an intruder. In that case, "If the dog barks, there must be an intruder." This can also be stated, "The dog cannot bark unless there is an intruder." We are not saying that this statement is true about all dogs, but if you do say that this statement is true, then logically you must also agree that its equivalents are all true. Keep in mind that this statement does not ensure that the dog will bark *every time* there is an intruder. For all we know, the dog never barks, and that would be fully compatible with the statement "The dog barks only if there is an intruder." All this statement is saying is that if the dog is barking, then there must be an intruder. It is impossible, in this situation, for the dog to bark simply because the kids are playing, or because the dog wants to go out. At a minimum, there would also have to be an intruder for the dog to be barking. To convey this set of ideas, you would want to say, "The dog barks only if there is an intruder," or one of its equivalents.

In Table 2.2, all of the statements on the left have the same meaning as each other, and all of the statements on the right have the same meaning as each other' however, none of the statements on the left share a meaning with the statements on the right.

Very often, people treat sentences like Statement 1 in Table 2.2. as though they are identical to Statement 2. This usually takes the place of a mistaken reversal or mistaken negation argument. Let's start by looking at Statement 1 and writing out the various valid arguments that you could make from it, and then by writing out the various invalid arguments that people might attempt to make from it. Review formal logic for a refresher on valid and invalid argument patterns of conditional reasoning.

Table 2.2. Mistaken Reversal and Mistaken Negation	
Statement 1	**Statement 2**
(All of these statements are equivalent to "The dog barks if there is an intruder.")	*(All of these statements are equivalent to "The dog barks only if is an intruder.")*
If there is an intruder, then the dog barks.	If the dog barks, then there is an intruder.
If the dog is not barking, then there is no intruder.	If there is no intruder, then the dog is not barking.
Only if the dog is barking is there an intruder.	Only if there is an intruder does the dog bark.
There cannot be an intruder unless the dog barks.	The dog cannot bark unless there is an intruder.
The dog must be barking or else there would not be an intruder.	There must be an intruder or else the dog would not be barking.

Table 2.2. Mistaken Reversal and Mistaken Negation

Either the dog is barking or there is no intruder.	Either there is an intruder, or the dog is not barking.
The dog barks if there is an intruder.	There is an intruder if the dog barks.
There is an intruder only if the dog barks.	The dog barks only if there is an intruder.
The presence of an intruder is sufficient to assert that the dog barks.	The dog's barking is sufficient to assert that there is an intruder.
The dog must bark in order for there to be an intruder.	There must be an intruder in order for the dog to bark.
The presence of an intruder ensures that the dog barks.	The dog's barking ensures that there is an intruder.
The presence of an intruder requires that the dog barks.	The dog's barking requires that there be an intruder.

Remember: In any LSAT argument, the premises are never in dispute and should therefore be accepted as factually correct. Your goal is simply to analyze whether the conclusion follows logically based upon the premises. Keep that in mind as we analyze the following arguments.

Statement 1

Remember, we can rearrange the sentence by moving the "If there is an intruder" clause to the beginning of the sentence, without changing the meaning of the sentence:

- The dog barks *if* there is an intruder.
- *If* there is an intruder, the dog barks. (I → D)

Valid Argument 1, Positive Argument:

Premise: If there is an intruder, then the dog barks. (I → D)

Premise: There is an intruder. (I)

Conclusion: Therefore, the dog is barking. (∴ D)

This is a valid argument because the truth of the sufficient condition (an intruder) ensures the truth of the necessary condition (the barking dog).

Valid Argument 2, Contrapositive Argument:

Premise: If there is an intruder, then the dog barks. (I → D)

Premise: The dog is not barking. [~D (this means "not D")]

Conclusion: Therefore, there is no intruder. (∴ ~I)

This is a valid argument because the absence of the necessary condition—the barking dog—ensures that the sufficient condition (the intruder) cannot occur. There is no way that there can be an intruder if the dog is not barking because we have made the absolute statement that if there is an intruder, the dog barks.

Invalid Argument 1, Mistaken Reversal:

Premise: If there is an intruder, then the dog barks. (I → D)

Premise: The dog is barking. (D)

Conclusion: Therefore, there is an intruder. (∴ I)

This is an invalid argument because there may be many other reasons why the dog is barking. Barking is necessary when there is an intruder, but barking is not sufficient to ensure that there is an intruder.

Invalid Argument 2, Mistaken Negation:

Premise: If there is an intruder, then the dog barks. (I → D)

Premise: There is no intruder. (~I)

Conclusion: Therefore, the dog is not barking. (∴ ~D)

This is an invalid argument because, as earlier, even though there is no intruder there might be other reasons for the dog to bark.

From the same conditional statement, these are two common valid argument patterns (positive and contrapositive) and two common flaws (mistaken reversal and mistaken negation). You will see these patterns on the LSAT. This concept is extremely important because many people do not recognize the error in a mistaken reversal or mistaken negation at first glance. If this concept is intuitive to you, then do not overthink it. Move on to the concepts that are more difficult for you. If this concept is not intuitive to you, then you should spend as much time as necessary changing the way that you use conditional reasoning. **You want to be able to distinguish a flawed argument from a valid argument.**

In the next set of examples, we will look at the valid and invalid arguments that can be made from the alternative statement: "The dog barks only if there is an intruder."

Statement 2

In this scenario, the dog barking ensures that there is an intruder. Unlike the earlier situation, which allows other things to be sufficient for the dog to bark, this scenario requires that the dog can only bark if there is an intruder; therefore, if the dog is barking, there must be an intruder. We can also rearrange the original statement:

- The dog barks *only if* there is an intruder.
- If the dog barks, then there is an intruder. (D → I)

Valid Argument 1:

Premise: If the dog barks, then there is an intruder. (D → I)

Premise: The dog is barking. (D)

Conclusion: Therefore, there is an intruder. (∴ I)

This is a valid argument because the truth of the sufficient condition (the dog barking) ensures the truth of the necessary condition (the intruder).

Valid Argument 2:

Premise: If the dog barks, then there is an intruder. (D → I)

Premise: There is no intruder. (~I)

Conclusion: Therefore, the dog is not barking. (∴ ~D)

This is a valid argument because the absence of the necessary condition (the intruder) ensures that the sufficient condition (the dog barking) cannot occur.

Invalid Argument 1, Mistaken Reversal:

Premise: If the dog barks, then there is an intruder. (D → I)

Premise: There is an intruder. (I)

Conclusion: Therefore, the dog is barking. (∴ D)

This is invalid because, in this case, the dog *does not have to bark* just because there is an intruder. If the dog is barking, then there must be an intruder, but just because there is an intruder does not mean that the dog will bark. Again, the presence of an intruder is *not sufficient* to ensure that the dog will bark, so even though the dog *may* bark when there is an intruder, one cannot logically conclude that the dog is barking just because there is an intruder.

Invalid Argument 2, Mistaken Negation:

Premise: If the dog barks, then there is an intruder. (D → I)

Premise: The dog is not barking. (~D)

Conclusion: Therefore, there is no intruder. (∴ ~I)

This is invalid for the same reason stated earlier: just because the dog is not barking does not mean that there is no intruder. This is as invalid as saying, "If I have a cold, then I sneeze. I don't have a cold right now. Therefore, I can't sneeze."

So why can't we say that when there is an intruder, the dog barks, and when the dog barks, there is an intruder? Why can't it go both ways?

Well, we can. Often, that is precisely what we want to communicate in day-to-day English, although logically we would need to say something like "The dog barks if, *and only if*, there is an intruder."

This is a combination: "The dog barks if there is an intruder" (meaning "If there is an intruder, then the dog barks") and "The dog barks only if there is an intruder" (meaning "If the dog is barking, then there is an intruder").

If and only if occasionally comes up in Logical Reasoning:

- When either of the two conditions is true, then the other must be true.
- If either condition is false, the other must be false.

When a father tells his son, "You can have your allowance if you take out the trash," the odds are that he really means "if, and only if." When the son takes out the trash, he is sure to get his allowance, but if the son does not take out the trash, he is sure *not* to get his allowance. Only by saying "if and only if" would the father actually be able to convey this message. If the father just says, "You can have your

Chapter 2 – Flawed Patterns of Reasoning

allowance if you take out the trash," then the son might still want to claim his allowance even if he does not take out the trash.

As you hear people use "if" and "only if" in their arguments, pay careful attention to whether they are saying what they mean, and watch out for mistaken reversals and mistaken negations. They are everywhere on the LSAT, in both simple and complex passages, and if you use a mistaken reversal or mistaken negation in your own reasoning, it will likely lead you astray on the Logical Reasoning sections of the exam.

Either-or Fallacy

In English, there are two meanings to the word *or*: a strong meaning and a weak meaning. In a sentence like "You can go either to Paris or to London," there is a strong *or*, because the choice between Paris and London is exclusive (by choosing Paris, you choose "not London," and vice versa). Thus, the statement "either A or B is true" is strong (i.e., it would prevent you from choosing both A and B).

Most of the time, however, English uses a weak *or*, which does allow both A and B to be true. Consider the sentence "You must take either French or Spanish in order to graduate." It is certain that you will choose either French or Spanish. But it is certainly possible that you may take both.

On the LSAT, you should assume that the weak *or* is used in all instances of the word *or*. Given the statement, "Either A is true or B is true," it is a fallacy to argue, "A is true, so B is false." The only valid arguments you could make are "A is false, so B is true," or "B is false, so A is true."

Note that this fallacy is different from false dilemma. A **false dilemma** may artificially *create* an either-or statement. The **either-or fallacy** occurs in an argument that takes an either-or statement as its premise and concludes that two alternatives are mutually exclusive merely because one of the two alternatives must be true.

> **Example:**
>
> "Burger Palace franchises are required to serve either Coke or Pepsi. The franchise in Miami is serving Coke. So, they must not be serving Pepsi." This is fallacious because the store might be serving both Coke and Pepsi.

This fallacy tends to occur within passages that do not accompany "argument flaw" Logical Reasoning questions. Understanding this fallacy is crucial to understanding the use of the word *or* on the Logical Reasoning portion of the exam, but this is perhaps the least common of the fallacies in this chapter.

The Undistributed Middle

When two groups share a characteristic, it is a fallacy to assume that the two groups must therefore have common members. Humans have ears and elephants have ears, but no human is an elephant.

In other words, when one group has members in common with each of two other groups, those two groups do not necessarily have members in common with each other. Things with ears include both humans and elephants, but no human is an elephant. These are two ways of thinking about this fallacy.

Sample LSAT answer options that reflect this fallacy include those that fail to recognize that one set might have some members in common with each of two other sets even though those two other sets have no members in common with each other.

> **Example:**
>
> "All roses are plants. Some plants are poisonous. Thus, some roses are poisonous."

This example takes the form "All A is B, some B is C; therefore, some A is C." This form is always flawed.

Contradiction

The final fallacy—contradiction—is the most straightforward of the fallacies. **Contradiction** is the assertion of two statements that cannot both be true at the same time. When you see the word *incompatible*, meaning that certain propositions cannot be simultaneously true, think "contradictory." Sample LSAT answer options that reflect this fallacy include the following:

- Those in which information is introduced that actually contradicts the conclusion.
- Those in which The conclusion contradicts the claim of the speakers.
- Those in which The results of an analysis are interpreted as indicating that the use of the substance both was, and was not, extremely restricted.

Example:

"The evidence that we caused a greater net increase in jobs than the previous administration is clear: we reduced the rate of unemployment growth per year from 10 percent to only 3 percent."

This is contradictory because the premise indicates that unemployment is still increasing, while the conclusion claims a net increase in jobs (i.e., a decrease in employment).

Practice Questions

20. *In order to keep dogs happy, you need to walk them at least once a day. If you love dogs, you want them to be happy; therefore, if you walk your dog at least once a day, you must love your dog.*

Which of the following MOST accurately identifies the main flaw in the above argument?
  A) The conclusion assumes that people who do not walk their dogs as often do not love their dogs.
  B) The conclusion fails to consider that different breeds of dogs have different exercise needs.
  C) The conclusion takes for granted that few people have enough time to take their dog for daily walks.
  D) The conclusion assumes that not every dog enjoys daily walks, and some prefer to be lazy.
  E) The conclusion fails to consider that there may be reasons beyond the dog's happiness that lead the owner to walk them frequently.

21. *A study states that in order to be healthy, people must exercise. Therefore, it follows that if you are not healthy, then you do not exercise.*

Which of the following MOST accurately identifies the main flaw in the argument above?
  A) It ignores the fact that other lifestyle factors beyond exercise contribute to a person's health.
  B) It fails to establish the exercise alone is sufficient to achieve good health.
  C) It does not consider that some people may be afflicted with genetic disease.
  D) It attacks the character of those who do not exercise.
  E) It uses arguments that only a person who accepts the conclusion would believe to be true.

22. *All whales are mammals. Some mammals are pets. Therefore, some whales are pets.*

Note: *The following question asks you to find an answer with an argument that commits the same fallacy as the argument in the preceding passage.*

Which one of the following arguments is flawed in a way MOST similar to the way in which the passage is flawed?
- A) All roses are flowers. Some flowers are red. Therefore, some roses are red.
- B) All roses are flowers. All flowers are red. Therefore, all roses are red.
- C) All roses are flowers. No flowers are red. Therefore, no roses are red.
- D) All roses are flowers. Some flowers are red. Therefore, some roses are not red.
- E) All roses are flowers. Some flowers are red. Therefore, all roses are red.

23. *A city plans to implement a new public transportation system that will reduce traffic congestion. The proposal claims that if every commuter used the new system, there would be no traffic congestion. However, it also states that even with the new system in place, there will be traffic congestion during peak hours.*

Which of the following MOST accurately identifies the main flaw in the above argument?
- A) The author assumes that all commuters will use the new public transportation system.
- B) The author appeals to conscience rather than reason.
- C) The author makes incompatible assumptions.
- D) The author mistakes an effect for a cause.
- E) The author overlooks the environmental impact of the new public transportation system.

ANSWER KEY

1. C: The environmental group's argument is the definition of "appeal to emotion"; therefore, option C is the correct answer. Rather than providing evidence that the factory will be detrimental to the environment or arguing against any of the assertions of the company concerning the benefits of the factory, the environmental group makes an emotional appeal by focusing on children and families. This argument is intended to tug on the heartstrings of the listener but makes no effort to appeal to reason.

2. B: Councilman Jones's argument fits the definition of an ad hominem attack—an argument against a person; therefore, option B is the correct answer. Mary's driving record is not indicative of her expertise in this area and is therefore irrelevant when considering whether her plan for reducing traffic congestion is well-formed and valid. In his argument, Councilman Jones does not address why it should matter that Mary has been fined for speeding in the past and makes no arguments about the subject matter of her proposed plan. His entire argument is an attack on Mary's character.

3. E: The advocates' argument is an example of false analogy; therefore, option E is the correct answer. The advocates do not present evidence that the methods that improve an athlete's performance would do the same for student learning, and they do not consider that athletic performance and academic achievement are two entirely different endeavors that require approaches tailored to their specific requirements. While option D touches on the idea that different approaches might be needed for different types of tasks, it does not directly identify the false analogy, which is the core flaw in the argument. Options A, B, and C all point out issues related to the flawed analogy offered by the advocates, but they do not pinpoint the main issue, which is the flawed analogy itself.

4. A: The manager's argument introduces a red herring in the form of irrelevant information about the award-winning performance of the store; therefore, option A is correct. Options B and C make false connections between the award and the issue of employee wages and do not address the fact that the two are not directly related. While options D and E may also be issues with the manager's argument, they do not point out the particular flaw that makes the manager's argument weak.

5. A: This technique of exaggerating the opponent's position is an example of a straw man argument; therefore, option A is the correct answer. The politician does not accurately outline the effects of his opponent's plan using evidence to back up his claims; he merely offers a doomsday prediction that neither employs nor can be combatted with logic. Options B, C, and D are all implicit assumptions made under the umbrella of this straw man argument, but they do not address the underlying issue. Option E likely reflects the opinions of our politician, but it does not necessarily point to a flaw in his argument.

6. D: The argument fails to consider the possibility that there may be more bicyclists than runners overall. The premise informs us that a percentage of each group has begun strength training. From this, we know that relatively more runners have implemented strength training exercises compared to bicyclists. If there were an equal number of runners and bicyclists, we would know that more runners have implemented strength training exercises, but what if there are only 100 runners but 1,000 bicyclists?

If the argument had included absolute numbers, then it could have avoided the fallacy and reached an absolute conclusion; however, the premises only includes proportions, and therefore does not support an absolute conclusion without further information.

7. C: The premise of the argument is that students perform poorly on comprehensive exams due to stress, and we should therefore focus on assessing students throughout the semester; however, it does not acknowledge that the main purpose of comprehensive exams is to evaluate a student's overall mastery of the subject. Because of this lack of acknowledgment, it misses the point of comprehensive exams and offers a solution that does not address this need.

While options A, B, and D are likely assumptions made by the student, they do not address the main flaw in the argument, which is that continuous assessment will not effectively evaluate a student's overall mastery of a subject. Option E is counter to the argument made by the student.

8. B: The scientist uses a lack of evidence that there is life on the planets that have already been explored as conclusive evidence that there is no life on any other planet in our universe. His conclusion suffers from the argument from ignorance fallacy. The premise is that we have no evidence of life on other planets; we cannot reach the conclusion that there is no life on other planets from this premise alone. Options A, D, and E point out reasons why we might not have found evidence of life on other planets; while they are related to the argument from ignorance fallacy, they do not directly address the main issue that absence of proof is not evidence of non-existence. Option C is incorrect because the scientist does not presume that we have already searched the entire universe.

9. E: The blogger's argument appeals to the authority of Dr. Smith, a heart surgeon, to make an argument that has nothing to do with heart surgery. Heart surgeons are not experts in general health and nutrition and would therefore be no more authoritative on this subject than a layman. The blogger makes an appeal to Dr. Smith's authority without considering that he is not an expert in the subject matter that is relevant to the conclusion she reached. Options A and D highlight potential issues with the argument that everyone should take vitamin supplements, but they do not point to the main flaw in the argument. Option C offers an alternative method for achieving good health, but once again, it does not address the primary flaw of Dr. Smith's lack of expertise in this particular area. Option E introduces a potential bias on the part of Dr. Smith, but once again, it does not directly address the appeal to authority fallacy in the blogger's argument.

10. C: The marketing analyst attributes the increase in sales to the introduction of green packaging without considering that there may be other factors at play. The fact that the introduction of green packaging occurred before the increase in sales does not imply a direct causal relationship. Options A and D introduce other factors that may have also had an effect on sales, but they miss the main issue with the argument, which is the unwarranted causal link between green packaging and increased sales. Option B is incorrect because the marketing analyst's argument assumes that customers prefer the green packaging, and this is the reason for increased sales. Option E is incorrect because it runs counter to the analyst's argument.

11. A: The student makes her argument based on the actions of one other student, generalizing the behaviors and habits of this one student to extrapolate her conclusion that studying does not matter and only natural intelligence does. Options B and C point out potential flaws with her argument in that the she does not have all of the information about the other student she is judging, but these options do not directly address the main flaw, which is that a person cannot draw general conclusions from the behavior of one individual. Options D and E similarly point out weaknesses in the student's argument, but once again, they do not address the main flaw.

12. D: Option D commits the same fallacy as the original argument. Based on the fact that, on average, paintings by famous artists are more valuable, it concludes that the most valuable painting must be by a famous artist. This conclusion fails to consider that the painting may be an outlier, just as the original argument fails to consider that Jacob may simply be an exceptional student, regardless of the platform

he uses. Both arguments incorrectly apply a general trend to a specific instance without sufficient evidence that it is relevant.

Option A uses the rules of probability to make its conclusion. It does not commit the same logical fallacy because it does not assume that the highest ranked individual must conform to the general trend. It merely makes a prediction of the likelihood that one individual will be more highly ranked than others.

Option B reaches a valid conclusion based on the information provided. According to the premises, the fire station with the most advanced equipment must have been built after 2000 in order to have the most advanced equipment.

Option C argues a probable outcome based on general trends. It does not reach a specific conclusion based on a general trend, and therefore does not commit the same fallacy.

Option E, like the original argument, draws a specific conclusion from general trends; however, it makes a valid logical conclusion based on the information provided. The highest-rated camera being in a new model follows logically given the premise about newer smartphones generally having better cameras.

13. B: Option B identifies the unjustified assumption in the passage and is therefore the correct answer. The argument says that achieving the goal requires knowledge about genes and their basic functions, gene interaction, and a delineation of the physiological processes. At present, only the first and third conditions are satisfied. The argument assumes, without justification, that the second condition will soon be true as well.

Option A is an example of a contradiction, which is not the fallacy here. Option C is not a fallacy; logic does not require a minimum level of detail. Option D is incorrect because the ethical implications are irrelevant to the argument. Option E is incorrect because the argument of the biologists does not assume that genetic explanations will replace all other explanations of aging.

14. E: The nutritionist's argument is circular because it states that the diet plan is effective because it results in weight loss, and then concludes that it is successful in helping people lose weight because it leads to weight reduction. The conclusion and premise are essentially the same, leading to a circular argument without providing independent support for the claim. Options B and C point toward a lack of detail in the nutritionist's argument but do not identify the circular reasoning flaw, which is a larger issue. Options A and D may be legitimate criticisms of the nutritionist's approach, but again, they do not identify the flaw in the logical structure of the argument.

15. A: Option A is the definition of a false dilemma and is therefore the correct answer. The argument assumes that one of two outcomes must occur. It addresses no other potential strategies for combating climate change, offering only two potential options in the immediate cessation of fossil fuel use or catastrophic environmental consequences. While Options B, C, D, and E are relevant to the subject of combating climate change, they are not directly related to the false dilemma fallacy, which is the central issue.

16. B: Option B highlights the main issue with the business consultant's argument, which is the incorrect assumption that the lessons learned from a small family-owned business can be applied to large multinational corporations. The business consultant fails to consider the starting point of each business and how this might affect the effectiveness of the management strategy. Options A, C, and E all touch upon this issue by pointing out potential differences between small family-owned businesses and multinational corporations, but they do not invoke the starting point fallacy that is the central issue with the argument. Option D is a valid criticism of the argument, considering that the only evidence the business consultant offers is the plan's efficacy in a different type of business. But although it nods at the central fallacy of the argument, it does not directly address the issue.

Chapter 2 – Flawed Patterns of Reasoning

17. C: Option C is the correct answer, and an exact match. *Tall* is the ambiguous term here: tall thrift stores and coffee shops are not generally tall buildings; even a two-story thrift store or coffee shop would be considered tall for the type of business it is. Two stories, however, is not considered tall when discussing buildings as a whole. This is the same issue as in the example: small dogs are not necessarily small pets. A small dog is still a lot larger than a hamster. The meaning of the adjective depends on the noun it is modifying.

Options A and D offer arguments based on correlation that do not provide proof of causation, which is also an issue, but not the same as the issue with the proffered argument. Option B takes a premise and exaggerates its implications, which although a flaw, is also not the same flaw. Option E does not exhibit flawed reasoning. If the two premises are true, then the conclusion here is true as well.

18. D: Option D is correct. The coach assumes that the students will be able to perform an entire fitness challenge in a single session because they were able to perform each of the tasks therein during a single session. The coach fails to account for the fact that each task will deplete the energy and abilities of the students, leading to more difficulty completing the subsequent tasks. To break it down, it is one thing for a student to run three miles; it is quite another for the student to run three miles, do a ten-mile bike ride, and a two-mile swim. Option A appeals to the coach's authority, which would not be a fallacy in this instance, as the coach would likely be more familiar with the athletic abilities of the students than their parents. Option B would be an example of an ad hominem attack if it were employed by the coach; however, the coach makes no such claims in his argument. Option C would be an instance of circular reasoning if employed; however, it is not. Option E is a good criticism of the coach's argument, but it is a sub-issue to the main flaw in the argument.

19. A: Option A, like the example argument, exhibits the fallacy of division by incorrectly assuming that because Paula is dedicated to environmental sustainability in most areas of her life, all of her actions are environmentally sustainable; however, driving an SUV is not generally considered an environmentally sustainable choice, and—just as Jane sometimes indulges in unhealthy foods—this is likely a place where Paula compromises her values in the name of balance. Just because a person generally approaches life with certain standards does not mean that their every action can be assigned those values.

Options B and C invoke value judgments as to how people should spend their time, but the options do not erroneously assign value to activities and behaviors that do not line up with the overall values of the people acting. Option D offers an argument that calls the equipment necessary to take professional photographs into question; however, it does not necessarily assign professional value to the smartphone. It can be argued that Emily's skill elevates the photography even if it is taken with a crude instrument that is not generally considered professional. Option E makes a leap from one of Sarah's interests to a conclusion about her enjoyment of another that does not follow the premises, but it does not commit the same error as the original argument.

20. E: The premises of the argument can be rearranged to be "if→then" statements: "If you love your dog, then you want them to be happy. If you want your dog to be happy, you must walk them at least once a day." Therefore, by the rule of syllogism, if you love your dog, you must walk them at least once a day. Logically speaking, the contrapositive of this statement would be presumed to be true (if you do not walk your dog every day, then you do not love your dog), even though in reality, as pointed out by options A and C, there may be other reasons a person does not walk their dog every day. Even though these options point to a flaw in the argument, they do not point to the main flaw, which is an error of logic. Options B and D also point out more minor flaws with the argument in that it does not take into account the differing needs of individual breeds and dogs.

The reversal of the above statement ("if you walk your dog daily, then you must love your dog")—does not follow the rules of logic. There are many reasons a person may walk their dog daily that have nothing to do with the dog's happiness, such as their own desire to get regular exercise for themselves or as a way to get out of the house. Therefore, Option E is correct.

21. B: Option B outlines the issue inherent in mistaken negation. While it is true that in order to be healthy, one must exercise, it does not follow that exercise is the only lifestyle factor necessary to achieve good health. This argument fails to consider other factors such as diet, sleep, and whether or not a person smokes. Options A and C nod toward this issue by mentioning that factors beyond exercise matter in a person's overall health; however, they do not directly address the root issue, which is the mistaken negation fallacy. Option D would be an example of an ad hominem fallacy if it were employed here; however, it is not. Option E would be an example of a circular logic policy if employed here, but again, this is not the fallacy made in the argument.

22. A: This passage is the form "All *A* is *B*. Some *B* is *C*. Therefore, some *A* is *C*." This is the classic formula for an undistributed middle. Just because some mammals are pets does not mean that all types of mammals can be kept as pets. The passage shows this obviously, as we all know that although whales are mammals, people do not keep whales as pets.

Option A is not as obviously flawed, as some roses are in fact red; however, if you look at the logical structure of the argument, it falls prey to the same logical fallacy as the argument about whales above, as it has the same form of "All *A* is *B*. Some *B* is *C*. Therefore, some *A* is *C*."

Options B and C show arguments where the conclusion logically follows from the premises, so they cannot be the correct answers as they do not contain any fallacies, let alone parallel ones. Option D is incorrect because, although the conclusion does not follow from the premises, the logical structure is different from the initial passage, as it has the form "All *A* is *B*. Some *B* is *C*. Therefore, some *A* is **not** *C*." This fallacy is similar, but not quite the same. Option E is another example that employs a similar flaw to the initial passage, and is another example of undistributed middle, but it, too, has a slightly different logical structure of "All *A* is *B*. Some *B* is *C*. Therefore, **all** *A* is *C*."

23. C: In the argument, the author states that the public transportation system will get rid of traffic congestion, and then asserts that there will still be traffic congestion at peak times. These statements cannot both be true. Options A and E point toward potential flaws in the argument in that it does not consider public interest in the transportation system or environmental factors, but they do not address the main flaw, which is the contradiction. Option B is the definition of an appeal to emotion, which is not an issue in this argument. Option D would be an example of a false cause, which is also not present in the above argument.

Chapter 3 – Logical Reasoning: Questions

Question Types: An Overview

There are eighteen types of Logical Reasoning questions on the LSAT, organized into four broader thematic families. The eighteen question types are as follows:

1. Main Conclusion
2. Inference (Must Be True/ Must Be False)
3. Inference (Most Strongly Supported)
4. Necessary Assumption
5. Point at Issue
6. Underlying Principle
7. Principle Application
8. Strengthen
9. Weaken
10. Justify (Sufficient Assumption)
11. Resolve
12. Method of Reasoning
13. Role of a Statement
14. Argument Flaw
15. Evaluate the Argument
16. Parallel Reasoning
17. Parallel Flaw
18. Parallel Principle

The four thematic families follow:

1. Passage-Based questions
2. Hypothetical questions
3. Critical Reasoning questions
4. Parallel Reasoning questions

Within each family, the same general strategies apply.

Over the next set of pages, we will examine each of the eighteen Logical Reasoning question types in detail and learn about the following:

- tips for solving the questions.
- how to identify the question type.
- how to read the passage that accompanies the question type.
- how to anticipate the answer.
- common misconceptions.
- an actual LSAT question, with an answer explanation.

As you work through these pages, read the information on each question type and then attempt to solve the question before checking the answer.

Once you have worked through the question types, try your hand at the full-length section of Logical Reasoning questions. You may choose to complete the section timed—in which case you have thirty-five minutes for twenty-six questions—or untimed, although **you should not take longer than fifty minutes to an hour under any circumstances.** Then review your answers and reread the portions of this book that are relevant to the questions you miss. You want to be able to use natural language to explain exactly why each incorrect answer is wrong and exactly why each correct answer is right.

Strategies for Solving Logical Reasoning Questions

Passages

Each passage consists of one sentence to one paragraph of text and is followed by one or two questions. In recent tests, each passage generally has its own question. There are twenty-four to twenty-six questions per thirty-five-minute Logical Reasoning section. Most passages are not mere information; instead, they are arguments in which you should identify the conclusion separately from premises and background information. The conclusion may be anywhere in the passage. Some passages (specifically those accompanying Inference or Resolve questions) may contain only a set of facts rather than an argument, but this is not the norm.

Questions

Many distinct types of questions are discussed in this chapter. Read the question carefully and answer exactly what is asked. For most students, it is best to know the question before reading the passage so that you know what to look for as you read.

Answer Options

Each question will have five answer options. One is correct; the other four are incorrect. On many difficult questions, you may find two answers that seem to be correct. Rather than choosing the answer that "sounds the best," look for why one of the two answers is incorrect and eliminate it.

For each question, the following method is suggested:

1. Read the question (five seconds).

2. Read the passage, paraphrasing to yourself as you read; identify any conclusions (ten to thirty seconds).

3. Stop and anticipate the answer (ten to twenty seconds).

4. Glance through the answers, looking for one that is similar to your anticipated answer (ten seconds).

5. Read the most plausible answer(s) more carefully, looking back to the passage, if needed, to confirm that your answer is correct and all the other options are wrong (ten to twenty seconds).

These steps are discussed in greater detail on the following pages. Before continuing, you may wish to attempt the sample question in Table 3.1., which will be explained along the way.

Read the Question

Practice reading the question before you read the passage. Some experts recommend reading the passage before the question. Their argument is that if you read the question first, you will end up having to read it again after you read the passage. This is true.

However, if you read the passage first, you will likely find yourself having to read the entire passage again after you read the question, which will take even more time. Unless you have an outstanding memory, you will likely have to read something twice; by reading the question before the passage, you will get more out of your initial reading of the passage, and you will minimize the quantity of material that you reread.

> **Helpful Hint**:
>
> The various question types are explained throughout this chapter. As you work through the chapter, develop a firm grasp of what each question is asking so that you can avoid potential traps.

Read the Passage

As you read, paraphrase what you are reading. Use the following strategies instead of focusing on every word of the passage:

- Pay more attention to the structure of the passage than to the content.
    - Your job is to assess the logical soundness of the passage, not the factual soundness.
    - Ignore factual truth.
- Identify the author's conclusion(s).
    - Read the conclusion, and then read the premises.
    - Do the premises support the conclusion? If not, why?
- Notice conditional statements, and diagram them in the margin as you read.
- Watch out for extreme language in conclusions.
- Look for language gaps between the premises and the conclusion.
    - For example, if the premises support a conclusion about monkeys, but the conclusion itself says primates, this may be a weak point that is relevant to answering the question.

Table 3.1. Paraphrasing Passages	
ORIGINAL PASSAGE	**YOUR (SILENT) PARAPHRASE**
Household indebtedness, which some theorists regard as causing recession, was high preceding the recent recession, but so was the value of assets owned by households. Admittedly, if most of the assets were owned by quite affluent households, and most of the debt was owned by low-income households, high household debt levels could have been the cause of the recession despite high asset values; low-income households might have been decreased spending in order to pay off debts, while the quite affluent ones might simply have failed to increase spending. But, in fact, quite affluent people must have owed most of the household debt, since money is not lent to those without assets. Therefore, the real cause must lie elsewhere.	• Some think debt caused the recession. Debt was high. • But assets were high too. • (Sounds like the author's conclusion is "Debt didn't cause the recession.") • If the rich owned the assets and the poor owned the debt, then debt might have been the cause. • [details, come back if necessary] • But the poor cannot acquire debt, so the rich must have owned most of the debt. • Therefore, the cause of the recession is something other than debt.

The question asks the reader to determine which conclusion can be made based on the structure of the argument. ("The argument is structured to lead to which one of the following conclusions?") This tells you that your task is to come up with the author's conclusion (review premise/conclusion). As you read the passage, notice the general structure of the passage:

- Some people think that *x* is true.
- But . . . [details].
- Also, *x* could be true if *y* were true. But *y* is not true; therefore, *x* is not true.

Frequently, Logical Reasoning passages follow the pattern of "Some people think *x*, but . . ." In almost every circumstance, regardless of what follows in the passage, the author's point in such an argument is simply that *x* is false.

Here, the author tells us that some theorists blame household debt for the recession, but [additional details]. This tells us, before we even get past the first sentence, that the author's point is very likely: "Household debt did not cause the recession." The author confirms this for us in the last sentence of the passage.

As you read, pay more attention to the structure and logical flow of the argument than to the factual details. Nobody is testing you on whether the poor can acquire enough debt to cause a recession. Whether that is true or false in real life is irrelevant to your task. You are to identify the argument's conclusion, so stay focused on the task at hand.

Stop and Anticipate the Answer

This is the most important step. Students who score high on the LSAT are almost always able to stop at the end of a question and express a possible answer in natural, everyday language. You will not necessarily be able to guess the correct answer word for word, but you must allow your brain to consider how the correct answer will probably look.

Chapter 3 – Logical Reasoning: Questions

If you skip this step, you risk becoming distracted by the five answer options, many of which may include enticing language and factual details from the passage. You will see language in the answer options that you will recognize from the passage. An irrelevant answer option can seem correct simply because of the way in which it is worded or because it includes facts from the passage. Take heed: **always stop and anticipate the answer.**

In the sample question in Table 3.1, you would anticipate "Debt did not cause the recession" as the answer.

Glance Through the Answers

Spend ten seconds or so glancing through the five answer options. Keep your eyes open for answers that resemble your anticipated answer. Crossing out obviously incorrect answers, while lightly marking those that appear correct, can also be helpful.

Select the Correct Answer

If you have two or three possible answers, do NOT pick an answer for any of the following reasons:

- It is the shortest.
- It is the longest.
- It has the most straightforward wording.
- It has the most complicated wording. (Incidentally, no LSAT answer is incorrect because it seems too easy.)
- It states a phrase, clause, or sentence word for word as it appears in the passage.
- It does not state a phrase, clause, or sentence word for word as it appears in the passage.
- It would give you an even number of C or D (or some other answer option letter) answers.
    - Out of twenty-five questions, there will not necessarily be five each of A, B, C, D, and E.
    - In fact, there might be as few as two or as many as ten of a given letter in any given question set.
    - Additionally, you might have up to four in a row of the same letter.
    - Do not base your answer on superstition.

> **Did You Know?**
>
> Some students find it helpful to make a list or spreadsheet of the different factors that make various answer choices incorrect.

In short, do not pick an answer just because it sounds or looks good; instead, look for reasons to eliminate answers that are incorrect. For example, you should eliminate an answer if it meets the following criteria:

- Its language is more extreme than it should be.
- You would have to bring in outside information to justify the answer as correct.
- It discusses a topic that is (even slightly) different from the topic at hand.

No LSAT questions will require you to pick the better of two good answer options. There will always be four answers that are clearly incorrect for identifiable reasons.

It may be extremely difficult to determine why an answer is wrong, so develop your ability to identify the reasons why answer choices are incorrect. If this seems difficult, try taking an LSAT prep test or two and simply read through the questions and answers (with the correct answers circled). Spend several hours studying each test until you can extract and explain why each right answer is correct and why each wrong answer is incorrect.

Time Management/Section Practice

You will have thirty-five minutes to answer between twenty-four and twenty-six Logical Reasoning questions. This allows you one minute and twenty seconds to one minute and twenty-seven seconds per question.

Within each section, the easiest questions tend to fall within the first ten questions, and the hardest questions tend to fall between questions 12 and 22. Do not mistake this for an easy-to-hard progression. The first question may be very difficult, and a later question may be very straightforward. This pattern has never been officially announced by LSAC, but observers have spotted it on modern LSAT exams since the early 1990s. Accordingly, the following guidelines can help you manage your time within each section:

- Aim to complete the first ten Logical Reasoning questions within ten minutes.
    - This will give you twenty-five minutes to complete the remaining problems.
    - Additionally, you might find it helpful to pause for fifteen to thirty seconds at the end of question 10.
- Go back, review your answers, and flag any that you might wish to come back to.

A Note About "EXCEPT" Questions

Several questions in each Logical Reasoning section will likely be EXCEPT questions; examples include the following:

- Each of the following, if true, strengthens the argument EXCEPT . . .
- If all of the statements in the passage are true, each of the following statements must also be true EXCEPT . . .

The word *EXCEPT* will always be capitalized so that you do not overlook it. You might also choose to underline or circle the word in order to focus your mind.

Be careful with these questions. In the first example above, you should not assume that the correct answer will weaken the argument. The question is telling you that four of the five answers will strengthen the argument, and that one will not. It is not saying that the right answer will weaken the argument—it might simply not add anything at all, or it might be completely irrelevant.

The best approach is to simply find and eliminate the four answers that actually do strengthen the argument. Whatever remains is the correct answer.

The same logic applies to the second example above. Do not look for an answer that must be false; instead, eliminate those four answer options that must be true. Your correct answer is one that *could* be false, not one that must be false.

Passage-Based Questions

This family of questions tests your ability to read a short passage and identify what the author is saying or arguing. These questions ask you to assess only the author's statements and any reasonable assumptions they require or any inferences that follow from the statements.

The diagram accompanying this family (see Table 3.3.) shows an arrow pointing from the passage to the answers. This represents the idea that the correct answer option comes directly out of the passage. In the pages that follow, each of the seven Passage-Based questions will be discussed in greater detail. Generally, these questions are simple to understand, although they may be very difficult to solve. They gauge your ability to use deductive reasoning to choose an answer that either restates part of the passage or follows from the passage as a logical consequence.

Table 3.2. Passage-Based Questions		
QUESTION TYPES	**GENERAL STRATEGIES**	**FAMILY DIAGRAM**
1. Main Conclusion 2. Inference (Must Be True/Must Be False) 3. Inference (Most Strongly Supported) 4. Necessary Assumption 5. Point at Issue 6. Underlying Principle 7. Principle Application	1. Your answer comes from the passage, so stick to the facts. 2. Ignore outside information. 3. Watch for extreme language.	Passage → Answers

Main Conclusion Questions

These questions use key phrases and words like *main point* and *conclusion*. Questions may include the following:

- Which one of the following most accurately expresses the main conclusion of the argument?
- Which one of the following most accurately restates the main point of the passage?
- Which one of the following most logically completes the argument?

When reading these passages, put yourself in the author's shoes. Read the passage as though you were really arguing with someone—not just reciting words on a page. Then, if you had just one clause to make your point, what would you say?

Practice articulating conclusions in this way as you work through Logical Reasoning questions. You may notice yourself using words like *because* or *since* in your paraphrased conclusions. Try to avoid those words. As soon as you say *because*, you have left conclusion territory to state a premise. Your task is to isolate the conclusion of the argument as separate from the premises.

Review common patterns of reasoning, including the "Some people think [x is true], but . . ." pattern; cause and effect; and argument by analogy, advocacy, and prediction. Also review the concepts of premise and conclusion.

Specific Tips for "Must Be True"/"Must Be False" Questions

1. Separate the conclusion from the premises.

2. The answer will not be a summary of the whole passage. It should just be a paraphrase of the clause of the sentence that is the author's conclusion.

3. When you see the "Some people think [x is true], but . . ." pattern of reasoning, the conclusion is "x is false."

Look for the clause or sentence that is the author's conclusion, and expect the answer to restate it. In questions that ask you to fill in the blank by completing an unfinished passage, come up with a conclusion that is safely supported by all the facts presented.

Look for conclusion indicators like *thus*, *therefore*, *so*, *consequently*, and *hence*. Additionally, look for words like *probably*, *must have*, and *should*, which are often found in conclusion sentences even in the absence of a conclusion indicator.

Common Misconceptions

1. You do not need to summarize the entire passage; a single line or clause is sufficient.

2. The fact that the answer is stated in the passage does not automatically make it correct. It might well be a premise, in which case it is *true*, but incorrect.

Inference ("Must Be True"/"Must Be False") Questions

"Must Be True" questions feature key phrases and words like *must be true*, *drawn from the passage*, *inferred*, *properly concluded*, *follows logically*, and *inference*. Questions may resemble the following:

- Which one of the following conclusions can be properly drawn from the statements above?
- Which one of the following can be properly inferred from Dr. Z's statement?
- If the statements above are true, which one of the following must be true?

To identify "Must Be False" questions, keep an eye out for key phrases and words like *cannot be true*, *inconsistent*, *conflicts with*, *could be true*, and *EXCEPT*. "Must Be False" questions may look like the following:

- Those whose view is described are able to hold inconsistent beliefs if they also believe that . . .
- If the statements in the passage are true, each of the following could be true EXCEPT . . .
- If the statements above are true, then which one of the following must be false?

Read the passage as a plain set of facts, rather than as an argument. Do not worry about distinguishing premises and conclusions here. Your job is to consider each proposition as a true fact and to discover what else must be true or false based on the facts stated.

These can be the hardest questions for which to anticipate an answer because many plausible inferences can arise from a set of facts; however, look for conditional statements and seek to make inferences from them. Frequently when conditional statements are in the passage, the answer is an inference that follows from those statements. Master the common patterns of deductive reasoning so that you can distinguish between valid and invalid inferences.

Specific Tips for "Must Be True"/"Must Be False" Questions

- The answer does not need to summarize the passage.
- Do not worry about conclusions here. Treat the entire passage (and all its implications) as factual truth.
- The answer can paraphrase (or contradict) any single fact or clause of the passage, even in a long and convoluted passage.

Chapter 3 – Logical Reasoning: Questions

- Must Be True: The answer must come directly from the facts. Prefer safe language over extreme language.

- Must Be False: The answer must directly contradict the facts.

NOTE: In the context presented, **safe language** refers to wording that is cautious, moderate, and directly supported by the text, as opposed to **extreme language**, which tends to be more absolute, sweeping, and speculative. In "Must Be True/Must Be False" questions, it is best to choose answers that use safe language, which means selecting options that are conservative; avoiding making broad, unqualified generalizations; and using moderate terms such as *some*, *often*, or *can be*, rather than extreme terms like *always*, *never*, and *must*.

Common Misconceptions

- You do not need to summarize or refute the entire passage.

- You are not looking for the author's main point, so a single fact from the passage is sufficient.

- You should not have normative language in your answer unless there is normative language in the passage.

Inference ("Most Strongly Supported") Questions

These questions contain straightforward key phrases, such as "most strongly supported" (i.e., by the passage). Some examples include the following:

- The statements above, if true, give the most support to which one of the following?

- The passage provides the most support for which one of the following?

- If the statements above are true, which one of the following conclusions is most strongly supported by them?

"Most Strongly Supported" (i.e., Inference) questions are similar to "Must Be True" questions: read the passage as a bare set of facts rather than as an argument, even if the author has premises and a conclusion.

Many times, the answer to a "Most Strongly Supported" question will be an answer that must be true. In other words, answer these questions the way you would respond to a "Must Be True" question; therefore, the same advice applies:

- When you see conditional statements, make inferences and anticipate a possible answer that follows deductively from the conditional statements in the passage.

- If the passage has no conditional statements, it can be difficult to anticipate an answer, so just do your best to think through the logical consequences of the facts presented.

> **Helpful Hint**:
> Do not confuse a "Most Strongly Supported" question with a "Strengthen" question. "Most Strongly Supported" questions ask you which answer is supported by the passage. "Strengthen" questions, however, ask you which answer would *hypothetically* support the passage.

Unlike "Must Be True" questions, the answers to "Most Strongly Supported" questions can have some wiggle room:

- The answer might not be a statement that follows conclusively from the passage.
- Instead, you may need to pick an answer which, if it were the conclusion of an argument that took the passage as its premises, would produce at least a reasonably strong argument.
- Only one of the five answer options will plausibly do this.

Specific Tips for Most Strongly Supported Questions

- The answer should be almost certainly based on the passage.
- Do not worry about conclusions here. Treat the entire passage (and all its implications) as factual truth.
- Look first for an answer that absolutely must be true. If you do not see one, then choose the answer that, based on inductive reasoning, is very likely to be true.

As with must be true/must be false questions, with "Inference" questions

- you do not need to summarize or refute the entire passage;
- you are not looking for the author's main point, so just a single fact from the passage is sufficient; and
- you should not have normative language in your answer unless there is normative language in the passage.

Necessary Assumption Questions

Necessary Assumption questions feature key words and phrases like *assumes, presupposes, required assumption,* and *depends on*. Questions may look like the following:

- The argument assumes which one of the following?
- Which one of the following is an assumption upon which the argument in the passage depends?
- The argument presupposes that which one of the following assumptions is required by the argument?

When reading Necessary Assumption questions, look for two things:

- holes in the argument
- possible objections to the argument

Holes in the argument are actual gaps between the language of the premises and the language of the conclusion. For example, analyze the following assertion:

- "Europeans have a lower risk of heart disease than North Americans. Therefore, Europeans are healthier than North Americans."

Here, there is a gap between "lower risk of heart disease" and "healthier." The author must be assuming that "no factors other than risk of heart disease affect the relative health of Europeans and North Americans."

Arguments like this commit the fallacy of **missing the point**; many Necessary Assumption questions commit this fallacy. Your job is to identify how the author is "jumping to conclusions" and articulate what the author must believe in order for the stated premises to actually support the stated conclusion.

Even in arguments that do not have clear disconnections between the premises and the conclusion, look for **potential weaknesses**, also known as **possible objections to the argument**. An author must necessarily assume that any potential weakeners are false; therefore, you can identify a necessary assumption by finding an answer that rules out a potential weakener.

For example, consider the following statement:

- "Laura drives a blue Ford Focus and gets twenty-five miles per gallon. A car's make and model tend to indicate its gas mileage; therefore, if Jordan buys a blue Ford Focus, he will also get twenty-five miles per gallon."

Here, there is no obvious gap between the language of the premises and the language of the conclusion. But is this a perfect argument? No. All we know is that make and model tend to indicate gas mileage; we do not know that they *guarantee* identical gas mileage.

Possible objections might therefore include the following:

- "What if Jordan uses a lot more air conditioning than Laura?"
- "What if Laura drives on country roads, and Jordan drives only in city traffic?"

Surely, if the author thought these objections were true, he would not be able to make the original argument. That is why the author must necessarily assume that these potential weakeners are false in order for the argument to be plausible.

Possible Necessary Assumption answer options for this example could include the following

- "It is not the case that Jordan uses a lot more air conditioning than Laura."
- "Jordan's highway-to-city driving ratio is not substantially lower than Laura's."

When answering Necessary Assumption questions, keep the following in mind:

- If you notice a "hole" or language gap, anticipate an answer that connects the premises to the conclusion using safe language.
- Consider possible objections to the argument and construct an assumption that defends the argument against those possible objections, especially in cause-and-effect arguments.
  - If the author is arguing based on a correlation between *x* and *y* that *x* is the cause of *y*, then the author must necessarily assume that *y* is not the cause of *x* and there is no third factor that causes both *x* and *y*.
  - Adding either of these two statements as a necessary assumption defends the causal conclusion against alternate possible conclusions.

Specific Tips for Necessary Assumption Questions

- The answer is something the author must absolutely believe to be true in order to make the argument.
  - If the correct answer were false, then the argument would be destroyed.
- Be careful not to assume the answer along with the passage.

- o In many cases, the necessary assumption is so obvious that the reader simply assumes that the author has stated it.
- o Remember, a necessary assumption is an unstated premise in an argument.
- The answer must be true based on the passage. Treat these questions as Inference/Must Be True questions.

The Negation Test

Use the negation test to confirm that your selected answer is indeed a necessary assumption:

- **If you negate the correct answer and add it into the passage, it will destroy the argument.**

This test holds true on every necessary assumption question. It can be time-consuming to negate lengthy answer options and evaluate how they would affect the passage, so do not apply the negation test to every answer option; rather, once you have settled on one or two answers that could be correct, use the negation test to confirm that your answer is necessary.

Here is how the negation test works: A **necessary assumption** is defined as a premise that the author must believe to be true in order for the argument to be sound. We could state this as a conditional statement:

- "If the argument is sound, then the necessary assumption must be true."

The negation test is the contrapositive of the above statement:

- "If a necessary assumption is false, then the argument will not be sound."

This means that four of the answer options could be negated while still being fully consistent with the argument in the passage; however, the correct answer's negated form is inconsistent with the argument in the passage. That is why the correct answer, in its positive (non-negated) form, is an assumption required by the argument.

Common Misconceptions

The correct answer does not need to justify the conclusion.

There may be many (even infinite) necessary assumptions in a given argument, but your job is simply to identify one necessary assumption. Consider the following example:

- All adult male citizens of Athens could vote; therefore, Socrates could vote.

Here, a valid answer would be "Socrates was male." Another answer would be "Socrates was a citizen of Athens." Another answer would be "Socrates attained adulthood." You could get an answer like "Socrates was an adult male citizen of Athens," and this would be correct, but that type of answer (which is both a necessary assumption and a sufficient assumption) is not required.

Language that appears "outside the scope" of the argument may be exactly what you want in the correct answer.

In the earlier Ford Focus argument, for example, a valid answer could be "It is not the case that Jordan drives only on three-lane roads, which are notoriously bad for fuel economy." You might see the bit about three-lane roads as beyond the scope of the argument, but it is not: the answer is ruling out a potential weakener. How? If it were the case that Jordan drives only on three-lane roads that are notoriously bad for fuel economy, then it would certainly weaken the argument that Jordan will get twenty-five miles per gallon. The answer option negates this potential weakener and is therefore a necessary assumption.

Chapter 3 – Logical Reasoning: Questions

Point at Issue Questions

Point at Issue questions feature key phrases and words like *point at issue*, *disagree*, and *committed to disagreeing*. Some examples include the following:

- The point at issue between Jones and Smith is . . .
- On the basis of their statements, Shanna and Jorge are committed to disagreeing about the truth of which one of the following statements?
- The dialogue most supports the claim that Tony and Raoul disagree about whether . . .

Passages accompanying Point at Issue questions always feature two speakers or authors. Identify each speaker's conclusion. Sometimes, the point of disagreement will be the speaker's conclusions. Other times, the speakers might agree with each other's conclusions but disagree with a premise or assumption.

To answer Point at Issue questions, think of a complete sentence for which one of the speakers must say, "Yes, that is true," and the other speaker must say, "No, that is false." This can simply be a clause or sentence taken from either one of the speaker's arguments.

Specific Tips for Point At Issue Questions

- Apply the "yes-no" test. For your answer, one of the two speakers must be committed to saying, "Yes, that is true," and the other must be committed to saying, "No, that is false."
- If there is any possible way for the two speakers to agree that the answer is true or that the answer is false, it is a wrong answer.

Common Misconceptions

The answer can restate a premise or a conclusion directly from one of the speaker's arguments. Even if the other speaker does not directly negate that proposition, the answer is correct if the other speaker would be committed to disagreeing with the proposition based on what is stated.

Underlying Principle Questions

To identify Underlying Principle questions, keep an eye out for key words and phrases along the lines of *the argument appeals to/is based on/conforms to/expresses a principle*. Questions may read as follows:

- The argument tacitly appeals to which one of the following principles?
- The person's reasoning could be based on which one of the following principles?
- The reasoning in the argument most closely conforms to which one of the following principles?
- Which one of the following expresses a general principle that could underlie the argument?

As you read the passage, think, "What is this passage an example of?" For example, consider the following argument:

- "Bob had four weeks to make the slideshow presentation that he was assigned to complete by this afternoon. The topic was simple, and he could have asked us questions if he didn't know how to proceed. His email this morning telling us that the presentation was beyond his ability and that he would not be able to complete it is therefore inexcusable, and he should be sanctioned."

The underlying principle here could be "Failure to complete a task for which one has ample time to seek help is inexcusable and worthy of sanctions." This is a general principle which could broadly apply to any number of situations; the preceding passage is one such possible situation.

To answer Underlying Principle questions, generalize from the subject matter detail of the passage to a broader, more generic statement. In the preceding example, step back from slideshow presentation and emails, and craft a broader statement that applies to the passage and can also apply to other analogous situations.

Specific Tips for Underlying Principle Questions

- Your answer should be a general principle that could guide the author's reasoning. Often, it is a principle that could serve to connect the argument's premises with its conclusion.
- The passage should be an example of your chosen answer.

Common Misconceptions

The correct answer does not need to mention any specifics from the passage. It can be very vague, broad, murky, and poorly worded.

Principle Application Questions

Principle Application questions often feature the following phrase type:

- Judgment below conforms to the principle above.

Principle Application questions may read as follows:

- Which one of the following judgments conforms to the principle stated above?
- Which one of the following judgments most closely conforms to the principle cited above?

Here, the passage is a principle, and the answer will be an example of the passage. Compare that to underlying principle questions, where the answer is a principle and the passage is an example of the answer. Very frequently, you will see conditional statements in the passage; these should be diagrammed.

If you have a conditional statement in the form "If A is true then B is true," expect the answer's conclusion to be "A is false or B is true."

Specific Tips for Principle Application Questions

- Here, the passage is the principle, and the answer is an example of the principle.
- Diagram conditional statements.
- Do not confuse "if" statements with "only if" statements.
- A principle in the form "If A is true then B is true" can never support the conclusion that A is true or that B is false. It can only support a conclusion that B is true (because A is true) or a conclusion that A is false (because B is false).

Common Misconceptions

Your answer does not need to be an example of the entire passage; it can be an example of just one sentence or conditional statement from the passage so long as it remains *consistent* with the whole passage.

Practice Questions

1. *The community center has instituted a new policy that all volunteers must undergo background checks. Joel has been volunteering at the community center for the past five years without incident, and therefore believes that he does not have to submit to a background check; however, the new policy applies to all volunteers, regardless of their histories, and is required in order for them to continue their volunteer work.*

What is the main conclusion of the argument?
   A) Joel has been volunteering at the community center for five years.
   B) Joel believes that he does not need a background check.
   C) The new policy applies to all volunteers.
   D) There should be some exceptions to the new policy.
   E) Joel must comply with the background check requirement in order to continue to volunteer at the community center.

2. *Studies have shown that a diet high in processed sugars can lead to various health issues, including obesity, diabetes, and heart disease; however, not all sugars have the same impact on health. Natural sugars found in fruits, for instance, come with essential nutrients and fiber that help mitigate their negative effects. Furthermore, people who consume diets rich in whole fruits tend to have lower rates of obesity and heart disease. It is crucial to distinguish between processed and natural sugars when considering dietary impacts on health.*

Which of the following statements MUST be true based on the information above?
   A) Diets high in processed sugars are the sole cause of obesity and heart disease.
   B) Consuming natural sugars in fruits does not lead to any health issues.
   C) All sugars have the same impact on health.
   D) People who eat a lot of whole fruits are less likely to be obese than those who consume a lot of processed sugars.
   E) Processed sugars provide essential nutrients and fiber that natural sugars do not.

3. *There is an increased trend of urbanization, leading to a rise in the number of people living in cities. This urban growth is accompanied by several challenges, such as increased pollution, higher costs of living, and greater demand for resources such as water and electricity. However, urbanization also offers benefits like better access to health care, education, and employment opportunities. Studies indicate that urban areas tend to have more efficient public transportation systems, which can reduce reliance on personal vehicles and lower greenhouse gas emissions.*

Which of the following MUST be false based on the information above?
   A) Urbanization leads to a decrease in the demand for resources such as water and electricity.
   B) Urbanization has contributed to increased pollution in cities.
   C) People living in urban areas have better access to health care and education.
   D) Urban areas tend to have more efficient public transportation systems.
   E) People living in urban areas tend to be happier.

4. *A recent study found that regular exercise significantly reduces the risk of chronic illnesses such as heart disease and diabetes. Participants who engaged in at least 150 minutes of moderate exercise per week had significantly lower rates of these conditions compared to those who were sedentary. Additionally, the study revealed that the mental health benefits of regular exercise, including reduced symptoms of depression and anxiety, were evident regardless of the participants' age, gender, or socioeconomic status.*

Which of the following is MOST strongly supported by the information above?
   A) Only moderate exercise can reduce the risk of chronic illnesses; vigorous exercise does not have the same effect.
   B) Regular exercise may contribute to a decrease in health care costs by reducing the prevalence of chronic illnesses.
   C) Sedentary individuals are more likely to develop mental health issues than those who exercise regularly.
   D) The study found that age and gender are significant factors in determining the mental health benefits of exercise.
   E) Participants who engaged in less than 150 minutes of moderate exercise per week showed no health benefits.

5. *In order to reduce traffic congestion, a city plans to implement a new bicycle-sharing program. The program will provide affordable access to bicycles at key locations through the city, making it easier for residents to choose biking over driving. The city expects this program to significantly decrease the number of cars on the road during peak hours.*

For the above argument to be logically correct, it must make which of the following assumptions?
   A) The bicycle-sharing program will be affordable for all residents.
   B) Traffic congestion is primarily caused by residents driving their cars during peak hours.
   C) Residents will choose biking over driving if it is made easier and more accessible.
   D) The city will provide sufficient funding to maintain the bicycle-sharing program.
   E) Bicycles are a safer and more efficient mode of transportation compared to cars.

6. **Emma:** *Organic farming is better for the environment than conventional farming because it avoids the use of synthetic pesticides and fertilizers, which cause harm to the environment.*

Lisa: *Although organic farming avoids synthetic chemicals, it often requires more land to produce the same yield as conventional farming, which can lead to deforestation and loss of wildlife habitats.*

Emma and Lisa disagree on which one of the following?
   A) Organic farming avoids the use of synthetic pesticides.
   B) Synthetic pesticides harm the environment.
   C) Organic farming requires more land to produce the same yield as conventional farming.
   D) Organic farming is better for the environment than conventional farming.
   E) The environmental impact of farming is primarily determined by pesticide and fertilizer use.

7. **Economist:** *Implementing a universal health care system would not only ensure that everyone has access to necessary medical care, but also reduce the overall cost of healthcare in the long term. Preventative care and early treatment are more cost-effective than emergency care and the treatment advanced diseases.*

This argument tacitly appeals to which of the following principles?
A) Health care should be accessible to everyone regardless of their financial situation.
B) The long-term benefits of preventative care justify the initial costs of implementing universal health care.
C) Preventative care and early treatment are more important than emergency care.
D) Reducing health care costs should be the primary goal of any health care policy.
E) A universal health care system is the only way to ensure cost-effective health care.

8. *A law is only considered just if it promotes the welfare of the community and was enacted with that intention. However, a law that causes harm to any group is unjust if such harm were intended or if reasonable forethought would have shown that the law was likely to cause harm.*

Which one of the following judgments MOST closely conforms to the principle cited above?
A) The city council passed a noise ordinance intended to reduce nighttime disturbances, benefiting the entire community. The law was unjust, though, because it inconvenienced late-night businesses, and this outcome was reasonably foreseeable.
B) Because a member of the city council disliked cyclists, a law was passed requiring all cyclists to wear helmets. Even though the motive for the law was to upset cyclists, it was just because it led to reduced injuries and promoted community welfare.
C) The government implemented a curfew to curb youth crime, intending to create a safer environment. However, it led to increased tensions and protests from the youth community, showing that well-intentioned actions can have bad consequences.
D) A traffic regulation was enacted to decrease congestion during rush hour, benefiting most commuters, but making it difficult for delivery services. The law was therefore unjust.
E) A new tax law was enacted to increase government revenue, resulting in a higher burden on low-income families. The law was unjust because it harmed a vulnerable group, and this outcome was foreseeable.

Hypothetical Questions

This family of questions tests your ability to read a short passage and bring in new information to answer the question asked. Hypothetical questions include variations of the following question stems:

Which of the following, if true (or, if assumed), would

- strengthen the reasoning above?
- weaken the reasoning above?
- justify the conclusion above?
- resolve the apparent paradox above?

Table 3.3. Hypothetical Questions

QUESTION TYPES	GENERAL STRATEGIES	FAMILY DIAGRAM
1. Strengthen 2. Weaken 3. Justify ("Sufficient Assumption") 4. Resolve	1. You are adding an answer choice into the argument in order to answer the question. 2. Extreme language can be ideal. 3. Never eliminate an answer because "it isn't true" – the question told you to assume that all of the answer choices are true!	Passage ← Answers

General Tips for Hypothetical Questions

- You are bringing in new information (a new premise if the passage is an argument) to answer the question.
- Extreme language can be ideal.
- Never eliminate an answer because "it is not true." The question says to assume that *all* the answer choices are true.

Strengthen Questions

To identify Strengthen questions, look for key words and phrases like *supports*, *strengthens*, *bolsters*, and *provides the strongest evidence for*. Questions might look like this:

- Which one of the following, if true, would most strengthen the argument?
- Which one of the following, if true, supports the conclusion in the passage?
- Which one of the following, if true, most strongly supports the explanation given in the argument?

When reading the passage, your primary goal is to identify the conclusion. Put yourself in the author's shoes and think about what other evidence you would like to have to make your conclusion more likely.

When answering Strengthen questions, stop and think about possible factors that would strengthen the argument if true. Do not confine yourself to the factors discussed in the premises: anything that would make the conclusion more likely is a strengthener.

Specific Tips for Strengthen Questions

- Rule out an alternate possible cause of an effect to strengthen a cause-and-effect argument.
- Anything that strengthens the conclusion is fair game, even if it seems to go beyond the scope of the stated premises.
- The answer options cannot negate a premise of the argument. If an answer appears to negate (and thus apparently weaken) the argument, stop to see how the answer might work with the premises of the argument to produce a strengthening inference.

Common Misconceptions

As discussed above, an answer option cannot actually negate a premise of an argument. Look for answer options that appear to be contradicting a premise of the argument but are actually narrowing the scope of the premise in a way that strengthens the argument.

Look for assumptions. An answer option that states (and thereby validates) an assumption by affirming that the assumption is true closes up a possible hole in the argument.

For cause-and-effect arguments, anticipate an answer that rules out an alternate possible cause of the effect as explained by the argument. (See "Condition, Correlation, and Causation" in Chapter 1.)

Do not confuse a Most Strongly Supported question with a Strengthen question:

- Most Strongly Supported questions ask which answer is supported by the passage.
- Strengthen questions ask which answer would hypothetically support the passage.
- The words *most strongly support* can appear in either type of question, so pay attention to whether the passage is supporting the answer or the answer is supporting the passage.

Weaken Questions

To identify Weaken questions, look out for key words and phrases like *undermine*, *weaken*, *call into question*, and *cast doubt upon*. Some examples of Weaken questions include the following:

- Which one of the following, if true, would best challenge the conclusion of the passage?
- Which one of the following, if true, most seriously weakens the argument?
- Which one of the following, if true, casts the most doubt on the author's hypothesis?
- Which one of the following, if true, most undermines the conclusion above?

When reading the passage, be critical. First identify the conclusion, and then look at and identify why the premises do not support the conclusion. Look for possible fallacies. Raise objections to the argument as you read.

To answer these questions, first state the counterargument by negating the conclusion, and then anticipate an answer that strengthens the counterargument. Additionally, in cause-and-effect arguments, the answer often presents an alternate possible cause of an effect that the argument is trying to explain. Finally, think about the author's assumptions, and anticipate an answer that negates an assumption in order to weaken the passage. (See "Weakening Assumptions" on the pages which follow.)

Specific Tips for Weaken Questions

- Bring in an alternate possible cause of an effect to weaken a cause-and-effect argument.
- Anything that weakens the conclusion is fair game, even if seems to go beyond the scope of the stated premises.
- Weaken the argument by either (1) presenting an alternative conclusion or (2) weakening the logical connection between the stated premise(s) and the conclusion.

Common Misconceptions

As previously discussed, an answer option cannot negate an argument's premise. Accordingly, you will never have an answer option that weakens an argument simply by contradicting a premise that has already been stated. Consider the following example:

- Politician: Pollution in North Dakota is now higher than it has ever been in recorded history. If we do not take action to curb pollution emissions in North Dakota, it will not be long before our citizens begin to suffer grave health-related consequences. Therefore, the new proposal to cap pollution at pre-2005 levels must be adopted.

Here, you will never have an answer option that says something like "Pollution in North Dakota is actually at its lowest point in recorded history" because all of the premises of the argument remain in full effect as you apply the answer options. This is what we mean when we say an answer will never negate a premise of the argument. Your goal in weakening the argument is to make the conclusion less likely. You can do this either by affirming an alternative conclusion or by weakening the logical connection between the premise and the conclusion. Here are two possible weakeners for this argument:

1. "An alternate proposal to work with neighboring states to reduce their pollution would be more effective in preventing pollution-related health disorders in North Dakota."

This weakens the argument by presenting an alternate conclusion. If this is true (and remember, the question tells you to assume it is true), then this undermines the argument's conclusion that the pre-2005 proposal should be adopted.

2. North Dakota has the lowest pollution rate in the country, and even citizens of the states with the highest pollution rates have not experienced any health-related consequences because of pollution.

This weakens the argument by weakening the logical connection between the premise and the conclusion. Notice that this answer option does not actually negate the premise of the argument. It is not contradicting the statement that pollution in North Dakota is higher than ever; rather, if this answer is true (and remember, the question says to assume it is true), it shows that the pollution in North Dakota is not really a problem. Although pollution is higher than ever, it is still relatively low, and there is no cause for concern over the health issues mentioned by the politician.

Weakening Assumptions

You can also think of the second weakener above as an attack against one of the author's implicit assumptions. In making the argument, the author's necessary assumption is "The fact that North Dakota's pollution is higher than ever is cause for health concern." By bringing in a sentence that effectively says, "No, it is not," you negate the assumption, weakening the argument.

Justify (Sufficient Assumption) Questions

To identify Justify (Sufficient Assumption) questions, watch for key words and phrases like *if assumed*, *if valid*, *if established*, *would enable*, and *justify*. Questions may look like the following:

- The conclusion is properly drawn if which one of the following is assumed?
- Which one of the following is an assumption that would serve to justify the conclusion above?
- From which one of the following does the conclusion logically follow?

- Which one of the following is an assumption that would permit the conclusion above to be properly drawn?
- Which one of the following principles, if accepted, most strongly justifies drawing the conclusion above?

When reading the passage, first identify the conclusion and then discover why it is not fully supported by the premises. Think about completing the following equation:

- **Stated Premises + Your Sufficient Assumption = Fully Justified Conclusion**

That is, you want to come up with a sentence that, combined with a premise (or premises) of the argument, would allow you to say, "Therefore, [conclusion]" with 100 percent logical certainty. Your goal is to justify the conclusion, turning the passage into a strong argument.

> **Did You Know?**
>
> Do not confuse Sufficient Assumption questions with Necessary Assumption questions. Necessary Assumption questions ask *what the author is assuming* whereas Sufficient Assumption questions ask you to *use outside assumptions* to justify the passage. These questions require entirely different strategies.

Watch out for language that appears only in the conclusion. Your answer choice must fully justify the entire conclusion; it should usually include the same language as any new language in the conclusion. If you have a normative conclusion, for example, you must have a normative premise; if you do not, then the sufficient assumption must include normative language.

Specific Tips For Justify/Sufficient Assumption Questions

- No matter how implausible or extreme, you want an answer that, if assumed, would make the argument airtight.
- Read the conclusion of the argument, and then say "This has to be true because . . ."; then read the premises and your selected answer.
  - The conclusion of the argument should be inescapably valid based on the premises plus your chosen answer.
- Sufficient assumptions are not actually assumptions. You are not identifying what the author is assuming. You are bringing in an extrinsic assumption to justify the author's reasoning.

Common Misconceptions

- Your answer needs to do more than strengthen the argument. It needs to completely connect the premises to the conclusion in a way that removes any possible "hole."
- Your answer does not need to be reasonable. It can be something completely absurd, in ridiculously extreme language. The point is that if we assume the answer to be true, then the conclusion of the argument is inescapably true as well.

Resolve Questions

To identify Resolve questions, look out for key words like *resolve, explain, reconcile, conflict, paradox,* and *discrepancy*. Resolve questions may read as follows:

- Which one of the following, if true, most helps to resolve the paradox?
- Which one of the following, if true, best reconciles the discrepancy described above?
- Which one of the following, if true, does most to explain the apparently paradoxical outcome?

When reading the passage, expect to find an apparent paradox (i.e., a situation where you have two facts and it does not seem like both could be true at the same time). Do not worry about premises and conclusions here; in many cases, the passage that accompanies Resolve questions will be a fact set rather than an argument.

To answer these questions, identify the apparent paradox or discrepancy, and then consider what would cause the paradoxical situation to make sense. Let's look at the following example sentence:

- "Saturated fat leads to heart disease. The French eat lots of butter, which is high in saturated fat, but have very low rates of heart disease."

Possible answers might include the following:

- "The French also eat lots of fish, which counteracts the negative effects of saturated fat."
- "The degree to which saturated fat leads to heart disease is minimal compared to almost every other food present in the diets of people in countries with high rates of heart disease."

Specific Tips for Resolve Questions

- First, identify the apparent paradox.
- Stop and think: What would cause this to make sense?
- Remember, not all of these passages are arguments. Some are mere fact sets and will not have conclusions.

Common Misconceptions

Remember that you should assume the answer options to be true. Never cross out an answer option as incorrect because it is either untrue in real life or unstated/not implied within the passage. The answer is, by nature, outside information that you are bringing into the passage to make things right.

Practice Questions

9. *Research shows that students who participate in extracurricular activities tend to perform better academically. Some educational theorists argue that this is because these activities teach students valuable skills, such as time management and teamwork. Therefore, schools should prioritize funding for extracurricular programs to improve overall student performance.*

Which one of the following, if true, MOST strengthens the argument?
A) Schools with extensive extracurricular programs have higher student GPAs on average than schools without such programs.
B) Participation in extracurricular activities is voluntary, and students who choose to participate are generally more motivated than students who choose not to.
C) The majority of students who participate in extracurricular activities report enjoying them more than their regular classes.
D) Research shows that students who participate in extracurricular activities are less likely to drop out of school.
E) Schools that have cut funding for extracurricular programs have seen a decrease in overall student performance.

10. Recent studies suggest that implementing flexible work hours can lead to higher employee productivity. Proponents argue that when employees can choose their own work hours, they are more likely to work during their productive times, leading to better overall performance; therefore, companies should adopt flexible work-hour policies to maximize productivity.

Which one of the following, if true, MOST strengthens the argument?
   A) Research shows that employees are more productive when they can work during their preferred hours.
   B) Employees with flexible work hours take fewer sick days compared to those with fixed schedules.
   C) Companies with flexible work hours report higher employee satisfaction than those with fixed schedules.
   D) Employees are more likely to prioritize their personal life over their work life if they have flexible work hours.
   E) Companies that have implemented flexible work hours have seen a decrease in employee turnover rates.

11. *Studies in Japan have shown that implementing mandatory physical education (PE) classes in schools significantly reduces childhood obesity rates; therefore, if mandatory PE classes are introduced in schools in the United States, childhood obesity rates will decline significantly.*

Each of the following, if true, would weaken the argument EXCEPT which of the following?
   A) The dietary habits of children in Japan are significantly healthier than those of children from the United States.
   B) Many schools in the United States lack the funding and facilities to implement effective PE programs.
   C) In Japan, mandatory PE classes are supplemented by extensive public health campaigns that promote healthy eating.
   D) Other countries that have implemented mandatory PE have not seen the same results as Japan.
   E) Physical education classes alone cannot address all of the factors contributing to childhood obesity in the United States.

12. *Increasing the minimum wage will lead to greater economic prosperity for low-income workers. Proponents argue that higher wages will give those workers more disposable income to spend on goods and services, thereby boosting the economy. Therefore, raising the minimum wage is beneficial for the overall economy.*

Which of the following, if true, MOST weakens the argument?
   A) Increasing the minimum wage has historically led to higher levels of consumer spending.
   B) Some workers may use their additional income to pay off debts rather than spending it on goods and services.
   C) Small businesses will likely need to reduce the number of people they employ if the minimum wage is increased.
   D) Larger businesses can absorb the cost of increased wages more easily than smaller businesses.
   E) Higher wages will result in increased tax revenues, which can be used for public services.

13. *In the tech industry, all innovative products are developed by companies that foster a creative work environment. The companies that have had the most success in creating innovative products have encouraged collaboration, resulting in a more creative work environment; therefore, in the tech industry, companies that do not encourage collaboration will not develop innovative products.*

The conclusion follows logically from the premises if which of the following is assumed?
   A) Encouraging collaboration is a necessary condition for fostering a creative work environment in the tech industry.
   B) Companies in the tech industry prize innovation above all else.
   C) Collaboration among employees is more important than individual talent in developing innovative products.
   D) The most successful companies in the tech industry have creative work environments.
   E) Companies in the tech industry that develop innovative products sometimes fail to encourage collaboration.

14. *A recent health study revealed that individuals who consume green smoothies regularly report feeling healthier and more energetic. Surprisingly, national sales data show that bottled green smoothies sell far less than sugary sodas.*

Each of the following would, by itself, help to resolve the apparent paradox described in the passage EXCEPT which option?
   A) Green smoothies are often made at home using fresh ingredients rather than purchased pre-made.
   B) The study was conducted in a region with higher health consciousness than the national average.
   C) Sugary sodas are much cheaper than bottled green smoothies.
   D) People do not typically consider health implications when purchasing a beverage.
   E) It is widely understood that soda is unhealthy and should be consumed infrequently.

Critical Reasoning Questions

This family of questions tests your ability to describe, using logical terms, how the author is making an argument (see "LSAT Logic Vocabulary" in Chapter 1). In Method of Reasoning questions, you describe a strategy the author uses to make the argument. In Role of a Statement questions, you describe the function of a particular clause or sentence, usually by describing it as a premise, conclusion, example, analogy, or intermediate conclusion. In Argument Flaw questions, you identify fallacies within the author's reasoning. In Evaluate the Argument questions, you assess what would be needed to determine whether the argument's conclusion is sound.

Table 3.4. Critical Reasoning Questions	
QUESTION TYPES	**GENERAL STRATEGIES**
1. Method of Reasoning	1. Focus on how the author argues, not what the author says.
2. Role of a Statement	
3. Argument Flaw	2. Paraphrase the structure of the argument as you read.
4. Evaluate the Argument	

General Tips for Critical Reasoning Questions

- Focus on how the author argues, not what the author says.
- Paraphrase the structure of the argument as you read.

Method of Reasoning Questions

To identify Method of Reasoning questions, look for key phrases and words like *argumentative strategy* and *the author does*. Sample wordings from actual LSAT tests include the following:

- In the passage, the author…
- In order to advance her point of view, the author does each of the following EXCEPT…
- The passage employs which one of the following argumentative strategies?
- Sims does which one of the following?

When reading the passage, identify the components of the argument:

- premise
- intermediate conclusion
- conclusion

If any of the premises are examples or analogies, identify those as well. Do not worry at all about subject matter detail; in fact, it is best to paraphrase these passages as you read in a such way that omits subject matter detail entirely (see answer explanation below).

The correct answer is anything that describes something the author does within the argument. These questions are testing your ability to describe the structure of the argument, rather than its content.

Specific Tips for Method Of Reasoning Questions

- Identify each component of the argument as you read, look for premises, intermediate conclusions, and conclusions.
- Be aware of examples and analogies.
- Review "LSAT Logic Vocabulary" in Chapter 1.

Avoid Common Misconceptions

No two answers will say the same thing. In these answer options, every word is important. If you are about to choose an answer that says, "presents evidence to refute a hypothesis," you should be able to identify the portion of the passage that matches up to the evidence, and you should be able to identify a specific hypothesis refuted by the author. If any element of the answer option is missing, then the answer is incorrect.

Role of a Statement Questions

To identify Role of a Statement questions, look for key phrases and words like *plays which role* and *performs which function*. Role of Statement questions may look like the following:

- The phrase *certain traits like herding ability risk being lost among pedigreed dogs* serves which one of the following functions in the argument?
- The statement that adolescents and adults are not the same plays which one of the following roles in the argument?

The question will present a phrase or sentence from the passage and ask you to identify the phrase's function. Is it the argument's conclusion? Premise? Intermediate premise? Underline or bracket the phrase or sentence that the question is asking you about; that way, it stands out as you read the passage.

As you read the passage, identify the conclusion. If it matches the underlined phrase or sentence, then your answer should be some variant of "It is the conclusion," such as "It is the claim that is supported by the remaining propositions in the argument." If the phrase or sentence does not match the conclusion, then consider the premise and whether the phrase serves as an example or analogy. If it is not a premise, then is it just background information? If so, then it essentially plays no role in the argument other than to introduce the topic. Any of these functions are possible answers to the question. Ideally, you should be able to identify the role of the statement without looking at the answers. Spend your time on the passage, not the answers.

Specific Tips for Role Of A Statement Questions

- Always stop and fully consider what role the statement plays before you even glance at the answer options.
- If the statement is simply a premise or a conclusion, then pick the answer that reflects that. Do not shy away from "easy" answers.

Common Misconceptions

As with Method of Reasoning questions, no two answer options will say the same thing, even if they look similar. Every word in the answer option is important. Review the "LSAT Logic Vocabulary" in Chapter 1 and add any new words found in these answer options to your vocabulary list if you have trouble with them.

Argument Flaw Questions

To identify Argument Flaw questions, look for key words and phrases like *error in reasoning*, *vulnerable to criticism*, *weakness*, and *flaw*. Argument Flaw questions may look like the following:

- A major weakness of the argument is that it...
- A questionable technique used in the argument is to...
- A reasoning error in the argument is that the argument...
- The reasoning in the argument is not sound because it fails to establish that...
- Which one of the following describes a flaw in the argument?

When reading the passage, be critical. Identify the conclusion, and then look at the premises and identify why the premises do not support the conclusion. Raise objections to the argument as you read.

Assuming you have thoroughly mastered the fallacies in Chapter 2 of this book, you should be able to identify the fallacy committed by the argument. Even if you do not call the fallacy by its name, you should be able to find a logical reason why the premises do not support the conclusion. Note that there are generally two forms in which the answers might be worded:

1. Logical terms: Sometimes the answers use wording that is similar to the actual definitions of the fallacies (e.g., "draws a generalization on the basis of an unrepresentative sample").

2. Factual terms: Other times, the answers use wording that is heavily laden with the factual content of the passage (e.g., "draws a generalization about all college students on the basis of a survey conducted at one college").

Specific Tips For Argument Flaw Questions

- Read the argument critically. Look for weaknesses.
- Do not simply say, "That doesn't sound right"'; finish the thought: "That doesn't sound right because [fallacy]."
- Review the fallacies frequently to stay fresh.

Common Misconceptions

Just because the answer option describes a fallacy that the author could have committed does not make it the correct answer. Be sure that your answer describes something that the author is actually doing.

Evaluate the Argument Questions

To identify Evaluate questions, look for key words and phrases like *evaluate* and *most helpful to know*. Evaluate questions may look like the following:

- Which one of the following would be most useful to know in evaluating the argument?
- Clarification of which one of the following issues would be most important to an evaluation of the skeptic's position?

These questions are rare, appearing at a frequency of less than one question per LSAT. When reading the passage, identify uncertainties in the argument so that you can identify the kind of information that would help evaluate whether the conclusion is actually likely or not.

To answer these questions, pretend that you have been called upon to evaluate the conclusion's likelihood. You get to ask for additional information and additional premises. What extra information would you **seek**? Generally, the answers to these questions are themselves in the form of a question, so this is a good way of anticipating the answer.

Additionally, you need an answer that makes the conclusion strong or weak, depending on whether it is true or false. It would be useful to know if an answer has this sort of effect on the argument and would therefore be a good answer choice.

Specific Tips for Evaluate The Argument Questions

- Read the argument very critically, in the same way that you would read the passage accompanying a Flaw question.
- Answer options usually start with the term *whether*. As you read these options, drop *whether*, and read the rest of the answer only. If the answer would strengthen the argument if it were true and weaken the argument if it were false (or vice versa), then it is exactly what you are looking for.

Practice Questions

15. *Many people claim that taking vitamin C supplements can prevent the common cold; however, numerous scientific studies have shown that vitamin C has no significant effect on preventing colds. The claim that vitamin C can prevent the common cold is therefore false.*

Which one of the following MOST accurately describes the method of reasoning used in the argument?
   A) drawing an analogy
   B) arguing that a correlation implies causation
   C) assuming that what is true of the parts is true of the whole
   D) appealing to scientific evidence to refute a commonly held belief
   E) relying on anecdotal evidence to support a claim

16. **Argument:** *Implementing stricter fuel efficiency standards in new cars is critical in reducing carbon emissions. Some argue that these standards will drive up the cost of vehicles; however, the savings on fuel will more than make up for the initial expenses. In addition to being beneficial to the environment, it is therefore in the best financial interests of the consumer to implement stricter fuel efficiency standards.*

Statement: *Some argue that these standards will drive up the cost of vehicles.*

What role does the statement, "Some argue that these standards will drive up the cost of vehicles" play in the above argument?
   A) It provides supporting evidence for the argument's main point.
   B) It explains the reasoning behind the argument's conclusion.
   C) It introduces an objection that the argument aims to refute.
   D) It highlights an unintended consequence of the proposed standards.
   E) It presents an alternative solution to reducing carbon emissions.

17. *The number of people who wear sunglasses has increased significantly over the past decade. During the same period, there has been a sizable increase in skin cancer cases. Therefore, the increase in skin cancer cases must be due to the increased use of sunglasses.*

What is the primary flaw in the above argument?
   A) It mistakes correlation for causation.
   B) It does not consider that people who wear sunglasses likely spend more time in the sun.
   C) It assumes that skin cancer cases are accurately reported and tracked.
   D) It fails to consider the role of genetics in skin cancer.
   E) It fails to consider that wearing sunglasses might reduce the risk of eye damage.

18. **Parent:** Childhood obesity is a health crisis, and measures need to be taken to improve public health. My daughter's school banned the sale of junk food two years ago, and she lost thirty pounds, going from clinically obese to a healthy weight. If we ban the sale of junk food at all of our schools, we can solve the crisis once and for all!

Which of the following would be MOST useful to know in evaluating the argument?
- A) what the students are eating at home
- B) whether the rate of obesity in the student body as a whole declined
- C) whether the school made other changes to encourage a healthier lifestyle for its student body
- D) what types of food the school has started serving since the ban was enacted
- E) what types of food the school was serving before the ban

Parallel Reasoning Questions

This family of questions, described in Table 3.6., tests your ability to isolate and match a pattern of reasoning, argument flaw, or underlying principle between two arguments. One of the skills that you will need as a law student and attorney is to be able to argue by analogy, and these questions test your ability to recognize when two arguments are actually analogous to each other. These questions tend to be long and time-consuming, but the concept of finding a matching argument is generally straightforward. The diagram accompanying this family shows a double-sided arrow, indicating that the passage will match an answer.

Table 3.5. Parallel Reasoning Questions

QUESTION TYPES	GENERAL STRATEGIES	FAMILY DIAGRAM
1. Parallel Pattern of Reasoning 2. Parallel Flaw 3. Parallel Principle	1. Identify the pattern of reasoning, argument flaw, or underlying principle of the passage as you read. 2. Match only the pattern of reasoning, not the content.	Passage ↔ Answers

General Tips for Parallel Reasoning Questions

- Identify the pattern of reasoning, argument flaw, or underlying principle of the passage as you read.
- Match only the pattern of reasoning, flaw, or principle—not the subject matter detail of the passage.

A Note About Parallel Reasoning and Parallel Flaw

Parallel Pattern of Reasoning questions are separated from Parallel Flaw questions because of the actual question that appears on the test. Sometimes it asks you to match the pattern of reasoning, and other times it asks you to match a flaw, indicating that the passage is flawed. However, even if it is a Parallel Pattern of Reasoning question, the argument might still be flawed. In such a case, you may be looking at a question that is effectively a Parallel Flaw question (i.e., you will only have to match the flaw in an answer). Or, you may need to match more than just the flaw. For example, you may also need to match up extreme language in the conclusions.

Parallel Pattern of Reasoning Questions

To identify Parallel Pattern of Reasoning questions, look for key words and phrases like *parallel*, *logical features*, *pattern of reasoning*, and *most similar*. Questions may be worded as follows:

- Which one of the following most closely parallels the reasoning used in the passage?
- Which one of the following has a logical structure most like that of the argument above?
- Which one of the following exhibits a pattern of reasoning that is most parallel to that used by the novelist?

Untangle the passage as you read:

- Place the premises first, and then read the conclusion last.
- Diagram any conditional statements alongside the passage.
- If you have categorical statements, use Venn diagrams or concentric circles to diagram the premises only, and then see whether the conclusion is apparent from the premises; if it is, then the argument is valid; if it is not, the argument is flawed.
    - Focus on the logical components of the passage.

To answer these questions, diagram the passage whenever possible, and preemptively think of an analogous argument. That way, when you read the correct answer, its similarity to the passage will stand out.

Specific Tips for Parallel (Pattern Of) Reasoning Questions

- Diagram conditional statements.
- Do not confuse "if" statements with "only if" statements.
- Use Venn diagrams or concentric circles to depict all/some/none statements.

Common Misconceptions

Do not worry about the order of the sentences in the passage. This is not part of the structure of the argument, and it is not something that you have to match up in your answer. If the conclusion is first in the passage, it can be last in the correct answer.

Parallel Flaw Questions

To identify Parallel Flaw questions, look for key words and phrases like *similar flaw* and *similar error in reasoning*. Questions may resemble the following:

- Which one of the following contains an error of reasoning most similar to that made in the argument above?
- Which one of the following arguments contains a flaw that is most similar to the one in the argument above?

These questions are only testing your ability to match the logical fallacy in the argument with the logical fallacy in the correct answer; therefore, your primary focus when reading the passage should be to identify the fallacy.

Even if the passage is long and convoluted, the defining characteristic of the correct answer is that it will contain the same fallacy as the passage. If the passage commits the fallacy of mistaken reversal, all a correct answer will need is mistaken reversal. Perhaps the answer will be similar in other regards (such as the number of premises or the order of the sentences), but this is not required.

Specific Tips for Parallel Argument Flaw Questions

- Always stop at the end of the passage and determine the flaw.
- You only have to match the flaw. Even if the passage is long and convoluted, if the flaw is a simple mistaken reversal, you only need to find an answer with a mistaken reversal.

Common Misconceptions

Many students try to take a shortcut by matching the language of the passage to the language of the answers. That is, they will see the words *always* or *should* in the passage and look for answers with similar wording. **Do not do this!** While it may sometimes work, it will also sometimes cause you to eliminate the correct answer. Your job is to match the fallacy—not the wording of the argument. You only have to match the underlying principle, not the argument's structure or language.

Parallel Principle Questions

To identify Parallel Principle questions, read the question carefully. In these questions, the passage and answers will all be arguments, without any principle explicitly stated in either the passage or the answers. Instead, the question itself will tell you that you are looking for an answer that is based on the same principle upon which the passage is based. Parallel Principle questions may look like this:

- Which one of the following most closely conforms to the principle that the passage above illustrates?

As you read the passage, think, "What is this passage an example of ?" Come up with a general, broad principle for which the passage would be a good example, but which could also apply to a variety of other situations.

To answer these questions, come up with another situation to which your anticipated general principle could apply. This will help you spot the correct answer as you read the answer options.

Specific Tips For Parallel Principle Questions

- These questions are the parallel version of Underlying Principle questions. Your job is to identify the principle that guides the author's reasoning in the original passage.
- The principle is often a generalized form of "If premises like these are true, then a conclusion like this can follow."
- The passage and your chosen answer should both be examples or illustrations of the same underlying principle.

> **Did You Know?**
>
> Answers options B and C in question number 4 (LSAT example 1.1.20.) fall into the category of answer options that are *never* correct. On Inference questions, you will never find a correct answer that makes a hypothetical prediction about a future condition unless the passage specifically includes information that would justify such a prediction.

Practice Questions

19. *If a someone is a doctor, then that person has completed medical school. Since Rachel has completed medical school, she must be a doctor.*

Which of the following arguments is MOST similar in structure to the argument above?
   A) If a building is a skyscraper, it has more than fifty floors. Since this building does not have more than fifty floors, it cannot be a skyscraper.
   B) If a student is on the honor roll, he must be smart and have good grades. Mark has good grades, so he must be smart.
   C) If an animal is a bird, then it must have wings. This animal does not have wings; therefore, it cannot be a bird.
   D) Whenever it rains, the streets get wet. Since it rained last night, the streets must be wet this morning.
   E) If a book is a best seller, then it has been widely read. Since this book has been widely read, it must be a bestseller.

20. *My doctor is very knowledgeable and has studied nutrition extensively. He recommended that I follow a strict low-fat, low-cholesterol diet for my heart health. He has had three triple bypasses, though, so I do not think his advice can be very sound.*

Which of the following exhibits the logical fallacy employed in the above passage?
   A) Having a strong educational background in nutrition is meaningless if a person does not apply those principles in their own life.
   B) Mary takes very good care of her health and has the energy of someone half her age. She says that her secret is strictly following a keto diet, so that must be the best way to achieve good health.
   C) The mayor's proposal to build a new park should be rejected. He was recently found guilty of tax evasion, and someone who cannot be trusted to obey the law should not be entrusted with public projects.
   D) Running must be very good for you. My neighbor runs marathons, and he is the healthiest person I know.
   E) The scientist is very educated in the subject of climate change; however, his theory runs counter to the theories espoused by the leading experts in his field. Therefore, it must be incorrect.

21. *When deciding whether or not an action is moral, one should consider the lessons to be drawn from major moral codes. Ultimately, however, the only way to act in a truly moral fashion is to follow one's own intuition and do what feels right.*

Which of the following MOST closely conforms to the principle that the passage above illustrates?
- A) When choosing a new hobby, it is important to do your research and figure out what seems most practical and interesting. This will ensure that you choose a hobby that is right for you.
- B) When deciding where to go on vacation, one should first make a list of places they would like to see, and then look for expert advice on which is the best destination. Being informed will lead to a better vacation experience.
- C) When deciding whether or not to purchase an expensive item, it is critical to read reviews and get feedback from others to make sure the product performs as advertised and does not disappoint the buyer. This will prevent buyer's remorse.
- D) When choosing which type of food to feed your cat, it is important to consider the advice of your veterinarian as well as experts on feline health. In the end, though, it is important to do your own research and choose the food that best fits the needs of your cat.
- E) When deciding how to raise your children, it is best to look at the methods of other parents and see how their children turned out. This way you can choose the parenting method that will lead your children down the path you would like them to take.

Helpful Hint:

1. Read the question carefully; there have been a few LSAT questions that do not ask what the two speakers disagree about but rather what they *agree* about. If you see such a question, choose an answer to which both speakers are either committed to saying, "That is true," or to saying, "That is false."

2. Review "Principles and Applications" in Chapter 1 to ensure that you thoroughly understand how general principles can apply to facts in order to produce conclusions.

3. Many students struggle with becoming personally involved in the content of the argument or relating the content to what they know about the subject in real life. Reading the argument without the subject matter detail can break this habit and help in evaluating arguments dispassionately.

4. Remember, you do not need to diagram all the answer choices. When you see conditional statements, try to diagram the passage to see the pattern of reasoning more clearly. Then, as you read through the answer choices, compare the answer choices to your shorthand diagram, matching com- ponents of the answer choices to the statements written in shorthand.

ANSWER KEY

1. E: The main conclusion of the passage is that in order to continue to volunteer at the community center, Joel must comply with its policies. Options A, B, and C are premises that are introduced in the passage and factor into the author's conclusion, but they do not reflect the conclusion itself. Option D is an implication that is not made by the writer of the passage, although it is clearly what Joel believes.

2. D: The passage directly states that people who consume diets rich in whole fruits tend to have lower rates of obesity and heart disease and does not contradict this assertion in any other place. This means the statement must be true for the purposes of this question. Option A is incorrect because the passage does not assert that diets high in processed sugar are the only causes of heart disease; it merely asserts that diets high in processed sugar can lead to health issues including heart disease. Option B is incorrect because the passage argues that any negative health impacts from natural sugar may be mitigated by fiber and nutrients; it does not argue that consuming natural sugars does not lead to health issues. Options C and E are incorrect because they are both contrary to information from the passage.

3. A: The passage directly states that demand for utilities such as water and electricity will increase. It is impossible that demand will both increase and decrease. This assertion must therefore be false, so option A is correct. Options B, C, and D are all stated as true in the text, and therefore cannot be false, making these options incorrect. The passage does not address the assertion in option E at all, so there is no way of knowing whether it is true or false.

4. B: Option B takes the argument made in the passage and extends it to a logical conclusion that is not directly stated in the passage. Lower incidence of chronic illnesses such as heart disease and diabetes would undoubtedly lead to lower health care costs. Options A and E are not addressed in the passage, nor is anything tangential. These options are therefore incorrect. Option C is incorrect because, although the study points out that exercise can have a beneficial effect on existing mental health symptoms, it does not address the issue of whether exercise can prevent mental health symptoms. Option D is directly contradictory to the findings of the study.

5. C: The argument hinges on the assumption that residents will choose to use the bicycles over driving their cars if biking is made easier and more accessible. Without this assumption, the expectation of reduced traffic congestion would not hold; therefore, option C is correct. Option A is not necessary for the argument to hold. Although traffic is more likely to be reduced if a larger portion of the city's residents can afford to utilize the program, it is not necessary for every resident to be able to afford the program for it to affect traffic congestion. Options C and E are not necessary for the argument to hold, as the source of traffic congestion and the relative safety of bicycles as opposed to cars are not factors that are explored in the original argument. Although sufficient funding is important for the program's success, it is not addressed in the argument; therefore, option D is also incorrect.

6. D: Emma argues that organic farming is better for the environment, while Lisa argues that it can lead to deforestation and loss of wildlife habitats, indicating that she believes organic farming may have a larger and more detrimental effect on the environment. Option A is incorrect, as both Emma and Lisa agree that organic farming avoids synthetic pesticides and fertilizers. Option B is incorrect, as Emma makes this claim directly in her argument, and it is not disputed by Lisa. Option C is incorrect, as it is an argument of Lisa's, and not directly addressed by Emma. Option E outlines a broader issue that is relevant to the argument, but neither addresses this point directly.

7. B: This principle aligns with the argument that the long-term benefits of preventative care justify the initial costs of implementing universal health care. Options A and D are incorrect, as they focus solely on the cost aspect of the argument, ignoring that access is also a benefit to be considered. Option C is touched on by the argument in that it is stated that preventative care is more cost-effective, but this alone is not an argument that is it necessarily better in general. Option E is too absolute of a principle and is not necessary for the argument to be valid. Even if it can be argued that universal health care is one of many ways to address the issues of access and cost, this does not invalidate the argument that it is a potential way to achieve these ends.

8. E: The tax law was unjust because it harmed low-income families, and that harm was foreseeable with reasonable forethought. Options A and D both describe laws that were intended to promote public welfare and succeeded in doing so. The fact that they also cause inconvenience to some parties does not make them unjust, as inconvenience does not equal harm. Option B lacks the positive intentions the principle requires for a law to be considered just. Although it ended with positive outcomes, it was still enacted in bad faith. Option C is incorrect because it does not adhere to the principle above. The negative outcomes were not necessarily foreseeable with reasonable forethought, and there is no claim made as to whether the law is just.

9. E: The author's conclusion is that schools should prioritize funding for extracurricular activities to improve academic performance. Option E is the answer that most strengthens this argument by showing that when a school that formerly prioritized extracurricular activities changed its behavior, the result was an overall decrease in student performance. This answer adds evidence that is not presented in the passage that helps to strengthen its conclusion.

Option A may also seem like a good strengthener for the conclusion, but really, it is just a restatement of a premise. The passage already states that students who engage in extracurricular activities perform better academically; option A merely restates this using GPA as the marker for academic performance. With hypothetical questions, it is important to make sure that you are not choosing an answer based on what the passage has already stated, but instead based on what would make the passage stronger or weaker. The correct answer would necessarily have to add information to the passage.

Option B would actually weaken the argument. If students who choose to engage in extracurricular activities are more motivated, then the reason they are getting better grades may be due to their motivation and not because of any benefits that result from the activities in which they engage. Option C does not directly strengthen the conclusion because students' enjoyment of extracurricular activities is not relevant to student performance. Option D provides an additional benefit to extracurricular activities, but again, it is not directly relevant to the issue of student performance, which is the focus of the argument.

10. A: Option A introduces research that strengthens the conclusion that companies should implement flexible work-hour policies to maximize productivity. While options B, C, and E may appear to strengthen the conclusion of the passage, they do not. Each of these options introduces another reason that flexible work-hour policies may benefit both companies and employees, but they do not support the conclusion of the passage directly. The conclusion is focused on maximizing productivity, and while taking fewer sick days, having higher rates of employee satisfaction, and having a lower turnover rate may help to increase productivity, these factors would not affect it as much as employees being able to work when they are most effective and focused on a daily basis. Option D is a weakener: if employees are placing a greater emphasis on their personal lives at the expense of their work lives in the work-life balance, their productivity would likely decrease.

11. B: While option B points out an issue that would make it more difficult to implement effective PE classes in the United States, it does not weaken the conclusion of the passage, which is that implementing mandatory PE classes in the United States would cause childhood obesity rates to decline significantly. While it may not be feasible to implement such programs in the United States, this does not weaken the argument that such programs would significantly impact childhood obesity rates if they were present.

Options A and C point toward cultural differences between the United States and Japan that would significantly weaken the causal link between mandatory PE classes and declining obesity rates. Without the benefit of the diet or health programs of Japan, mandatory PE in the United States would likely have a much smaller impact on childhood obesity. Option E also nods toward this issue in stating that PE classes cannot address all of the factors leading to childhood obesity in the United States. Option D weakens the argument significantly by stating that mandatory PE has not worked when implemented in places other than Japan.

12. C: The author's conclusion is that raising the minimum wage would be beneficial for the overall economy. Option C subverts this argument by pointing out that increasing the minimum wage can potentially lead to job loss, which would be a negative economic outcome. Options A and E support the conclusion of the passage. Option A directly states that increasing minimum wage has historically increased consumer spending, providing historical evidence that the predictions of proponents of raising minimum wage are correct. Option E shows an additional economic benefit to increasing minimum wage. Option B weakens the argument slightly, as paying off debt would not stimulate the economy as much as increased consumer spending; however, it would still do some measure of good for the economic standing of low-income workers and would likely lead to increased spending once their debt has been paid down. Option D does not address the overall economic impact but rather the manner in which different types of businesses would be affected by raising the minimum wage. While this is a relevant issue, it does not address the central focus of the conclusion.

13. A: The passage argues that a creative work environment is necessary to create innovative products and follows that by stating that companies that have encouraged collaboration have fostered creative work environments as a result. However, it is not stated anywhere in the passage that encouraging collaboration is a necessary precondition to fostering a creative work environment. Without this assertion, the conclusion that tech companies that do not encourage collaboration will not develop innovative products is not fully supported by the premises. If it is possible that there are other ways to foster a creative work environment without encouraging collaboration, this would render the conclusion false.

Option B does not connect the premises to the conclusion; it is merely a statement of company values that does not speak to the conditions necessary to develop innovative products. Option C compares the merits of individual talents versus collaborative efforts, which is supported by the conclusion that collaboration is a necessary condition of developing innovative products; however, the reverse is not true. Although this statement is justified by the passage, it does not justify the conclusion of the passage. Option D is basically a generalization of the premise presented in the passage that states, "all innovative products are developed by companies that foster a creative work environment," and does nothing to justify the conclusion. Option E directly contradicts the conclusion of the passage and is therefore incorrect.

14. E: This option only strengthens the paradox presented in the passage. The contradiction lies in people reporting feeling healthier after drinking green smoothies but engaging in purchasing decisions that do not reflect this. One would assume that feeling better after imbibing a beverage would result in people purchasing that beverage more, but clearly this is not the case, just as knowing that soda is unhealthy does not typically deter people from buying it.

Option A points to a potential reason that sales do not reflect people's preferences. Someone whose main concern is good health would be more likely to make their refreshment at home, whereas your average soda drinker is more interested in convenience than health. Option B brings up the fact that the data from the study may be skewed, and that a broader study might reveal different findings if conducted nationally. Option C provides a good reason that someone may choose a sugary soda over a green beverage; budget is an important consideration for most people. Option D states that people often do not consider health implications when purchasing a beverage, which may account for the discrepancy between the study's findings and the sales data.

15. D: To figure out the method of reasoning, paraphrase the passage omitting the content of the argument. The author states the common belief, presents scientific evidence against this belief, and concludes that the common belief is false. In other words, the author appeals to scientific evidence to refute a commonly held belief. It is not important whether the author is correct in this assertion or not; what matters is the form the argument takes.

Option A is incorrect because the author does not use an analogy to make her argument. Option B is incorrect because nowhere does the author argue that a correlation implies causation. Option C is a fallacy of composition and is not employed in the passage. Option E is the opposite of the author's method, and arguably is the fallacy committed by those who hold the belief she refutes with her evidence.

16. C: Let's begin by breaking this argument down into its main components:

- **Premise One:** Implementing stricter fuel efficiency standards in new cars is critical in reducing carbon emissions
- **Counterargument:** Some argue that these standards will drive up the cost of vehicles.
- **Premise Two:** The savings on fuel will more than make up for the initial expenses.
- **Conclusion:** In addition to being beneficial to the environment, it is therefore in the best financial interests of the consumer to implement stricter fuel efficiency standards.

The sentence, "Some argue that these standards will drive up the cost of vehicles," introduces an objection to the implementation of stricter fuel efficiency standards, which the passage goes on to refute before reaching its conclusion.

Option A is incorrect because this sentence actually does the opposite; it opposes the argument's main point. Option B is incorrect, again, because this sentence does nothing to bolster the main conclusion of the argument. Option D sounds correct at first glance, as this sentence does in fact highlight an unintended consequence of the proposed standards; however, this is not the primary function of the sentence in this context. Option E is incorrect, as this sentence merely raises an objection to the standards and does not offer an alternative solution.

17. A: The argument draws its conclusion from the factors introduced in the premises without determining whether or not those factors are related. While there is an apparent correlation between the increased use of sunglasses and the increased incidence of skin cancer, this does not show a causal link between wearing sunglasses and getting skin cancer, and the author fails to introduce any evidence that such a link exists. Option B is incorrect. Although it nods at the flaw in the argument, it does not directly address it. It is possible that the correlation is due to the people feeling comfortable spending more time in the sun because of their sunglasses; however, the real problem with the argument is that there are many factors that could account for the increase in skin cancer that have nothing to do with sunglasses. Option C is also a potential flaw, but a minor one in comparison to the above. Option D is incorrect; genetics is irrelevant to the argument as presented. Option E is incorrect, as eye damage is also irrelevant.

18. B: The argument relies on a sample of $n = 1$, and therefore commits the fallacy of hasty generalization. The effectiveness of the school's junk food ban is impossible to surmise from the success of just one student. The daughter discussed in the argument might simply have had a change of heart and altered her habits for reasons entirely unconnected to the junk food ban. If we knew the effects on the entire student body, the parent's argument would be a lot more effective. It would be better still to draw data from multiple schools employing the same policy.

Option A is incorrect. While their eating habits at home would have an impact on the individual health of the students, it would not impact whether banning junk food at schools is an effective measure to induce weight reduction. Option C is incorrect, but only because it is secondary to the hasty generalization flaw. It does point to a secondary flaw with the argument, which is that a school that enacts a junk food ban might also be encouraging more physical activity or offering improved health education at the same time, or that the ban might have been coincidental and the weight loss was due to other factors. Options D and E are incorrect, as knowing the details of the type of food served before and after the ban would not increase the effectiveness of the argument.

19. E: The passage can be mapped as two conditional statements:

- "If someone is a doctor, then that person has completed medical school," becomes D → M
- "Since Rachel has completed medical school, she must be a doctor," becomes M → D

Notice that the logic here is flawed. The passage commits the fallacy of mistaken reversal, so the answer must do the same. Option E follows this same pattern:

- "If a book is a best seller, then it has been widely read," becomes B → R
- "Since this book has been widely read, it must be a bestseller," becomes R → B

Although neither of these passages is logically correct, they are structured in the same manner.

Options A and C are incorrect; however, they are both logically valid and parallel in structure to each other, as both employ the contrapositive correctly. Option B neglects the premise from the first sentence in the second and is therefore incorrect. Option D shows a particular instance from a generalization and is also logically sound, and therefore not the correct answer.

20. C: The passage uses an ad hominem attack on the doctor to discredit his advice. The speaker argues that his education is meaningless, as he has suffered the same heart problems that he is trying to prevent in his patient. However, it is fallacious to believe that someone does not have knowledge just because they do not apply that knowledge in their own life. The doctor is educated in this matter, so the knowledge is there. The reason for his poor health may not be due to his diet; or if it is, his poor dietary choices may be the result of stress or addiction rather than lack of knowledge. Similarly, the mayor in option C's character is under attack in the argument.

Option A most resembles the passage in content, and in fact summarizes the argument of the speaker; however, it does not employ an ad hominem attack directly. It is therefore incorrect. Option B uses the hasty generalization fallacy and is therefore incorrect. Option D is incorrect for the same reason. Option E is incorrect, as it employs the appeal to authority fallacy rather than an ad hominem attack on the scientist.

Chapter 3 – Logical Reasoning: Questions

21. D: The principle behind the passage is that when making a decision, one should consider the advice of experts but ultimately choose what feels right to them. Option D employs this same principle. Consider the advice of your vet and experts as a factor, but also do your own research and then make your own decision. Option A does not mention considering the advice of experts and is therefore incorrect. Options B and C both espouse the principle that when choosing something, it is helpful to seek the advice of others to have a better experience; therefore, both are incorrect. Option E almost looks correct; however, the conclusion is that you should follow the parenting style that results in the child you want. In order to parallel the principle from the passage, the conclusion would need to be that you need to trust your own judgment when it comes to raising your child.

Chapter 4 – Reading Comprehension

There are two major components of a Reading Comprehension section: the **passages** and the **questions**. Four sets of questions must be completed, with five to eight questions per set, for a **total of approximately twenty-seven questions per section**. You have thirty-five minutes to complete the section.

Reading Comprehension questions are very similar to Logical Reasoning questions. In general, students who master Logical Reasoning questions generally have few problems with the Reading Comprehension questions.

The primary difference between the Logical Reasoning and Reading Comprehension questions is that the Reading Comprehension passages are longer. Many students find it difficult to read the lengthy passage and answer its seven questions in under nine minutes. This chapter therefore focuses primarily on efficient and effective reading strategies to help you beat the clock.

The Passage

Four sets of questions will appear in the Reading Comprehension section:

- Three sets of questions will each follow a single, long passage that usually ranges from fifty to seventy lines of text (350 – 500 words).
- One set of questions is a comparative reading exercise. This set of questions follows a set of two shorter passages (200 – 275 words each) on the same or similar topics.

Comparative reading passages can appear at any point during the Reading Comprehension section.

Always read Reading Comprehension passages as arguments, never as mere informational summaries or explanations. Additional tips on how to read the passages are provided next.

The Questions

Following each passage (or set of Comparative Reading passages), you will have five to eight questions. Questions generally ask the following:

- What is the author's main point/main idea/main conclusion?
- What is the author's primary purpose?
- What is the purpose of a given paragraph, sentence, line number, or word?
- What is the author (or another party) committed to believing, based on the passage?
- What attitude must the author (or another party) hold toward a given proposition?
- Which of the following is stated in the passage? (These are called Detail questions.)

- Which of the following is implied by the passage? (These are called Inference questions.)
- Which of the following, if true, would strengthen or weaken the argument?

Five Tips for Effective Reading

Reading Comprehension passages generally fall into one of four broad categories:

1. humanities
2. social sciences
3. life sciences
4. issues related to the law

You are not expected to have any background knowledge of the passage content; in fact, background knowledge can be a hindrance when you subconsciously read additional outside information into the passage. Be careful to focus only on what the passage actually says.

A common misconception is that the Reading Comprehension passages are descriptive, informational articles. In reality, every Reading Comprehension passage is persuasive. This means that you will need to distinguish an author's premises from the conclusions. Do the following as you read:

- Keep your pencil in hand in order to get things out of your head and on paper.
    - When you read something that sounds like a conclusion, put it in brackets.
    - When you see extreme language, circle it.
    - When you notice two facts that work together to make an interesting inference, write it down.
    - See "Recommended Symbols for Annotation" in Table 5.1.
- **Read the passage for structure** (not to memorize the details), and focus on the logical components of the passage For example:
    - Where is the author's main conclusion (if there is one)?
    - Where are the intermediate conclusions?
    - Who are the different parties with their perspectives?
    - By focusing on the logical components, you can quickly identify the specific details needed to answer a question.
- At the end of the first paragraph, stop and make sure you thoroughly understand what the author has said. The first paragraph generally presents one of three things:
    - The **author's conclusion**, which will then be supported in the following paragraphs.
    - **Another person's point of view**, which the author will then accept or refute in the following paragraphs.
    - **A problem or situation**, which the author will attempt to solve or explain in the following paragraphs.

- o Note: **Understanding the first paragraph is crucial to understanding the function of the passage as a whole.** If you are confused by the first paragraph, read it again for understanding.
- After you finish reading each paragraph, take three to five seconds to write a few words about the paragraph.
    - o For example, if the author is comparing Tuscan art to Venetian art and decides that Tuscan art was more widely renowned in the eighteenth century, you might write "T > V" in the margin to summarize the author's thoughts.
    - o **Short margin annotations** can be instrumental in marking details you may need to find later.
    - o Annotations also help your brain analyze the big picture of the argument.
- At the end of the whole passage, stop and spend ten to twenty seconds thinking about the answers to these two questions:
    - o What is the **author's main point**?
    - o What is the **author's primary purpose**?

These questions are discussed in detail later in the chapter. Knowing the answers to them can save you several minutes when answering the passage's multiple-choice questions.

Table 4.1. Recommended Symbols for Annotation in the Margin		
SYMBOL	**MEANING**	**USAGE**
→	if...then	Diagram conditional statements. Just as in Logical Reasoning and Logic Games, you will be expected to make inferences, and conditional statements often lead to such inferences.
+ -	positive attitude negative attitude	Notice where the author makes his or her personal feelings known about a subject by using words with positive or negative connotations, such as: "This **inspirational** work..." or "Smith's study portrays an **alarming** phenomenon..."
V_{auth} V_B V_C	Viewpoint	Keep the various viewpoints in the passage distinct. Some questions ask you for the view of someone other than the author.
ex.	Example	Section off lengthy examples from the rest of the passage. Use an arrow pointing from the example to the sentence in the passage that the example is supporting. Remember: Examples are premises.
[ ]	Conclusion	Put brackets around all conclusions, whether the author's or another's.

Table 4.1. Recommended Symbols for Annotation in the Margin

SYMBOL	MEANING	USAGE
⬭	transitions premise/conclusion indicators	Circle transition words such as: **But**, **However**, **Nevertheless**, **Yet**, **On the other hand**, etc., as well as premise and conclusion indicators.

Question Types

Main Point

Often, the first question in the set of questions that follows the passage will ask you something along the lines of "Which of the following best expresses the main idea of the passage?"

When you stop to consider the main idea, put yourself in the author's shoes:

- If you were the author, and if you had to replace the entire passage with one sentence that would prove your point, what would you say?

Focus primarily on the author's conclusion, as opposed to the premises:

- What is the author trying to prove?

As discussed earlier, you should always stop to consider the author's main point after reading the passage, even if you are short on time or if there is not an explicit "main point" question. Identify the author's argument so that you can better answer the questions about what the author believes.

Primary Purpose

One of the questions that follows many of the passages will ask you something along the lines of the following:

- Which of the following describes the primary purpose of the passage? Which of the following most accurately characterizes the function of the passage?

> **Did You Know?**
>
> The main point and the author's primary purpose are distinct. The **main point** is the main idea of a passage—the author's thesis or main conclusion. On the other hand, the author's **primary purpose** is the function of the passage, or what the author intends the passage to accomplish.

When you stop to consider the primary purpose of the passage, put yourself in the position of a critic. Pretend someone has just asked you to describe why the author has written the passage. You should respond with a simple verb phrase, such as one of the following:

- to present new evidence
- to question a common assumption
- to refute a hypothesis
- to critique a recently released book
- to showcase the various viewpoints in a scholarly debate
- to evaluate a theory and the charges of its critics

Use Method of Reasoning language to describe the function of the passage. Whereas Main Point answers tend to be lengthy (e.g., thesis sentences), Primary Purpose answers can be as short as four words.

Purpose of a Paragraph, Lines, or Words

These questions are similar to Primary Purpose questions, except that they focus on a specific paragraph, certain lines, or certain words in the passage. Answer questions about a specific paragraph just like you would answer a question about the primary passage as a whole:

- Consider, in one verb phrase (with an infinitive verb and a direct object), why the author is writing that paragraph.
    - Do this before you look at the answer options so that they do not distract you.

Be careful with questions that ask about specific line numbers, as in the following example:

- The author most likely refers to birds (lines 31 – 33) in order to do what?

First, go back to the passage to find the reference that the question mentions. But do not simply read the lines mentioned. Read one sentence before and one sentence after. Realize that the question is not asking you to define what the author is saying in lines 31 – 33; rather, the question is asking you why the author has included the sentence in lines 31 – 33. Usually, the answer is something like one of the following:

- "It is an example of [the point the author is trying to make in lines 29 – 30]."
- "It is offered in support of [the point the author is trying to make in lines 34 – 35]."

Very often, one of the incorrect answers will look like an interpretation of whatever the author has actually said in lines 31 – 33. Beware: Explaining the meaning of the author's sentence does not answer the question of the purpose of the author's sentence. Always read up one and down one additional sentence, and look for the logical connection between the line numbers in question and the remainder of the passage. Many questions ask you about a specific word, for example:

- The use of the word *deviation* (line 24) serves primarily to
- The author uses the word *transitory* (line 8) to most closely mean

First, go back to the passage and see how the word is used in context. In these two sample questions, the first asks for the word's purpose (i.e., look before and after the word for clues as to its logical function), while the second asks for the word's definition.

Author's Belief

Consider this question:

- It can be inferred from the passage that the author most likely believes which of the following?

Here, the key is to treat this question as a simple "What must be true?" question. Very frequently, students pick an answer that is consistent with the passage, but not an answer that follows from the passage.

If you treat these questions like Must Be True questions, you will find it easier to eliminate four answer options and choose the remaining answer; otherwise, you might find that two or three of the answer options look equally plausible.

Author's Attitude

Consider this question:

- The author most probably holds which of the following attitudes toward spelunking?

Generally, these questions have five answer options that span the following spectrum:

A) wild enthusiasm

B) overt optimism

C) qualified approval

D) reluctant disapproval

E) intransigent scorn

In most cases, extreme answers, like options A and E are not correct; however, if a word or phrase in the passage indicates that one of these is the answer, then choose the extreme answer. This is where using the + and – in the margins to annotate attitude-indicator words comes in handy.

Questions about the author's attitude or what the author would agree with are not subjective. You should read these questions as saying, "Based on the passage, what does the author absolutely have to believe?" or "What attitude must the author hold because of what the author has written?"

Many students have trouble with Reading Comprehension because they feel that they are supposed to be able to read the author's mind. In reality, you only need to read the text and make the logical inferences that reasonably follow from what has been explicitly stated.

Detail Questions

Consider this question/prompt:

- All of the following are specifically mentioned in the passage EXCEPT _____.

This traditional Reading Comprehension exercise tests your ability to remember where to find specific details in the passage. Frequently, these are EXCEPT questions that require you to find four of the five answer options in the passage before choosing the remaining answer.

Inference Questions

Consider this question/prompt:

- It can be inferred from the passage that _____.

These are the Reading Comprehension equivalent of Must Be True questions, and they should be treated accordingly by basing your answer entirely and only on the facts stated in the passage. Watch out for extreme language in the answer options, and pick an answer that is modestly worded.

Strengthen and Weaken Questions

Consider these questions:

- Which of the following, if true, would lend the most support to the author's hypothesis?

- Which of the following, if true, would most seriously undermine the validity of the author's research?

Just as in Logical Reasoning Strengthen and Weaken questions, you will be asked to bring in outside information to bolster or attack the author's argument. Remember that every LSAT Reading

Comprehension passage is an argument. Also, remember to never cross out an answer option because it "is not true"; the questions here tell you to assume that the answers *are* true.

Other Questions

Although not as common, other questions will ask you to describe the organization of the passage or a specific paragraph. These questions are similar to Role of a Statement or Method of Reasoning questions, but you must choose an answer that lists the correct sequence of components that appear in the passage.

Additionally, some questions ask you to complete an analogy by identifying which of the five answer options is most analogous to a situation in the passage. These questions are similar to Parallel Principle questions.

Recognize that you may see new and different questions on test day. Still, the vast majority of questions will be the types described above. Because there are five to eight questions (of a generally predictable nature) following each passage, it is not worth your time to read all the questions before you read the passage. Just read the passage, annotate as you go, and follow the tips presented earlier to ensure that you are looking for relevant information as you read.

Comparative Reading: Passages and Questions

Sometimes, the two passages come from authors who are writing on the same issue. In such a case, they may either be writing opposing arguments, or they may be arguing the same conclusion but for different reasons. Alternatively, you might have two authors whose passages are related because they cover a common subject, but they do not actually argue the same specific issue. For example, one might be writing about teaching law, while the other might be writing about teaching history. Identify the authors' relationships to each other as you read because you will likely be asked about how one of the authors views the other, or about the relationship of one passage to the other.

Time Management

There are generally two strategies for time management on Reading Comprehension:

1. **Attempt to read all four passages and answer all the questions.**

This is the path you should take if you have little or no trouble reading the passages and answering the questions within thirty-five minutes:

- Plan to spend eight minutes and forty-five seconds on each of the four passages—a little less if the passage only has five or six questions, and a little longer if the passage has eight questions.

- Generally, it is a good idea to spend three minutes to three minutes and forty-five seconds reading the passage, and then ten to twenty seconds considering the main point and primary purpose.

- Use the remaining four minutes and thirty seconds to five minutes and thirty seconds to answer the questions.

2. **Choose the three passages you prefer, and aim for near–100 percent accuracy on the questions for those.**

If you find that reading through the passage in four minutes or less is difficult, then you might aim to answer only three of the four sets of questions (all of them correctly). If you do this, you should try to reduce the number of questions you would miss by skipping either the passage that has the fewest questions or the passage that looks the most difficult. You may find that completing three passages well can earn you more points than you would be able to earn by attempting all four passages poorly.

Finally, as with Logical Reasoning, work efficiently on the questions. You will likely be asked about a specific fact from the passage, an inference about a topic that was discussed, or a specific paragraph or line number. Before you start sifting through answer options, be sure to do the following in order to have a better grasp of what the answer should look like, greater confidence in choosing an answer, and less difficulty in choosing between two answers that both look right:

- Go to the passage.
- Consider the question.
- Anticipate the answer.

Learning to Read Difficult Material

If you are not accustomed to reading difficult articles and find yourself unable to digest the content of LSAT Reading Comprehension passages, then spend several weeks (ideally, three to four months) reading dense, scholarly material. For example, you might consider reading the online version of the Harvard Law Review. Read quickly, paraphrase as you read, and practice typing out 350- to 500-word articles (in the style of LSAT Reading Comprehension passages) on the material that you read. Additionally, consider using the Reading Comprehension Worksheet on non-LSAT reading materials to practice your ability to identify arguments in day-to-day readings.

It is extremely important for you to understand the material you are reading; you cannot simply let your eyes pass over the page. Use the following strategies to help you best understand the material you will read:

- Engage with the passages.
- Pretend you are arguing against the author.
- Become personally involved, and wrap your mind around the passage.

If you fail to understand a sentence, you may very well lose the meaning of the paragraph, and you cannot afford to do this. Be diligent, keep your focus, and keep your pencil on the page.

Practice Questions

Social media has become ubiquitous and is now a routine part of teenage life, as common as attending school and engaging in extracurriculars. Although this innovation comes with benefits, such as opportunities for connection, creativity, and self-expression, the negative effects social media has on our youth cannot be ignored. Constant exposure to "highlight reels" taken from the lives of models and famous people has taken a significant toll on the self-esteem and mental health of the population as a whole; even more so on those in their most vulnerable years. Many of the negative outcomes associated with social media use are due to a phenomenon known as social comparison.

Social comparison is a natural human tendency wherein individuals determine their social and personal worth based on their observations of others. Even before social media, this could be very damaging, as we tend to compare ourselves to those we feel are better than us rather than engaging in a fair, balanced comparison. As a result, we often end up feeling that we are not good enough. These days, this issue is exacerbated by the fact that we are constantly bombarded by idealized images of beautiful people and their impossible lifestyles. For teenagers, who are at a critical stage in developing their identities, this can be particularly damaging.

Constant feelings of inadequacy have led to a steep decline in the self-esteem of teenagers. Studies show that self-esteem and the amount of time spent on social media apps have an inverse relationship, likely stemming from the perception that others are more successful, attractive, and happy than we are. This perception breeds feelings of worthlessness and insecurity that can lead to negative mental health outcomes.

Studies show that anxiety and depression rates have skyrocketed, especially among teenagers. Eating disorders are more common now than ever before. And the dopamine-fueled high of receiving likes, comments, and followers can lead to obsessive behaviors that cause people to prioritize their online presence over their real-world interests, responsibilities, and relationships. These behaviors mirror those in people suffering from substance abuse disorders and other addiction issues.

The negative impacts social media has on our youth can, however, be ameliorated. Education is a key factor. Ensuring that teenagers are aware of the curated nature of social media content and encouraging critical thinking can help lessen the adverse effects of social comparison. Teaching healthy online habits and directing teenagers to use social media in ways that enhance their lives rather than detract from them can also be helpful.

The most important way to mitigate the damage caused by social media, though, is not education. It is setting limits—limiting the amount of time teenagers spend on social media and ensuring that they are paying attention to their real-world lives. Continually learning new skills, developing satisfying social relationships, and improving themselves will go far in reducing the harm to their self-esteem that is inflicted by constant exposure to unrealistic standards.

1. Which option BEST expresses the main point of the passage?
    A) Social media can be a healthy part of a teenager's life if used responsibly.
    B) Social comparison has always been an issue for teenagers, as it is a part of human nature to compare ourselves to others, particularly those we perceive as doing better than we are.
    C) Education can help to counter the negative effects of social media.
    D) Social media has had a profound negative effect on the mental health and well-being of teenagers, and measures should be taken to limit this impact.
    E) No one should ever use social media.

2. What is the author's purpose in writing the passage?
    A) to warn of the dangers of social media on teenagers' mental health and offer ways to lessen the impact
    B) to encourage teenagers to spend more time outside and with their families
    C) to convince people to stop using social media
    D) to argue that social media can be a positive influence on teenagers if used correctly
    E) to complain about teenagers and modern technology

3. Which one of the following does the author offer as an argument in favor of limiting social media use in teenagers?
    A) Social media can allow for greater connection, creativity, and self-expression.
    B) Social comparison was never an issue before the advent of social media.
    C) Rates of anxiety and depression in teenagers have skyrocketed.
    D) There is no other way to mitigate the negative effects of social media.

   E) Teenagers are the only ones who suffer the adverse effects of social media. Adults are savvy enough to protect themselves.

4. What is the purpose of the fourth paragraph?
   A) to offer ways to mitigate the negative effects of social media on the mental health of teenagers
   B) to draw parallels between social media use and addiction issues
   C) to discuss the way that social comparison can affect teenagers' mental health
   D) to shock the reader into believing the author's assertions
   E) to offer evidence that social media is detrimental to teenagers' mental health by providing specific examples

5. Which of the following is likely a belief held by the author?
   A) Parents should monitor their children's social media usage closely and impose strict limits.
   B) It is more important to spend time with family than to spend it on social media.
   C) Nobody should use social media, especially not teenagers.
   D) Social media can be beneficial if used correctly.
   E) Real-world hobbies, like painting, are better than digital hobbies, like filmmaking.

6. Which of the following, if true, would MOST strengthen the author's argument?
   A) Real-world hobbies and socialization are far more rewarding than spending time on social media and lead to positive mental health outcomes.
   B) Social media was introduced to a remote tribe in Africa, and the teenagers there experienced the same mental health symptoms despite having no prior history of such issues.
   C) Teenagers who spend less time on social media grow up to be more successful in their adult lives.
   D) Many people who are unable to work traditional jobs make their livings off of social media.
   E) Social media causes harm to everyone who uses it, not just teenagers.

7. Which of the following, if true, would MOST weaken the author's argument?
   A) Only teenagers in westernized countries have the mental health issues she describes.
   B) Social media was introduced to a remote tribe in Africa, and the teenagers there did not experience the same mental health symptoms.
   C) A new study shows that the reason for the sharp decline in teenagers' mental health is almost entirely due to their dietary choices of ultra-processed foods and sugary beverages.
   D) Many people believe that social media has had a positive impact on their mental health due to their ability to connect with others and share their stories with people around the world.
   E) Social media has created opportunities for people who have previously been unable to support themselves due to disabilities.

The following passages concern climate change and how we should address this issue. Passage A was written by a climate scientist. Passage B was written by a representative of an oil company.

Passage A

Climate change is one of the most pressing issues facing humanity at this point in time. In the past century, the average temperatures have increased markedly; indeed, the past few decades have been record-breaking. Because of this rapid warming, severe weather events have become more and more frequent. The incidence of hurricanes, tornadoes, droughts, and heatwaves has soared, and people are struggling to adapt to this new normal.

Human activity is the driving force behind these changes, primarily due to the burning of fossil fuels such as coal, oil, and natural gas. This releases large quantities of carbon dioxide into the atmosphere, trapping heat and causing temperatures to rise. Deforestation has exacerbated this issue, as trees naturally reduce the amount of carbon dioxide in the atmosphere, and our planet has far fewer trees than in the past.

The consequences of inaction are dire. Rising sea levels threaten coastal communities, and hurricanes are more frequent and devastating every year. Changing weather patterns disrupt ecosystems and agricultural practices, leaving us more vulnerable to shortened growing seasons and decreased harvests that can potentially lead to famine. Economically, the costs of coping with climate-related disasters are staggering.

Addressing climate change requires immediate action. It is crucial to reduce our greenhouse gas emissions by replacing fossil fuels with alternate energy sources, such as wind and solar. Global cooperation and decisive changes are essential to protect our planet and ensure that it is habitable for future generations.

Passage B

As a key player in the global energy sector, we recognize the urgent need to address climate change. While oil and gas continue to play a significant role in providing reliable energy, the environmental challenges we are facing today cannot be ignored. We are acutely aware of the complications surrounding this issue and committed to immediate and sustainable action.

The oil industry is essential for energy security, supporting transportation, heating, and industrial processes. We have intensified our efforts to mitigate our environmental impact in an effort to sustainably serve the population's energy needs. Our efforts include investing in cleaner technologies such as carbon capture and storage and committing to the research and development of alternative energy sources.

However, the transition to renewable energy is complex and requires a strategic approach. While these technologies hold great promise, they are challenging to enact on the necessary scale. A sudden shift from fossil fuels could disrupt energy stability, affecting economies and employment. It is necessary to enact changes gradually in order to reduce any collateral damage from the transition to a more sustainable energy model.

Our commitment to the environment extends beyond the basics, and we are continually improving our practices. Corporate social responsibility initiatives are integral to our operations, ensuring that we contribute to the communities we serve and are part of the broader global effort to combat climate change. By investing in cleaner technologies and fostering collaboration, we strive to adapt to and mitigate the impacts of climate change while ensuring energy security and economic stability. Together, we can forge a sustainable future.

8. Both passages explicitly mention which of the following?
    A) the development of alternative energy sources
    B) the importance of fossil fuels on energy stability
    C) the costs of coping with climate-related disasters
    D) the negative effects of deforestation
    E) the importance of corporate social responsibility

9. Each of the passages contains information that is sufficient to answer which of the following questions?
    A) What are some alternative energy sources that could replace fossil fuels?
    B) What are some examples of the impact of climate change?
    C) What is the role of the oil industry in the face of climate change?
    D) What are some examples of technologies that can be employed to mitigate the effects of climate change?
    E) What are the costs of coping with climate-related disasters?

10. It can be inferred that the authors would likely disagree MOST strongly on which of the following?
    A) the likely effects of climate change if left unchecked
    B) the intensity and immediacy of the measures necessary to mitigate climate change
    C) whether or not we need to reduce greenhouse gas emissions
    D) the importance of addressing climate change
    E) whether human activity is the driving force behind climate change

11. Which option BEST describes the attitude the author of passage B likely has toward the arguments made in passage A?
    A) She is in full agreement with the premises of the argument and supports the conclusion wholeheartedly.
    B) She cautiously agrees with the content of passage A and tentatively supports its conclusion.
    C) She is neutral toward the author's arguments.
    D) She fully disagrees with the premises of the argument, and therefore finds the conclusion to be false.
    E) While she agrees with the premises of the argument, she considers the author's conclusion to be extreme and alarmist.

12. It can be inferred that both authors would be MOST likely to agree with which of the following statements?
    A) Solar and wind power are the energy sources of the future.
    B) It is important to consider the economy and employment concerns when working to decrease the impact of climate change.
    C) Fossil fuels can be environmentally friendly with the right safeguards, such as carbon capture and storage.
    D) Reforestation is a viable option for reducing atmospheric levels of carbon emissions.
    E) The impact of stricter environmental standards on low-income populations must be considered.

13. Which of the following is TRUE about the relationship between the two passages?
    A) Passage B presents evidence that directly counters claims made in passage A.
    B) Passage B argues for more serious action than passage A.
    C) Passage B downplays the seriousness of the claims made in passage A.
    D) The passages are in direct contradiction to each other on all points.
    E) Passage A displays an awareness of the arguments presented in passage B.

Although Option B downplays the seriousness of the claims made in passage A, it does not directly counter any of the claims made therein. Therefore, Option A is incorrect. Option B is the reverse of the actual relationship between the passages; passage A clearly argues for more serious action. Option D is incorrect, as the passages do agree on a few key issues, namely that climate change is an important issue that must be addressed. They merely differ on how this should be accomplished. Option E is incorrect, as the author of passage A does not consider the economic concerns of an oil company in making their argument.

14. Which of the following, if true, would strengthen the argument in passage B but weaken the argument in passage A?
    A) The ecological impacts of climate change have been greatly exaggerated.
    B) Economic considerations are important when considering how to address climate change.
    C) The impact of stricter environmental standards on the oil industry would be devastating.
    D) Climate change is a crisis that must be dealt with immediately and by any means necessary.
    E) The damage from climate change is irreparable at this point.

ANSWER KEY

1. D: This is a main point question. The author is trying to prove that social media is profoundly harmful to the mental health of teenagers and steps should be taken to mitigate this harm. Option A is not necessarily supported by the passage. Options B and C are both stated in the passage, but neither encompasses the main idea of the test. Option E is not stated in the passage. The author merely suggests ways to lessen the damage caused by social media rather than advising that it be avoided entirely.

2. A: The author's purpose is to highlight a problem with the way social media impacts teenagers and provide solutions to this problem. Option B is incorrect. Getting outside and spending more time with family would be a consequence of taking the author's advice; however, it is not the primary purpose of the passage. Option C is incorrect. The author never advocates for completely getting off of social media and even allows that there are some positives. Option D is incorrect, as it is contrary to the main point of the passage. Option E is also incorrect. The author does not complain about teenagers, but rather worries about their mental health.

3. C: The author directly argues this in the passage. Option A is incorrect. Although the author does state that this is the case, it is not an argument in favor of limiting social media use. Option B is incorrect, as it directly contradicts the passage. Option D is incorrect. Although the author argues that limiting social media is the most important way to mitigate the negative effects of social media, she offers other alternatives. Option E is contradicted by the passage and is therefore incorrect.

4. E: Paragraph four offers specific examples of the manner in which social media has been shown to impact teenagers' mental health. Option A is incorrect; that is the purpose of paragraphs five and six. Option B is incorrect. Although the author does draw this parallel in the paragraph, it is not the main point of the paragraph. Option C may seem correct at first glance and would be if option E were not a choice; however, it is not just the author's intent to "demonstrate" the effects but to use them as evidence of her assertions. Option D is incorrect, as the author is not going for shock value but rather offering evidence for her claims.

5. A: In the last paragraph, limiting social media use is recommended as the most important way to protect teenagers' mental health, and although the author does not specifically state that parents should monitor their children's use of social media, it is likely something she would also endorse. Option B could be a belief held by the author, but we do not know her opinions on family. Option C also seems like a possibility, but this is never stated outright by the author. Option D runs counter to the entirety of the passage. Option E is not supported by the passage, as the author makes no comment about digital hobbies or the internet in general and focuses her arguments solely on social media.

6. B: If the same negative mental health outcomes appear with the introduction of social media in a population that has never experienced such mental health symptoms before, it is compelling evidence for the author's argument. Option A would also strengthen the author's argument but not as much and not as directly. The author's argument is more focused on the negative impacts of social media on teenagers' mental health than the positive impacts of real-world experiences. Option C would also strengthen the argument slightly but not as much as directly observing the same negative outcomes on a new population. Options D and E are irrelevant to the author's main point.

7. C: If the mental health effects the author uses to support her argument can be attributed almost entirely to another source, her argument falls apart. Option A is incorrect, as teenagers in westernized countries are more likely to have higher exposure to social media and are therefore more likely to experience the mental health issues the author describes. Option B is incorrect. Although this would weaken the author's argument somewhat, it is not nearly as detrimental as Option C, as there may be other reasons this particular tribe is resistant to the mental health issues. Options D and E both highlight positives of social media; however, these positives do not take away from the author's argument that social media has been shown to have severe effects on teenagers' mental health.

8. A: This is a detail question. The development of alternative energy sources is mentioned in both passages. The climate scientist specifies wind and solar power, and the representative from the oil company mentions that they are working on alternatives but does not specify exactly what this means.

9. D: The first passage, by the climate scientist, highlights alternative energy sources, such as wind and solar. The second, by the representative of the oil company, mentions carbon capture and storage. Option A may be tempting, as both passages mention alternative energy sources, but the second does not specify examples. Option B can only be answered with information from the first passage. Option C can only be answered with information from the second passage. Option E is not answered by either passage, but merely mentioned in the first.

10. B: It is clear from the passages that the climate scientist feels that we need immediate, decisive action. While the representative from the oil company agrees that measures need to be taken, the representative is far less urgent in her call to action. She mentions factors such as employment and the economy as reasons that a transition to sustainable energy needs to be taken slowly and with caution. Options A, C, and E also point toward areas where there is the potential for disagreement; however, the representative does not specifically outline her beliefs on these points. Option D is a point on which both the climate scientist and the oil company representative seem to be in agreement, based on their writings.

11. E: This is an attitude question. The author of passage B states that she agrees with the premises argued in passage A—that climate change is a serious threat and must be addressed accordingly; however, the measures proposed in passage B are far less urgent and are tempered by warnings that we need to consider the economic ramifications. As a representative of an oil company, the author of passage B likely considers the measures proposed in passage A to be extremist.

12. D: The author of passage A directly mentions that deforestation is a contributing factor in climate change. The author of passage B does not explicitly talk about this point; however, based on the passage, it can be inferred that she would be a proponent of any measure to combat climate change that does not interrupt her company's ability to continue using fossil fuels as a primary energy source.

Option A is not going to be supported by the author of passage B, as the author does not want to switch energy sources. Option B would not be supported by the author of passage A, as this author sees the existential threat of climate change as paramount. Option C, which is clearly supported by the author of passage B, is in direct contradiction to the apparent beliefs of the author of passage A, who claims that fossil fuels are a huge factor in climate change. Neither author addresses the impact on stricter environmental standards on low-income populations, so we have no information on their beliefs concerning Option E.

13. C: While both passages agree that climate change is a serious threat, the author of passage B does not take the threat nearly as seriously as the author of passage A. The author of passage B is more concerned with protecting her company's interests than with mitigating the effects of climate change, whereas the author of passage A states that addressing climate change is imperative.

14. A: If the ecological effects of climate change have been exaggerated, then the crisis is not as urgent as the author of passage A claims, and the more conservative approach to addressing it, as proposed in passage B, would be appropriate.

Option B is incorrect. While the importance of economic considerations would strengthen the arguments in passage B, it would not necessarily weaken the arguments in passage A, as passage A is also concerned with the economic ramifications of *not* dealing with climate change. Option C looks correct at first glance; however, it does not actually weaken the arguments in passage A any more than option B. Devastating effects on the oil industry can be considered worthwhile collateral damage in the fight against the existential threat that is climate change. Option D would strengthen passage A and weaken passage B, which is the opposite of what we're looking for. Option E does not strengthen or weaken either passage: it does not matter that irreparable damage has been done if future damage can still be mitigated.

Chapter 5 – Argumentative Writing Sample

What Is the LSAT Argumentative Writing Sample?

The final section of the LSAT is the "Argumentative Writing Sample." The Argumentative Writing Sample portion of the exam requires you to develop a convincing argument using numerous sources of evidence. You will be given an issue that is being debated and no more than four different perspectives in relation to that issue. Your task is to decide your position on the issue. As the name of this portion of the test implies, you must also *argue* in favor of your position by addressing the opposing viewpoints.

The majority of people taking the LSAT will be given just under an hour—fifty minutes—to complete this portion of the exam. Fifteen of these minutes can be devoted to completing prewriting analysis questions and notetaking in preparation for your written response. The remaining thirty-five minutes are dedicated to writing the argument that will serve as your Argumentative Writing Sample.

The Argumentative Writing portion of the exam can be accessed through your LSAC JD account eight days prior to your exam date for the multiple-choice portions of the test.

Is the Writing Sample Scored?

No. This portion of the exam does not count toward your LSAT score; however, this does not mean that you should dismiss this section of the exam altogether. A copy of your writing sample from every LSAT you take will be forwarded to every law school to which you apply, so you should not leave the Writing Sample section blank, write in a foreign language, respond to a different topic, or do anything else that would indicate your disregard for this portion of the test.

Why Complete an Unscored Writing Sample?

Many students perform very well on the LSAT but cannot compose a proper paragraph or write a simple argument in which they state applicable rules, discuss the relevant facts, and then draw conclusions. This act of applying rules to facts in order to draw conclusions is the absolute essence of law school and lawyering, and law schools want to be sure that you have at least a fundamental understanding of what that entails.

While an excellent writing sample will not help a student overcome a poor LSAT score, it could make the difference between an admission and a waitlist (or denial) when you are up against several other candidates who appear otherwise similar on paper.

Tips for the Writing Sample

- Write your answer as though your reader is not intimately familiar with the goals and facts stated in the prompt/issue. In other words, do not be afraid to restate the goals and facts verbatim.
- Do not use quotation marks or citations when citing facts from the prompt.

- Avoid first-person narrative (which often sounds unprofessional).

Recommended Structure

- Start with a one- to three-sentence introductory paragraph in which you describe the decision to be made, the relevant goals, and your recommendation.

- In the next paragraph, discuss your (factual) reasons for the option you recommend, and refute the strongest counterarguments against your option.

> **Did You Know?**
> Very minor errors in grammar and spelling are acceptable as long as the overall response is clearly structured and appropriately addresses the prompt.

- In the third paragraph, factually refute the strongest argument for the option you did not choose.

- End with a one-sentence conclusion, restating your recommendation and its factual basis.

Practice Writing Sample

Prompt: *A local health center has received a grant to improve public health in the community that it serves. The center's staff is deciding whether to use the money to implement a community health and wellness program aimed at preventative care or expand their existing health care services so that they can be more effective in servicing those with preexisting health conditions. Using the facts below, write an essay in which you argue for one choice over the other based on the following two criteria:*

1.   The organization wants to improve overall community health.

2.   The organization wants to make the best use of their limited resources.

The proposed community health and wellness program would offer free exercise classes, nutrition workshops, and health screenings. Its aim would be to address lifestyle-related health issues before they become severe and require medical treatment. Studies show that preventative care can reduce long-term health care costs and significantly improve quality of life; however, the program requires initial funding for equipment, instructors, and marketing, and its success relies on community participation.

Expanding its existing health care services will allow the health center to provide more comprehensive care for those currently in need of medical attention. This includes hiring new staff, increasing the center's capacity for medical appointments, offering new specialties, and improving facilities. The demand for health care services in the area is high, and this expansion could help to meet an immediate need in the community. It does not, however, address the root causes of the health issues suffered by the majority of its patients and without preventative measures, long-term health care costs will continue to rise.

Writing Sample: Based on the criteria offered in the prompt, it is advisable that the health center use the grant money to implement a community health and wellness program aimed at preventative care. This program would do more to advance the health center's goal of improving overall community health by educating the public on the effects that certain lifestyles can have on disease risk, leading to better health outcomes for the population and decreased health care costs over time. The significant improvements in quality of life that such a program can have on members of the community would be invaluable for improving public health.

While expanding the services currently offered by the health center would serve an immediate need in the community, doing so would not significantly improve overall health in the long term. Those seeking medical care are often already suffering from chronic illnesses likely induced by poor lifestyle choices. The health and wellness program aims to prevent these conditions from developing in the first place. Additionally, the program can educate those who are already ill on lifestyle interventions as part of their treatment, thereby decreasing the need for standard health care services and resolving the issue of limited availability of care.

Given the health center's limited funds, it is critical that they make the best possible use of this grant. The expenses associated with beginning a health and wellness program may appear steeper than those of expanding existing services; however, with expanded services comes an expanded staff, new equipment, and improved facilities, which are also substantial expenses. Focusing on illness prevention in the community rather than pouring more resources into expanding services for those who are already unwell would be the best strategy for the health center to reach its goals of improving community health and making the most of the grant money.

Ultimately, the long-term benefits of a community health and wellness program will outweigh the immediate advantages of expanding the health center's current services. By prioritizing disease prevention, the health center can create a healthier population, reduce health care costs, and ensure the sustainability of its services.

Explanation: The above writing sample clearly adheres to the given criteria and effectively argues for the implementation of a community health and wellness program over expansion of current services. The argument is well structured and logically sound; the author states their argument clearly in the first paragraph and then serves to strengthen it with each successive paragraph. Every point supports the author's conclusion. The writing style is clear, concise, and persuasive.

The sample addresses potential counterarguments and provides a balanced analysis of the financial and social implications of both options. It acknowledges the immediate benefits of expanding existing services but counters with a case for the greater long-term benefits of preventative care. This nuanced approach demonstrates critical thinking skills and the ability to weigh competing considerations, making it a strong writing sample.

LSAT Practice Test #1

Section I – Reading Comprehension

Passage 1

Discovered at the end of the nineteenth century, the Amarna letters provide historians with a precious glimpse into the realities of political conflict during the Late Bronze Age. They document the conflicts of personality between rulers of major Near East polities, thus illuminating how psychological factors and interpersonal relationships shaped the ancient world.

These documents were discovered at *el-Amarna* in modern Egypt. The pharaoh Akhenaten, a religious reformer, built a new capital city for the ancient state to separate himself from the traditional social and religious structures of Egyptian life. For Akhenaten, the sun disk Aten was the supreme deity. Venerating the Aten above the traditional deities centralized power within Akhenaten's court by reducing the influence of other priesthoods and temples (e.g., the priests of Ra or Osiris). However, Akhenaten's son and heir Tutankhaten lacked the political capital to retain these changes, in no small part due to his youth. Consequently, the city at *el-Amarna* was abandoned. The transition of political power back into the hands of the traditional priests was substantial enough that the pharaoh's name was changed. Tutankh*aten* became the now-famous Tutankh*amun*, discovered by Howard Carter in the early twentieth century. However, the city's demise was fortuitous for the study of history in that it preserved the Amarna texts for future generations.

Only a handful of the texts were discovered *in situ.* Much of the archaeological context is, alas, lost due to the looting that alerted authorities to the site's location and importance. They are clay tablets written primarily in Akkadian, the *lingua franca* of the Bronze Age. Although Akkadian's viability as a spoken language had diminished by the Late Bronze Age, its cuneiform script remained prominent among scribes. It is unlikely that the rulers who sent the Amarna letters understood Akkadian in either written or spoken form. Rather, scribal annotations and commentary suggest that, in almost all circumstances, political letters were dictated to a scribe and then sent by an illiterate messenger to the foreign court. There, the local scribe would translate the letter from Akkadian into the language of that nation for their liege.

The picture we get from these letters is of family relationships writ large upon the landscape. The pharaoh calls his Hittite, Assyrian, and Babylonian counterparts "brother." Rulers of lesser courts address Akhenaten as "father," placing themselves in a subordinate position. It's not clear to what extent these formalities were understood to be political realities—even during Akhenaten's reign! The "brother" kings conspired regularly against one another. Minor lords seeking political independence often wrote facile assurances while continuing to act against the pharaoh's interests.

1. Which of the following most accurately expresses the central idea of the passage?
   A) Religious differences were a significant cause of conflict and war between major powers during the Late Bronze Age.
   B) Ancient rulers utilized the structure of family dynamics in their communications because this assured the kings that all parties understood their political responsibilities.
   C) The Amarna letters are especially precious for the study of history because they not only reveal official correspondence between rulers, but also demonstrate that they had personal friendships.
   D) Understanding the context of where ancient texts were found and when they were written provides essential information for interpreting the relationships expressed in the documents.
   E) Although historians are grateful that the Amarna letters have survived, they are severely limited in terms of how much they can learn from them due to their unscientific discovery through looting.

2. Which of the following best describes the meaning of *"lingua franca"* in paragraph 3?
   A) common tongue
   B) French language
   C) scholarly language
   D) political discourse
   E) diplomatic etiquette

3. This passage provides sufficient information to answer which one of the following questions?
   A) In what city did looters sell most of the Amarna letters?
   B) Why did Akhenaten call King Suppiluliuma his "brother"?
   C) How many different languages are found in the extant Amarna texts?
   D) Was the Aten worshiped as a deity of traditional Egyptian religion?
   E) Have all of the Amarna letters been translated by modern scholars?

4. What is the most likely reason that the author mentions "scribal annotations" in the third paragraph?
   A) to support their position that the Amarna letters provide insight into the personality of ancient political figures
   B) since this is evidence that most Bronze Age rulers were illiterate and reliant upon their court's scribes
   C) because these types of notes contextualize the situations within which international communications were conducted
   D) because referencing the lower-status scribes rhetorically emphasizes stratifications in ancient society
   E) to imply that scribes truly had diplomatic power because they could alter the ruler's words in a message.

5. Which of the following best describes the relationship between the first paragraph and the second paragraph?
   A) The first paragraph describes what the Amarna letters are, and the second paragraph describes how archaeologists discovered them.
   B) The first paragraph argues that the Amarna letters contextualize history, and the second paragraph presents Akhenaten's religious beliefs as evidence.
   C) The first paragraph claims why the Amarna letters are valuable, and the second paragraph provides background information about their owner and discovery.
   D) The first paragraph describes Akhenaten's relationship with the Amarna letters, and the second paragraph describes how the letters were found in modern times.
   E) The first paragraph claims that we understand the psychology of Akhenaten due to the Amarna letters, and the second demonstrates this using a story from the actual texts.

6. Which of the following claims is most strongly supported by the information in the passage?
   A) Legitimate political authority was conceived within a framework of familial relationships during the Late Bronze Age.
   B) The pharaoh Akhenaten used terms such as "brother" in the Amarna letters as political rhetoric to convince other rulers to work with him.
   C) The Amarna letters provide significant insight into how unstable and insecure Akhenaten's psyche was during his reign.
   D) Without this cache of Akkadian texts, it is unlikely that historians would know anything at all about the pharaoh Akhenaten.
   E) Akhenaten's religious reforms suggest delusions of grandeur; therefore, one cannot trust that the letters he wrote are sincere.

7. Which of the following hypothetical discoveries would be most analogous to the discovery of the Amarna texts?
   A) discovering a diary by Abraham Lincoln devising policy ideas prior to his inauguration as president
   B) detecting the existence of a sunken island in the Mediterranean Sea using deep-sea radar
   C) learning why a close friend never proposed to their significant other during college
   D) encountering an unrecorded pathogen that may have mutated to become the Black Death of the 1300s CE
   E) finding new personal correspondence between Adolf Hitler and Joseph Stalin prior to the outbreak of World War II

Passage 2

Everyone knows water is largely absent from a desert. One might even suggest that its scarcity is a defining feature of such an environment. However, it's a common misconception that this resource is wholly absent. Water doesn't just play a vital role in enabling plants, animals, and humans to thrive in these arid wastelands; it is also a force that *shapes* the desert. Understanding the role water plays in a desert's geography improves one's understanding of where to find water and how to manage it.

The most dramatic method by which water shapes the desert is through flooding. Riverbeds and lakes—often called *playas*—lay dry for much of the year. When rain arrives, the hard, arid ground struggles to absorb the moisture. The water is channeled into these dry beds with astonishing rapidity. Such a flash flood can produce a rushing wall of water 10 feet tall, or even higher. Desert flooding is caused by rain or thunderstorms. While rainfall is more common than one may expect in a desert, heavy storms most commonly occur in adjacent mountains. The rainfall then pours into the desert and along the dried-out paths. This shapes the desert through erosion along the water's path. The development of dams and other structures mitigates flood risk near settlements. These structures also make it possible to catch water in cisterns for use, rather than allowing it to evaporate under the scorching heat.

Groundwater in the desert may be less thrilling but is only moderately more stable. Desert regions tend to have very deep groundwater reservoirs, if they have any at all. The environment's dry heat pulls water out of the ground through capillary action. This type of motion seeks equilibrium between the humidity of the air and the soil. If absorbed deeply enough, groundwater is protected from this action by the mass of soil above it. This depth, however, makes it more challenging to access the groundwater. Such groundwater reservoirs are also at risk of not refilling naturally since the water must penetrate to a greater depth to reach the reservoir.

Most human water needs exceed what is available as desert groundwater. Consequently, desert communities often rely on fossil water retained far below ground. This resource is only accessed by humans because its depth requires drilling. The water is called "fossil" because it is a remnant from prior geological epochs. Despite the massive volume of most fossil water reservoirs, they are indeed finite. Reclaiming water, storing water, and restricting water usage are important techniques to preserve sources of fossil water for when no other sources of water are available.

8. The phrase "mitigates flood risk" (paragraph 2) is best interpreted by which one of the following?
    A) Floods are more likely to occur in those areas; thus, it is appropriate to build dams there.
    B) Dams should be built so that floods are less hazardous for local communities.
    C) The primary benefit of dam construction is to catch water for use by human communities.
    D) Constructing dams reduces flooding along riverbeds and *playas*, even if they are not near a major city.
    E) Flash floods no longer erode our deserts due to the construction of water management systems, like dams.

9. In this passage, the author's primary motive is to do which one of the following?
    A) inform the reader about how water erosion shapes deserts
    B) advocate for the immediate construction of new dams to protect desert communities
    C) describe the dangers of flash floods in the desert and how to avoid them
    D) emphasize the importance of water to the desert despite the environment's lack of it
    E) educate the general public about how the changing climate is impacting desert water management

10. Why did this passage's author feel it was necessary to describe capillary action in paragraph 3?
    A) because it describes why water does not remain for long on the surface of the desert
    B) because it is key to understanding the fragility of groundwater as a resource
    C) because it explains how fossil water ended up collecting so deep under the surface
    D) because it strengthens their argument that desert communities ought to use fossil water instead of groundwater
    E) because it is one of several mechanisms by which water shapes and changes the desert environment

11. The author's concern for the cautious use of water by desert communities is most accurately reflected in which one of the following words?
    A) remnant (paragraph 4)
    B) scarcity (paragraph 1)
    C) protected (paragraph 3)
    D) exceed (paragraph 4)
    E) equilibrium (paragraph 3)

12. Which one of the following reasons does the passage give for why humans should NOT rely on sources of fossil water for their communities?
    A) Fossil water is often unclean due to its depth and the length of time it has been under the ground.
    B) There is scientific value to be obtained from studying fossil water, so it should be preserved for future research.
    C) Groundwater is replenished easily, so communities should use it first.
    D) Fossil water replenishes slowly because it takes a long time for capillary action to leech water down to that level.
    E) This resource is limited in quantity and therefore should be used sparingly, analogous to oil or coal.

13. Which one of the following best explains why the author organized this passage so that flash floods are described before other types of water in the desert?
    A) Due to the danger of flash floods on riverbeds and lakebeds, this is the most important information for the author to impart to travelers.
    B) Flash floods are the most common form of water in the desert, while fossil water is the least common.
    C) Describing flooding first provides a rhetorical hook that draws the reader into the author's discussion of water management.
    D) Understanding flash floods is necessary for comprehending the later paragraphs in the passage.
    E) It's most important that humans learn to control floodwaters in the desert, because this source of water is the most consistent.

14. Some desert plants, such as the velvet mesquite, are capable of sinking taproots 50 feet or more in length. Based on the information in the passage, which of the following statements is most likely true?
    A) The velvet mesquite primarily grows where there is a source of fossil water deep below the surface.
    B) This plant survives in the desert due to its ability to reach water via its roots even during drought.
    C) Deep roots, like those of the velvet mesquite, are an adaptation necessary to endure the desert's harsh flash floods.
    D) Plants can only sink roots so deeply when they are in deserts due to the dry, sandy composition of a desert's soil.
    E) The taproot is a thick root that stores water in proportion to its length, thus allowing a plant to endure long droughts.

Passage 3

Are there circumstances that don't merely justify, but *demand* that a moral person performs a heinous deed? This troubling question permeates Dietrich Bonhoeffer's *Ethics*. A Lutheran pastor, Bonhoeffer nonetheless became embroiled in Operation Valkyrie: a plot to assassinate Hitler. Yet Exodus 20:13 states quite clearly "Thou shalt not kill." *Ethics* is Bonhoeffer's attempt to reconcile his feelings of what *must* be done with both theological and moral principles that argue otherwise.

The fulcrum of Bonhoeffer's analysis lies in the internal character of a moral agent. By studying different approaches to ethical theory—such as the rationalizing quantification of happiness of Mill's utilitarianism—through the lens of internal character, contradictions between value and principle are unveiled. Explicit principles, such as those sought by most philosophers and theologians, are necessarily inflexible. The example closest to Bonhoeffer's own heart, naturally, was Exodus 20:13. This mechanistic way that moral principles operate is necessary to explicate ethics. Ethical theory attempts to catch and express a person's values through stated rules. Thus, two persons who generally agree on the same code of ethics, like the Ten Commandments, might act in contradictory ways while asserting their adherence to that code.

Bonhoeffer sought a firm foundation for value, for internal character, in order to vouchsafe ethical action. He sacrificed ethical theory because concrete rules fail when confronting the world. In Bonhoeffer's own life, he felt this in confronting evil as expressed by the actions of the Third Reich. One of the Bible's most solemn and explicit rules was insufficient to grapple with evil. What, then, made it possible for a person to act ethically? The person's internal character. Virtuous people are capable of moral choice and good action not based upon following a moral law but rather through remaining internally consistent in how their acts express their values and beliefs.

15. Which one of the following does the passage list as a failing of ethical theories?
    A) Ethical theories care about a person's actions without regard to their internal self.
    B) It is not possible for a code of ethics to remain 100 percent consistent with someone's personal values.
    C) Most theories fail because they do not address the existence of good and evil as real cosmic forces.
    D) The lack of education about how to become virtuous is why ethical behavior continues to deteriorate in public.
    E) A code of ethics is only valid if it is supported by an external, eternal source, such as a belief in God.

16. What is the primary purpose of the author's quotation from Exodus?
    A) The quote indicates that Bonhoeffer was Christian and took his faith very seriously.
    B) The quotation provides an example of a rule that is almost always impossible to follow consistently.
    C) Exodus is the central focus of Bonhoeffer's argument, so the quotation is necessary in order to present the argument honestly.
    D) By quoting from Exodus, the author exemplifies good ethical rules, which nonetheless may be insufficient.
    E) Bonhoeffer believed that the Bible is a reliable source of ethical advice, especially the book of Exodus.

17. Which one of the following best describes the organization of this passage?
    A) The passage begins with a short biographical summary, describes Bonhoeffer's ethics, and concludes by applying his ethics to his life.
    B) The passage describes the composition of *Ethics* and the central point of Bonhoeffer's argument, and then it discusses the book's historical impact.
    C) The passage outlines Bonhoeffer's ethical principles, provides further detail on how he drew those conclusions, and then it gives an example from Bonhoeffer's life choices.
    D) The passage first describes the Bible's ethical teachings in Exodus, and then it provides Mill's utilitarianism as a counterexample and concludes by showing Bonhoeffer's synthesis of the two moral codes.
    E) The passage starts with explaining how Bonhoeffer impacted history, and then it describes how his own *Ethics* convinced him to join Operation Valkyrie.

18. In this passage, what is the author's primary goal?
    A) to recognize and praise Bonhoeffer as a moral hero of the twentieth century because of his involvement in Operation Valkyrie
    B) to explain why Bonhoeffer's argument is interesting but ultimately does not eliminate codes of ethics
    C) to show that Bonhoeffer's *Ethics* is an important text for students to read because of its impact on understanding right and wrong actions
    D) to describe Bonhoeffer's ethical theory so that persons of all ages can improve their behaviors
    E) to present Bonhoeffer's argument in favor of virtue ethics in order to persuade readers that morality should not be codified

19. The trolley problem is a philosophical thought experiment in which a trolley is rolling down a track and will kill multiple people on the rails; however, a bystander is able to pull a lever so that it goes down a different track and kills only one person. Based on this passage, which option best describes how Bonhoeffer would believe that a virtuous bystander should respond?
    A) The bystander should pull the lever because doing so will kill the fewest people.
    B) The bystander should not pull the lever because they do not know the value of the lives of the different people on the rails.
    C) The bystander should not pull the lever because by taking action the bystander is morally responsible for the consequences.
    D) The bystander should pull the lever because it is the most compassionate action given the information available.
    E) The bystander should not pull the lever because killing someone with a trolley would be inconsistent with the person's moral character.

20. Which one of the following positions about ethics is most similar to Bonhoeffer's position as described in this passage?
    A) Immanuel Kant's categorical imperative states that people should act as if the principle of their actions could be applied universally without contradiction.
    B) Utilitarian theory argues that in all circumstances we ought to act in whatever way will create the greatest happiness for all persons involved.
    C) For many, the statement "treat others as you would want to be treated" is at the heart of being a good person.
    D) Stealing is always wrong because, by definition, it is an act that causes harm; however, causing harm may sometimes be justified (e.g., if you are starving).
    E) The "virtues" Aristotle describes in the *Nicomachean Ethics* teach how to identify virtues as the mean between the extreme of two vices.

21. Which word would best replace the word *fulcrum* in paragraph 2?
    A) heart
    B) context
    C) lever
    D) bridge
    E) center

Passage 4 (Parts A and B)

Part A

TO ALL FREE MEN OF OUR KINGDOM we have also granted, for us and our heirs forever, all the liberties written out below, to have and to keep for them and their heirs, of us and our heirs:

If any earl, baron, or other person that holds lands directly of the Crown, for military service, shall die, and at his death his heir shall be of full age and owe a "relief,", the heir shall have his inheritance on payment of the ancient scale of "relief." That is to say, the heir or heirs of an earl shall pay 100 pounds for the entire earl's barony, the heir or heirs of a knight 100 shillings at most for the entire knight's "fee," and any man who owes less shall pay less, in accordance with the ancient usage of "fees."

But if the heir of such a person is underage and a ward, when he comes of age he shall have his inheritance without "relief" or fine.

The guardian of the land of an heir who is under age shall take from it only reasonable revenues, customary dues, and feudal services. He shall do this without destruction or damage to men or property. If we have given the guardianship of the land to a sheriff, or to any person answerable to us for the revenues, and he commits destruction or damage, we will exact compensation from him, and the land shall be entrusted to two worthy and prudent men of the same "fee."

For so long as a guardian has guardianship of such land, he shall maintain the houses, parks, fish preserves, ponds, mills, and everything else pertaining to it, from the revenues of the land itself. When

the heir comes of age, he shall restore the whole land to him, stocked with plough teams and such implements of husbandry as the season demands and the revenues from the land can reasonably bear.

Heirs may be given in marriage, but not to someone of lower social standing. Before a marriage takes place, it shall be made known to the heir's next-of-kin.

Part B

When in the Course of human events, it becomes necessary for one people to dissolve the political bands which have connected them with another, and to assume, among the Powers of the earth, the separate and equal station to which the Laws of Nature and of Nature's God entitle them, a decent respect to the opinions of mankind requires that they should declare the causes which impel them to the separation.

We hold these truths to be self-evident, that all men are created equal, that they are endowed by their Creator with certain unalienable Rights, that among these are Life, Liberty, and the pursuit of Happiness. That to secure these rights, Governments are instituted among Men, deriving their just powers from the consent of the governed, That whenever any Form of Government becomes destructive of these ends, it is the Right of the People to alter or to abolish it, and to institute new Government, laying its foundation on such principles and organizing its powers in such form, as to them shall seem most likely to effect their Safety and Happiness. Prudence, indeed, will dictate that Governments long established should not be changed for light and transient causes; and accordingly all experience hath shown, that mankind are more disposed to suffer, while evils are sufferable, than to right themselves by abolishing the forms to which they are accustomed. But when a long train of abuses and usurpations, pursuing invariably the same Object evinces a design to reduce them under absolute Despotism, it is their right, it is their duty, to throw off such Government, and to provide new Guards for their future security.—Such has been the patient sufferance of these Colonies; and such is now the necessity which constrains them to alter their former Systems of Government. The history of the present King of Great Britain is a history of repeated injuries and usurpations, all having in direct object the establishment of an absolute Tyranny over these States. To prove this, let Facts be submitted to a candid world.

22. The word *Rights* in the second paragraph of passage B is most closely related to which one of the following words in passage A?
    A) relief
    B) liberties
    C) reasonable
    D) guardianship
    E) entrusted

23. Both passages use the concept of "freedom" or "liberty" in order to do which one of the following?
    A) describe why all people have rights given by God
    B) list which actions are considered permissible and which are not considered permissible
    C) claim that people who are free accordingly have certain rights or privileges
    D) argue that no ruler may govern without the people's consent
    E) define who is considered a citizen of the nation and who is considered foreign

24. Based on what can be inferred from the passages, which one of the following is most likely to be explicitly asserted by passage A but not by passage B?
    A) Widows have a freedom from forced remarriage.
    B) Government may not seize a debtor's land.
    C) The ruler's ability to levy taxes shall be restricted.
    D) Sons shall have the same rights and privileges as their fathers.
    E) All free persons have a right to trial before judgment.

25. Given the specific concerns listed, which one of the following is most likely to correctly describe the expected audience of each passage?
    A) Passage A is directed at an entrenched nobility protecting its rights, while passage B is directed at negotiating the rights of all people under an established government.
    B) Passage A is directed at all males in the kingdom, while passage B is directed at justifying secession from the government.
    C) Passage A is directed at bishops and other members of the clergy, while passage B is directed at informing the general public.
    D) Passage A is directed at persons concerned with their children's inheritance, while passage B is directed at persuading the general public.
    E) Passage A is directed at the king of his kingdom, while passage B is directed at the whole world.

26. Both passages refer to which one of the following?
    A) the duties of a legal guardian
    B) the king of Great Britain
    C) acts of governmental overreach
    D) the creation of a new social order
    E) the rights of the governed

27. Unlike passage A, passage B, is structured how?
    A) so that its assertion of rights is rhetorically supported by the king's violation of those rights
    B) so that the specific rights given by God to all people are enunciated clearly and precisely defined
    C) so that it builds a definition of rights and liberties prior to asserting the use of those rights and liberties
    D) so that the rhetorical emphasis is on the king's "usurpations" rather than on the people's actions
    E) so that the audience's freedom is used as the cause of the passage's rights and liberties

Section II – Logical Reasoning

1. The manufacturer is recalling some cars of their A250 model. The recall was ordered because one version of the A250 has airbags that do not work correctly. Rachel is not sure if her A250's airbags work correctly. She sent her car in to the manufacturer just in case.

Which of the following best identifies Rachel's conclusion?
    A) If the airbags aren't working, then I should send my A250 to the manufacturer.
    B) My car's airbags don't work, so it must be a faulty model.
    C) It's best to be safe and send my A250 to the manufacturer for inspection.
    D) I need more information to determine if my A250 is included in the manufacturer's recall.
    E) I shouldn't drive my A250 until the manufacturer has replaced the airbags.

2. In baseball, getting hits consistently is the best way for a team to score runs. Some teams emphasize home runs because they excite the crowd; however, trying to hit a home run is more difficult than making any hit that gets the player on base. In the long run, hitting singles scores more runs. This strategy gives a team the best chance to win baseball games.

Based on the statements above, which of the following must be true?
- A) Defensive skills in baseball are less important than being able to hit the ball consistently.
- B) If a strategy results in more runs over a period of time, then it's better than other strategies.
- C) Home runs are less exciting for the team's crowd than being able to win the game.
- D) If it were easier to hit a home run, then baseball games wouldn't be as exciting.
- E) A professional baseball team's goal ought to be to win as many games as possible each year.

3. Napoleon's victory at the Battle of Austerlitz may be the most successful feint in the history of warfare. He weakened his right flank, and then retreated from the Pratzen Heights to give the semblance of defeat. Indeed, this nearly resulted in a true defeat! After the Coalition's army took the Pratzen Heights, a well-timed French counterattack caught them off-guard. Napoleon's strategic gamble routed the Coalition and won the battle.

Which of the following is most strongly supported on the basis of the information above?
- A) Napoleon was the most skilled military tactician of his historical period.
- B) It's unlikely that any other "great general" could have won the Battle of Austerlitz.
- C) Napoleon won this battle because the Coalition's generals underestimated his strategy.
- D) There has never been a military mind as devious and clever as Napoleon's.
- E) Although Napoleon's strategy was clever, it nearly lost him this battle.

4. Nancy: I don't understand what you see in him. Your boyfriend may have a good job, but why doesn't he ever want to hang out and have fun?

Linda: Ralph just has a different idea of what "fun" means. I don't mind if he wants to take it easy, since we'll spend time together later.

Based on the dialogue, we can infer that Nancy and Linda disagree about which one of the following?
- A) Linda's boyfriend, Ralph, is a supportive and caring partner.
- B) It's important for a partner to participate, even if they don't want to.
- C) The best partner is someone who can financially provide for a family.
- D) "Fun" is defined as activities that the participants enjoy doing.
- E) A significant other ought to be someone you can have fun with.

5. If a house has a basement and a good roof, then it is well-built. All fabricated homes or trailers lack a basement; therefore, fabricated homes or trailers are not well-built. When buying a house, you should only buy a well-built home; therefore, you should not buy a fabricated home or trailer.

Which of the following describes a technique of reasoning used in the above argument?
- A) The author uses a defined premise to support both their intermediate and final conclusions.
- B) The author uses the word *or* to argue that, if the reader excludes one option, then they have to pick the other.
- C) The author uses an intermediary conclusion to refute a counterexample to the premise.
- D) The author uses definitions to claim that the reader ought to take a particular course of action.
- E) The author uses evidence to demonstrate that their premise is true and to support their conclusion.

6. Eddie: Let's go to Yellowstone next year. It's the last big National Park we haven't visited, and I know seeing Old Faithful is on your bucket list.

Janessa: I'm not sure if we can afford it. It'll take a long drive to reach Yellowstone. We would spend most of the vacation traveling there, not actually hiking around.

The claim that it's a long drive for Eddie and Janessa to reach Yellowstone is used to do which one of the following?
- A). describe why the couple can't afford the trip.
- B) explain why it has taken so long for them to visit Yellowstone.
- C) explain why the couple visited other big National Parks first.
- D) refute spending vacation time to visit the park.
- E) demonstrate why seeing Old Faithful is on Janessa's bucket list.

7. All journalists have their access to a nation restricted due to a war in that nation's region. One journalist, Bob, sneaks into the nation. Bob gets caught by local police. In court, he acknowledges that he is guilty of violating the temporary rule. Bob argues that it's more important to tell the true story of the war than to obey the rules.

Which of the following principles, if valid, most helps to justify Bob's reasoning?
- A) It is OK to break this rule because Bob is a legitimate journalist with a professional interest in telling the truth.
- B) A journalist can break rules put in place for the safety of other people but is not justified in breaking actual laws.
- C) People are justified in pursuing causes they believe are moral, even if doing so gets them in trouble with the government.
- D) Rules and regulations are only valid if they were voted on by a nation's constituents or their representatives.
- E) Respecting authority is the most important moral duty, even above telling the truth.

8. Apples keep doctors away. Doctors are necessary to stay in good health. If someone doesn't have a doctor, then they won't stay in good health. Therefore, apples are not healthy.

Which of the following arguments is most closely parallel in its reasoning to the argument above?
- A) Cats improve happiness because they're fluffy. Therefore, if a dog is fluffy it also improves happiness.
- B) Trucks are better for hauling than cars. Cars are cheap vehicles. If someone wants to haul things, then they should buy a truck. Therefore, they won't buy a cheap vehicle.
- C) All mice hate rats. Some rats carry disease. If a mouse is near a rat, then it will get a disease. That's why mice hate rats.
- D) Newspapers provide knowledge that people need to make informed decisions. If someone doesn't read the newspaper, they aren't knowledgeable. Therefore, they will make uninformed decisions.
- E) Some gases are breathable. Some gases are flammable. If a gas is breathable, then it is flammable; therefore, all breathable gases are also flammable.

9. There is a Geneva Convention that bans the use of tear gas in warfare; however, tear gas is commonly used by police to control riots. If a Geneva Convention bans tear gas, we should stop using it on civilians too.

Which of the following conforms most closely to the principle illustrated in the above argument?
- A) It's important to set an example for others to follow; that's why we decided to ban the dumping of industrial waste into public waters.
- B) Small businesses are required to pay property tax, but our town gave an exemption to the new factory. If we have to pay it, then the factory ought to pay it too.
- C) Our competitors have begun serving better food during flights. They are getting more customers. If it's worth the expense, then we should do the same.
- D) We get water from the lake. Some people dump trash in the lake; therefore, some water we drink is polluted.
- E) It's illegal to hold civilians prisoner without a trial. Some enemy soldiers are captured during war; therefore, we should put soldiers on trial after capture.

10. John Smith was reported missing this morning by the director of his new movie following a failure to appear for the day's filming. Since Smith disappeared just days after marriage to his third wife, it can hardly be surprising that many people suspect foul play. For now, the police chief claims "We have no suspects in this case."

Which of the following best describes a logical flaw in the above passage?
- A) The author assumes that John Smith was murdered, despite being reported missing.
- B) The author uses a broad generalization to support a claim of foul play.
- C) The author implies that the police were involved in John Smith's disappearance.
- D) The author claims that John Smith's third wife knows of his whereabouts.
- E) The author has insufficient evidence to conclude that the police have no suspects.

11. If we have enough rain this spring, then there will be flowers in my garden. I did not plant flowers this year. Therefore, we did not have enough rain this spring for flowers.

Which of the following arguments is most similar in its flawed reasoning to the argument above?
- A) Some years have enough rain for a good harvest. I had a good harvest this year; therefore, this year had enough rain.
- B) Some flowers require fertilizer to bloom. I did not fertilize my garden. All of my flowers bloomed; therefore, some of my flowers did not require fertilizer.
- C) When we go to the beach, I bring an umbrella so I won't get a sunburn. I came home from vacation with a sunburn; therefore, we went to the beach.
- D) All pine trees are tall, slender, and have needles. Some trees in a forest are evergreen; therefore, all trees in that forest are pine trees.
- E) Whoever broke the window must have been in the room. There are glass shards on the ground outside; therefore, whoever broke the window is still inside the room.

12. A farmer keeps a bull in a fenced-off field so that it will not chase people. During the night, the farmer hears someone shouting for help. When the farmer goes outside, he sees that a person is up the tree in the bull's field while the bull stands at the bottom of the tree. The farmer goes inside and calls the police.

Which of the following assumptions best explains the farmer's actions?
- A) Only the police have authority to put down the bull.
- B) If the bull chased someone, then that person injured the bull.
- C) The bull can discern between strangers and familiar people.
- D) The farmer does not have the authority to arrest the person.
- E) If someone crosses the bull's fence at night, then they are trespassing.

13. Paul is a trained scuba diver. During a dive, his partner's oxygen tank malfunctions. Paul does not attempt to share oxygen with his partner. Paul swims to the surface alone and reports the incident.

Paul's action is most strongly supported if which of the following is assumed?
- A) Paul was not trained well.
- B) Paul's tank was low on oxygen.
- C) Paul's tank also malfunctioned.
- D) Paul did not like his partner.
- E) Paul used a different brand of tank.

14. Julie is deciding whether to buy a desktop or a laptop for her new work computer. Desktops have better processing power and are not portable. Laptops have worse processing power and are portable. Desktops cost more than laptops. Julie buys a laptop.

Which of the following, if true, most strengthens the support for Julie's decision?
- A) Some laptops have a long battery life.
- B) Julie needs a computer for her home office.
- C) The employer will pay for half of Julie's new computer.
- D) Julie travels frequently to visit family.
- E) Desktops are more durable than laptops.

15. Wetlands are an environment that can absorb a lot of water. Heavy rainfall causes flooding; therefore, wetlands can absorb water from floods. Floods are dangerous due to the sudden increase in a river's volume of water; therefore, wetlands reduce danger during floods. If preserving the environment reduces danger, then that environment should be preserved; therefore, we should not develop the local wetland into housing.

Which of the following, if true, most seriously weakens this argument?
- A) The local area does not receive heavy rainfall.
- B) Wetlands are not the only environment that can absorb a lot of water.
- C) Floods in the local area cause a lot of damage.
- D) The local area uses dams to relieve flooding.
- E) Wetlands can absorb water from floods but not from rainfall.

16. Historically speaking, bombing campaigns do not weaken a population's resolve. Germany was heavily bombed during WWII and refused to surrender. Common-sense psychology supports this; if someone's home or livelihood is destroyed, they feel angry. It is natural that they are even more driven to fight against the enemy.

Which of the following would be most useful to help evaluate this argument?
- A) the frequency with which Germany was bombed during the war
- B) the number of people who lost homes due to the bombing campaign
- C) the percentage of total war deaths caused by the bombing
- D) the impact of leaders in inspiring people who had been bombed
- E) the percentage of bombed German civilians who supported the war

17. Water is necessary for all life to survive. It rains very rarely in the desert, so there is very little water. Consequently, one might expect there to be very little life; however, many plants and animals have adapted to survive in the desert. Only the harshest deserts—like the sandy Gobi Desert—are totally absent of life.

Which of the following, if true, most helps to explain why there is life in the desert?
- A) Although deserts have little rain, they still have water due to rivers that flow through.
- B) It is difficult for plants to grow in sandy environments.
- C) Some animals only live in the desert for part of the year.
- D) Adaptations help animals find alternative water sources.
- E) Desert plants require less water than normal plants.

18. Dr. Lem: It's clear that this patient is suffering from dehydration. Her skin is dry, her heartbeat is irregular, and she is confused and having trouble walking and speaking clearly. Let's get an IV in to support rehydration.

Dr. Condo: Those symptoms are also consistent with a brain injury. We should get her an MRI right away. If we wait for symptoms to improve with the IV and it is not dehydration, then the actual cause of illness may worsen.

Which of the following, if true, best resolves the conflict between these doctors?
- A) Dr. Condo is a neurologist.
- B) It is a hot day, and the patient was not sweating.
- C) When asked if she drank water, the patient nodded her head "yes."
- D) Dr. Lem is a surgeon.
- E) The patient was brought to the hospital by two family members.

19. The first year a festival was held, the owner advertised it heavily, and it drew a large crowd. The second year, the owner did not advertise it, and it drew a small crowd. The third year, the owner advertised it a little and hoped to have a moderate crowd; however, the owner had a small crowd.

Which of the following is an assumption that, if believed by the owner, does the most to justify his actions?
- A) There is a relationship between the quality of the bands and the size of the crowd.
- B) The large crowd in the first year was due to excitement for the festival's opening.
- C) The size of the crowd is proportional to the amount of advertising.
- D) The amount of advertising has no relationship with the size of the crowd.
- E) If the festival draws a moderate crowd, then it should keep being held.

20. Winter is the best time for fishing because you can go ice fishing. Ice fishing is fun because being on a frozen lake is exciting: you can rest in a heated cabin, and you can use a snowmobile to reach the fishing spot. Because you can't do these activities during other seasons, ice fishing is better than other types of fishing.

This argument's reasoning is questionable in that the argument
   A)   is about winter activities, not about ice fishing itself.
   B)   relies on a faulty premise about the winter season.
   C)   fails to refute the counter-example about other types of fishing.
   D)   does not provide evidence that ice fishing catches more fish.
   E)   fails to provide evidence that the listed activities are fun.

21. The doctor recommended a surgical procedure to diagnose why I'm feeling abdominal pain. I'm scared about anesthesia. If something scares me, it may be painful; therefore, if something scares me, I shouldn't do it. But the doctor is an expert. If I'm feeling pain, I should try to prevent it. In the end, I consented to the procedure.

The situation described above conforms most closely to which of the following generalizations?
   A)   If something is painful, then it is always bad.
   B)   You should always follow an expert's recommendations.
   C)   If something is scary, then it is guaranteed to be painful.
   D)   Anesthesia is both scary and painful.
   E)   It is better to accept a mild negative than to take a major risk.

22. An organism is a new species if its physical or behavioral adaptations to the environment are substantially different from those of similar species. The classic example is Darwin's study of finches in the Galapagos Islands. Although the finches shared similarities in size, weight, and plumage, their beaks varied from one island to another. Through observation, Darwin concluded that different beaks improved a finch's ability to access different sources of food. Thus, he argued that . . .

Which one of the following most logically completes the passage?
   A)   the Galapagos finches exemplified a species that was in the process of diversifying into new species through adaptation.
   B)   only one variant factor is required to determine whether or not an organism is a new species.
   C)   the islands' biodiversity provides important examples of speciation for the study of taxonomy and evolution.
   D)   the finches had previously been all the same species and only later adapted to become different species.
   E)   though related, each island's finches were a distinct species due to differences in both beak shape and food sources.

23. Aristotle: The principle of your action must strive for the mean. Do not seek wholly to indulge in pleasures, nor to avoid them outright. Balancing your actions exemplifies self-mastery.

Alexander: That's a beautiful idea, but how can you achieve it? Some situations require extreme actions.

Which of the following best expresses the conclusion drawn by Aristotle in this dialogue?
- A) Real-world exigencies sometimes prevent a person from choosing the mean.
- B) Ethical principles ought to be preserved as much as possible, even if they can't be followed in all situations.
- C) It is not correct behavior to always be indulging oneself in enjoyable activities.
- D) A virtuous person is capable of ethical behavior because they intentionally choose how to act.
- E) The mean between pleasure and pain varies depending on the situation.

24. Laura: The new hospital ought to be built on Front Street because it's the biggest road with the best access for ambulances to travel quickly.

Cassie: Since Front Street is the biggest road, it also has the most traffic; therefore, we should build the hospital somewhere else. How about Second Street? It still has good access, but it has less traffic.

Which of the following is a technique of reasoning used in this dialogue?
- A) Refuting an argument by weakening its evidence
- B) Drawing a conclusion utilizing agreed-upon premises
- C) Creating an analogy between two types of evidence
- D) Using a metaphor to explain the context
- E) Appealing to expert authority to provide evidence

25. The night before an exam, it's more important to get rest than to study. Resting improves a person's energy and focus during the test. In contrast, last-minute cramming expends more energy and increases the student's anxiety.

Which of the following arguments is most similar in its reasoning to the argument above?
- A) I don't want to get sick because I have a job interview tomorrow. My sister has a cold; therefore, I should not visit my sister today.
- B) Consistent sleep improves energy and focus by letting the mind and body relax. Dreams help a person emotionally process their day and be ready for the next.
- C) Buying a new appliance doesn't have to be stressful. Use the internet to understand what features you want before you go shopping. Lack of preparation can result in indecision, which increases stress.
- D) If I go to the mall with friends, I'm probably going to buy something frivolous. I'm caught up on my bills, so it's OK to be frivolous. Therefore, it's OK for me to go to the mall with my friends.
- E) We think knowledge is mostly explicit; however, intuition plays a larger role in thought than you might expect. For example, answers often pop into our minds rather than being logically formulated.

Section III – Logical Reasoning

1. A particle is a fundamental object in quantum physics. Most particles are "building blocks" that constitute atoms. According to Heisenberg, if we perfectly know a particle's momentum, then we cannot know its position. If we perfectly know a particle's position, then we cannot know its momentum; however, if our knowledge is imperfect (i.e., an approximation), then we can imperfectly know both.

Which of the following statements can be inferred from the information above?
   A) If I approximate a particle's momentum, then I can know nothing about its position.
   B) If I know a particle's position, then I can approximate its momentum.
   C) If I know a particle's momentum, then I know it is probably in some atom.
   D) All particles can be found as parts of a molecule built out of several atoms.
   E) If I know a particle's position, then the particle does not have momentum.

2. Stuart: That old oak is getting dangerous. One good thunderstorm could blow it down. If it damages my roof, I'm going to sue you.

Ashlyn: My oak isn't anywhere near the property line. You let me worry about it.

The dialogue provides the most support for the claim that Stuart and Ashlyn disagree over whether
   A) the oak is likely to collapse in the next thunderstorm.
   B) Ashlyn is responsible for damage caused by the oak.
   C) Stuart's worries are reasonable based on the oak's age.
   D) a thunderstorm is likely to cause damage to both Stuart and Ashlyn's roofs.
   E) Ashlyn's oak poses a reasonable danger to Stuart's roof.

3. There is no single "best" type of cheese. Cheddar is great for a grilled cheese sandwich, while mozzarella is perfect for pizza and (of course) mozzarella sticks. Meanwhile, blue cheese is perfect for most salads, and Parmesan goes well on pasta. Some people might claim that you can choose one "best" cheese based on the cheese's taste on its own. Yet most cheese is eaten as an ingredient in another dish—surely this suggests a cheese's pairing with other foods is most important.

The claim that cheese is an ingredient plays which of the following roles in the argument?
   A) refuting the passage's hypothetical counterexample
   B) providing evidence that cheddar is used in sandwiches
   C) supporting the conclusion that there's no "best" cheese
   D) providing evidence that cheese is not often eaten on its own
   E) structuring the conclusion of a conditional statement

4. Lanesha's farm needs a new tractor. Her farm is small and has three crops. Of those crops, one is tall and the other two are short. Tractor A is best for large farms with tall crops. Tractor B is best for small farms with any crops. Tractor C is best for small farms with tall crops. Therefore, Lanesha ought to buy Tractor B.

Which of the following arguments is most similar in its reasoning to the passage?
- A) All cars are small and fuel-efficient. Jasper's vehicle is not small; therefore, it is a truck.
- B) Apples are either red or green. Only green apples are tart. Phillip doesn't like tart flavors; therefore, he ought to buy red apples.
- C) Some people believe Bigfoot lives in Washington. Other people believe Bigfoot lives in Oregon. If Bigfoot is real, then it lives somewhere; therefore, if Bigfoot is real, then it lives in either Washington or Oregon.
- D) If a window is broken, then it should be fixed. A storm broke John's window. The store has a window that fits John's frame; therefore, John bought a new window.
- E) If something is a necessity, then you should buy it. I need new shoes. If the shoes are not expensive, then I will buy them. The shoes are expensive; therefore, I did not buy them.

5. All stories have three parts: a beginning, a middle, and an ending. The beginning must grab the reader's attention. The middle must keep them interested. The ending must emotionally reward the reader. If the beginning is weak, then . . .

Which one of the following most logically completes the argument?
- A) the reader will not remain interested in the story.
- B) the reader will not start to read the story.
- C) the reader will not enjoy the emotional reward.
- D) the reader will not reach the emotional reward.
- E) the reader will not remember what the story is about.

6. The best way to hide from someone is to be inconspicuous in plain sight. If you're visibly nervous or watching for the seeker, you'll stick out. During hide-and-seek, I never try to physically conceal myself. Most seekers look in actual hiding places. Most seekers don't pay attention to crowds.

What is the conclusion drawn in this argument?
- A) Seekers ignore large bodies of people.
- B) Hide-and-seek is a game about psychology, not stealth.
- C) Hiders should avoid actual hiding spots.
- D) Some seekers check both hiding spots and crowds.
- E) It's easy to be inconspicuous.

7. A suspension bridge is built using steel cables for supports. Steel cables are flexible. When I tried to build a model bridge out of flexible materials, the bridge collapsed. The second time, I tried using metal wire, and that model bridge also collapsed. Therefore, bridges built with flexible materials are not safe, which means that suspension bridges are not safe.

Which of the following generalizations, if valid, best justifies this argument's reasoning?
- A) If a model bridge is unsafe, then the full-size bridge is also unsafe.
- B) An analogy comparing a controlled example to a real-world scenario is generally valid.
- C) If a test can be performed by any lay person, then that test is valid.
- D) The property of a material can be expressed in different ways for different materials.
- E) Physics is consistent; therefore, experiments at one scale produce relevant results for all scales.

8. Twelve men were in a clothing store when the power was cut. When the lights turned back on, eleven men remained. The cash register had been robbed. The store's manager asked the remaining customers to empty their pockets. One man had a large amount of money, so the manager called the police.

The manager's reasoning is questionable in that
- A) It is reasonable to infer that the thief is the man who left.
- B) The manager assumed that a customer robbed the cash register.
- C) The cash register was closed during the power outage.
- D) The large amount of money does not support suspicion.
- E) The manager did not call the police while the robber stole the money.

9. Janet: It's too late to call for delivery. Could you cook tonight?

Gene: If I cooked last night, then it's not my turn tonight. Let's figure something else out.

Which of the following assumptions is required for Gene's argument in this dialogue to make sense?
- A) Tonight is not Gene's turn to cook.
- B) Janet cooked last night.
- C) If it's too late to call for delivery, then someone must cook.
- D) Gene cooked last night.
- E) Either Janet or Gene must have cooked last night.

10. If I want to feel good, then I should go on vacation. Helping others makes me feel good. It feels good to be in a new place. Therefore, being on vacation in a new place feels better than being on vacation in a familiar place. If I go on vacation, I want to maximize how good I feel. Therefore, if I go on vacation, I should visit a new place. Therefore, during vacation I should both visit a new place and help others.

The principle underlying the argument above is most similar to the principle underlying which one of the following arguments?
- A) If eating pizza makes me feel good, then I should eat pizza. Eating pizza makes me feel good. Eating in excess makes me feel bad; therefore, I should eat pizza in moderation.
- B) Building a dam will secure water for 1,000 people; however, building the dam requires demolishing 10 houses. If we help those households relocate, then we should build the dam.
- C) Suffering is caused if I'm never satisfied. I'm never satisfied because only new things and experiences cause pleasure; therefore, I should seek new things and experiences to minimize suffering.
- D) Most dogs like to eat food off the floor. If food falls on the floor, it might be toxic to dogs; therefore, we should prevent dogs from eating food off the floor even if they like it.
- E) Government regulates industries. New regulations should be made if and only if an industry is causing harm. Windmill manufacturers are causing harm by not protecting employees; therefore, windmill manufacturers should be regulated.

11. If a drug causes sufficient harm, then it is banned. Sufficient harm is when the drug hurts patients more often than it helps them. Drugs cause harm by damaging the body, by being addictive, or both. Some drugs feel good. If something feels good, then it is not harmful; therefore, drugs that feel good do not cause harm, which means that drugs that feel good are both addictive and do not damage the body.

Which one of the following arguments is most similar in its flawed reasoning to the argument above?
- A) I can't remember if Jennifer likes apples or oranges. Dan says Jennifer likes apples; therefore, she doesn't like oranges.
- B) If medicine cures disease, then it is beneficial. A medicine is addictive and cures disease; therefore, that medicine is beneficial, which means that some beneficial medicines are addictive. If a medicine is addictive, then it might be beneficial.
- C) Lawrence is a secret agent. He needs to decide whether to bring a flashlight, night vision goggles, or both on a mission. If the mission takes place at night, then night vision will be beneficial; therefore, Lawrence will bring night vision goggles and not a flashlight.
- D) Cleaning windows requires being high up. Jobs in high places are dangerous; therefore, being a window cleaner is a dangerous job. Window cleaners should invest in life insurance.
- E) When it's hot outside, I always bring a water bottle on hikes. It's not hot outside; therefore, I never bring my water bottle on hikes.

12. If there is extraterrestrial life, then it is either similar to us or different from us. Similar life is life based on carbon and water (H_2O); therefore, if we find water on a planet, any life on that planet is similar to us.

Which one of the following, if true, most strengthens this argument?
- A) Scientists find a planet that has abundant carbon; therefore, any life is different from us.
- B) Scientists find a planet that has abundant H_2O; therefore, any life is similar to us.
- C) Scientists find a planet that has abundant ice; therefore, it does not have life.
- D) Scientists find consistent radio waves. If a radio wave is consistent, then it was made by living creatures.
- E) Scientists find a planet with moving creatures; therefore, any life is similar to us.

13. If there is a fuzzlewump, then it has colored fur. Blue fuzzlewumps are happy. Yellow fuzzlewumps are angry. If a fuzzlewump is angry, then it is not happy. Therefore, some fuzzlewumps are either blue or yellow.

The answer to which one of the following questions would LEAST help in evaluating this argument?
- A) How many colors of fuzzlewump exist?
- B) What are the properties of a fuzzlewump?
- C) Are all fuzzlewumps always the same color?
- D) What makes a fuzzlewump happy?
- E) Why are yellow fuzzlewumps angry?

14. Sam: Before you went to the bathroom, it was my turn in the board game. You took your turn, and then Fred took his turn. That means it's my turn.

Bridget: This game piece is in the same spot on the board. That means I haven't taken my next turn.

Which of the following, if true, most helps to resolve the apparent conflict in this dialogue?
    A) The game's turn order is Sam, Bridget, Fred.
    B) The game paused while Bridget was in the bathroom.
    C) The game continued while Bridget was in the bathroom.
    D) Bridget has multiple pieces on the game board.
    E) Sam is close to winning the game.

15. Devon: Number 23 fouled me! I dribbled up to the basket, jumped, and felt someone touch my left arm while I took my shot. Because his touch interfered with my shot, I missed. That means you should give me a free throw.

Referee: I didn't see Number 23 foul you. The shot was a miss without interference, so you don't get a free throw. When we continue the clock, the other team will get the ball.

Which of the following pieces of evidence most seriously weakens Devon's argument?
    A) No one was standing on Devon's left side.
    B) Number 23's arms were extended straight up.
    C) A teammate was standing on Devon's left side.
    D) Number 24 touched Devon's left arm.
    E) If a penalty is called, then the clock is paused.

16. I don't understand why I'm not losing weight. I'm following my meal plan exactly as the nutritionist ordered. I'm even making sure I snack *less* than the plan anticipates! That's reducing my calories even further than expected.

Which of the following, if true, most helps to explain why the speaker's meal plan is not working?
    A) By reducing calories more than expected, the speaker is consuming less food and not following the plan.
    B) Although this person is following the meal plan, the nutritionist also told the person to exercise daily.
    C) If the speaker is snacking less than the plan anticipates, then the meal plan is not being followed exactly.
    D) Reducing food consumption alone is not sufficient for the speaker to lose weight.
    E) The meal plan is incorrect and should have required the speaker to consume more calories.

17. When the *Mayflower* sailed from England in 1620, the pilgrims left a land where they had food, water, and shelter. They hoped for a life where the Church of England would not persecute them. Even if colonizing North America would be more difficult than life in Europe, they felt religious freedom was worth crossing the Atlantic Ocean.

The pilgrims' decision is strongly supported if which one of the following is assumed?
    A) The pilgrims were being persecuted by someone in England.
    B) No European nation in the seventeenth century had the right to religious freedom.
    C) King James I of England was both head of state and head of the Church of England.
    D) Neither the pilgrims nor King James I were members of the Roman Catholic church.
    E) The Church of England had authority to persecute heterodox Christian worshipers.

18. The city of Springfield requires a new water treatment plant due to an increase in population over the last 50 years. The city council calls for a referendum from the electorate to approve or deny an increase in sales tax to finance the plant. The referendum votes 64 percent "No," 23 percent "Yes," and 13 percent "Indifferent." The city council begins plans to build a second water treatment plant instead of replacing the old plant. This plan will be less expensive and will not require raising the sales tax.

Which of the following conforms most closely to the principle illustrated in the passage above?
- A) A Congressional representative introduces an act that will introduce term limits on representatives. This act will require them to not seek re-election, but it is overwhelmingly supported by their district.
- B) A pig farmer is disappointed with the weight of his new hogs. He tries three new food brands. The hogs eat 95 percent of the second brand, so he begins using that brand exclusively.
- C) An eighteenth century English caravel is running out of food. Despite the crew's complaints, the captain orders that the remaining supplies be locked away for the good of everyone aboard the ship.
- D) In a referendum about raising property tax to build a new school, the voters vote 70 percent "Yes" and 30 percent "No"; however, the city council chooses not to raise taxes and not to build the new school.
- E) A painter fears she will not complete her current commission by the project's deadline. First, she tries working overtime, and then she decides to cut corners to save time. The painting is delivered on time.

19. When John got on the bus, I knew he'd be trouble. From the sway in his step, the poor man had fallen back into the bottle. He gave the $0.50 fare, though, so I couldn't turn him away. It surprised me that John had anything left in his wallet. Sure enough, 20 minutes into the trip, old John began raising his voice at one of the other passengers.

What role does the third sentence of this passage play in the speaker's argument?
- A) If passengers pay the fare, then the bus driver must let them ride.
- B) The passenger's fare refutes the speaker's unstated argument that they should not let John ride.
- C) This provides a counterexample to the passage's premise in the first sentence.
- D) This sentence is supporting evidence for the conclusion stated at the beginning of the passage.
- E) This sentence is the premise for a conditional statement, which is concluded with the following sentence.

20. Harry: Our most important duty as parents is to discipline Ben. Good discipline will make him well-behaved. He might not like it now, but as an adult he'll appreciate why we were strict.

Sally: Discipline isn't enough for Ben to become a well-adjusted adult. He needs more than just to be able to follow the rules. If we nurture Ben, he will be empathetic and able to care for others. If he cares for others, he'll make the world a better place. Thus, our most important duty is to nurture him.

Sally responds to Harry's argument by doing which one of the following?
- A) She refutes his premise by providing evidence that it is not well-supported.
- B) She shows how Harry's proposed course of action will not improve their child's discipline.
- C) She argues that empathy is equal in value to discipline, thereby weakening Harry's argument.
- D) She demonstrates that Harry's claim about discipline is not sufficient to support his conclusion.
- E) She claims that Harry's argument is based on subjective values, while hers is based on objective values.

21. The Latin phrase *casus belli* means "cause for war." If the international community recognizes a particular reason as a just cause for going to war, then that reason is a *casus belli*. If Nation A is defending itself from Nation B, then Nation A has *casus belli*. Thus, we can conclude that . . .

Which of the following most logically completes the argument?
    A)   Nation A is not the aggressor, and Nation B is the aggressor.
    B)   Either Nation A or Nation B is the aggressor.
    C)   The international community does not agree that Nation B has *casus belli*.
    D)   Defending yourself is a *casus belli* recognized by the international community.
    E)   Going to war against Nation B is always considered *casus belli*.

22. It is never permissible to lie. It is always permissible to tell the truth. Further, one *must* tell the truth in all situations. If a statement is true, then it is not false. Wrong actions perpetuate more wrong actions. If a person tells a convenient lie, then that person is more likely to tell a serious lie. If a person tells a convenient lie, then society is more likely to be structured around lies.

If the above passage is true, then which of the following statements must be true?
    A)   You must tell the truth even to a person who wants to harm you.
    B)   You should perform good actions because good actions perpetuate more good actions.
    C)   If society is structured around lies, then a person is more likely to tell a serious lie.
    D)   Only serious lies truly matter; convenient lies are bad, but sometimes they are acceptable.
    E)   An action is either right or wrong; therefore, lying is right if and only if doing so prevents a more wrong action.

23. Moe: This bakery is never going to turn a profit if we don't get some customers in. Let's buy some advertising so that more people are aware of our products.

Larry: Are you out of your mind? We can't afford that! Let's just print some fliers and hand them out instead.

Over which one of the following do Moe and Larry disagree?
    A)   that they ought to advertise their bakery
    B)   that fliers are an effective means of advertising
    C)   that advertising will help the bakery get more customers
    D)   that the bakery can afford to buy an advertisement
    E)   that turning a profit requires advertising

24. The bank closes at 4:00 p.m. If we go to the grocery store first, then we might not make it to the bank. We have a lot of shopping to do at the grocery store; therefore, going to the grocery store will take a lot of time. Money management is more important than running errands; therefore, shopping is more important than going to the bank. For this reason, we'll go to the grocery store first, and then if it's still open, we'll also go to the bank. Otherwise, we'll go to the bank tomorrow.

Which of the following most accurately describes a flaw in this passage's reasoning?
    A)   The passage's conclusion does not account for the bank's closing time.
    B)   The passage forms a conditional statement but does not provide a premise that supports it.
    C)   The passage does not identify that going to the bank constitutes money management.
    D)   The passage does not recognize that running errands also includes going to the grocery store.
    E)   The passage cannot reasonably form a conclusion because the grocery store's closing time is not also stated.

25. If the bus is not available, then we will hire a taxi. If a taxi is not available, then we will rent a car. If a car is not available, then we will take the ferry. If the ferry is not available, then we will not be able to travel. If we are not able to travel, then I won't be able to go to work tomorrow; however, today I was able to go to work because I rented a car.

This passage's conclusion requires the assumption that
- A) the bus was not available.
- B) the bus and taxi were not available.
- C) the bus, taxi, and car were not available.
- D) no wheeled vehicles were available.
- E) no wheeled vehicles will be available tomorrow.

Section IV – Logical Reasoning (Unscored Section)

As discussed earlier in this book, the revised LSAT exam will include one <u>unscored</u> section that consists of either logical reasoning questions OR reading comprehension questions. These questions will be used by the creators of the exam to determine their appropriateness for future LSAT exams. This sample test uses logical reasoning questions.

1. Dr. Everson: Water is necessary for all life as we know it. If there is water on Mars, then there will be life. Our exploration rover recently found water in the form of ice. If we keep searching, we're sure to find life!

Dr. Holstrand: I wish that were true, but if there really is water, why haven't we found life already? Surely if there is life on Mars, our telescopes or rovers would have found evidence. Because we've found no evidence, it's unlikely that continuing to explore will find it.

Which of the following, if true, most helps to resolve the conflict between Dr. Everson and Dr. Holstrand?
- A) The presence of water makes life possible, but it is not sufficient to prove life necessarily exists on Mars.
- B) Water is only necessary in liquid form for life, not in its solid form as ice.
- C) Liquid water only exists under the surface of Mars, and it is not present on the exterior of the planet.
- D) Some life on Earth does not require water. Therefore, some life on Mars does not require water.
- E) An astronaut visits Mars and returns with Martian ice, thereby proving that Mars has water.

2. Football is a complex game because of the number of players on the field and the different ways they each might act or react to events. Each "play" of the game typically takes less than a minute. The clock is often stopped between plays for players to return to the line of scrimmage. This line is where each play begins. Typical options for the team's leader—the quarterback—include passing the ball, handing it to a runner, or running with it themselves. Further, athletes are impacted by outside influences such as weather, diet, personal lives, and so on. Consequently, it's little surprise that the "best" team doesn't always win a football game!

Each of the following, if true, contributes to an explanation of why the "best" football team does not always win EXCEPT for which statement?
- A) Athletes have to make split-second decisions without the ability to consult teammates.
- B) A team's budget is limited, so it can afford good players in some positions and saves money on other positions.
- C) Younger players have a distinct advantage in speed over older players, despite the latter's experience.
- D) Teams with great players do not necessarily have great coaches to create game-winning strategies.
- E) Quarterbacks who are good at one type of play—such as passing—are not usually good at other plays.

3. Cheerleaders have a higher rate of injury than other high school athletes. The cause of injuries is unknown. All cheerleaders participate in dance routines. Female cheerleaders usually participate in acrobatic routines by being lifted or thrown. Male cheerleaders usually participate in acrobatic routines by providing a foundation for lifts and throws. If one gender is injured more often than the other, then we can identify how most cheerleaders are injured.

The answer to which of the following questions would most help in evaluating the argument above?
- A) How many female cheerleaders were injured during the last year?
- B) What is the rate of injury while performing dance routines?
- C) How often are high school cheerleaders injured during acrobatic routines?
- D) Is the rate of injury higher when lifting or being lifted?
- E) Which sports have an injury rate comparable to cheerleading?

4. Organisms are living things. All bacteria are organisms. All bacteria are single-celled. Therefore, all single-celled organisms are bacteria. A virus is a single entity smaller than a cell. A virus is not a cell because it cannot reproduce itself through mitosis. If something cannot produce offspring itself, then it is not an organism. Therefore, viruses are not organisms and not bacteria.

The conclusion of the argument is strongly supported if which one of the following is assumed?
- A) All viruses cannot reproduce themselves through mitosis.
- B) If a living thing cannot reproduce, then it is not a living thing.
- C) All bacteria can reproduce through mitosis.
- D) If an organism can reproduce, then its offspring can reproduce as well.
- E) A virus reproduces by infecting a cell's reproductive process.

5. Jeremy only goes hiking when the weather is cool and sunny. If Jeremy does not go hiking, then he goes to the gym. Shana invites Jeremy to go hiking since the weather is sunny; however, Jeremy says he will go to the gym. Therefore, Shana will go hiking alone.

Which of the following, if true, most seriously weakens the argument?
A) If the weather is sunny, then Shana will go hiking.
B) Shana only hikes if the weather is cool.
C) Jeremy's weather forecast predicted the day to be hot and sunny.
D) Shana and Jeremy never go hiking together.
E) Jeremy is at the gym because the weather is cool.

6. There is an eldest human who is older than all other humans; therefore, that human's birthday is the date farthest into the past on which any living person was born. Therefore, that person remembers events farther into the past than any other living person. If someone remembers events from long ago, then they are probably wise. The eldest human remembers events from long ago; therefore, that person is probably wise.

The argument requires which assumption?
A) that the eldest human has not yet passed away
B) that events long ago are more important than current events
C) that the present is contingent on events that happened in the past
D) that the eldest human's memory is accurate
E) that wisdom is an attribute possessed only by the eldest human

7. Politician: Our state's roads are in deplorable condition. There are many potholes and other signs of deterioration. That's why I've introduced a bill imposing a new gas tax to finance road refurbishment.

Journalist: In the past, you claimed the state's most important infrastructure was our railways. Yet now you're supporting road construction instead! What do you say to your supporters who want better railways?

Which of the following, if true, most strengthens the politician's argument?
A) Potholes cause car accidents; therefore, repairing potholes will make the state's roads safer.
B) The state's roads are in worse condition than the railways; therefore, the roads should be repaired first.
C) The railways are more important, but repairing the roads will be cheaper, thereby saving the taxpayer money.
D) The politician's supporters care less about railways than about other concerns, like social issues.
E) The funds to repair railways have already been secured, which is why a new gas tax is required for the road repairs.

8. If you carry too much while going backpacking, your gear will slow you down. Think about your pack like a sailboat. You wouldn't want to overload a sailboat, right? If you did, the boat would be more likely to sink when caught in a storm. On the bottom, you're going nowhere.

Using parallel reasoning, the flawed nature of the argument above can most effectively be demonstrated by noting which one of the following?
   A) that pressing a car's brake pedal is analogous to getting in a car crash
   B) that if you increase weight slowly, you will never reach your weight-lifting goals
   C) that perseverance is more important for achievements than getting lucky
   D) that to avoid getting in danger, it is important to plan a travel itinerary
   E) that when dancing at a nightclub, you can drink if and only if a friend is the designated driver

9. Bananas from Brazil cost $.50 per pound, and bananas from Argentina cost $0.45 per pound. I prefer Brazilian bananas. Pork is cheaper than beef, but more expensive than chicken. I prefer pork. I only buy baked goods when they're on the discount rack. That's why today I came home with Brazilian bananas, chicken, and a muffin.

Which of the following conforms most closely to the principle illustrated above?
   A) Ivan went to the hairdresser and spent $21 for a haircut and coloring, since color was only $5 more.
   B) The city commissioner declined employee raises for the third year. He said he wanted to pay more, but taxes would have to go up first.
   C) My favorite treat is buying a new video game. They can be expensive, though, so I do not buy them very often.
   D) A $20 discount is not enough to justify buying a $300 TV—let's wait until the annual sale in a few months.
   E) Ronald likes chocolate muffins, Daisy likes blueberry muffins, and Jeff likes poppyseed muffins. Thus, their mother bought one of each muffin.

10. Timmy's bedtime is 8:00 p.m. If it is Saturday, then Timmy's bedtime is one hour later than during a weekday. Today, Timmy went to bed at 9:00 p.m.; therefore, tomorrow will be Sunday.

The argument's reasoning is questionable in that the argument
   A) does not provide evidence about what time Timmy went to bed.
   B) makes an invalid inference to conclude that today is Saturday.
   C) uses evidence about today to conclude about tomorrow.
   D) fails to use arithmetic correctly to analyze the evidence.
   E) uses an inappropriate analogy to draw an equivalence between Saturday and Sunday.

11. Either the weather is good or the weather is bad. If the weather is good, then we will go swimming. If the weather is bad, then we will play board games. Ricky likes swimming more than board games. Jan and Alex don't like swimming at all. I like both equally; therefore, I hope the weather is bad tomorrow because that will be the most fun for everyone.

Which of the following arguments is most similar in its reasoning to the argument above?
- A) If I buy apples, then I can make pie. If I buy oranges, then I can make juice. If I want both pie and juice, then I must buy both apples and oranges; therefore, I bought both apples and oranges.
- B) The weather is bad. Either we are going to play a board game or we are going to play video games. We decided to play video games during the rainy day.
- C) The director wants to maximize profits. He must pick between either Project P or Project Q. Project Q's sponsor has a history of unprofitable ideas; therefore, the director picked Project P.
- D) I think the weather is bad if and only if there is a thunderstorm that day. There was a thunderstorm in the morning and clear weather in the afternoon; therefore, that day had bad weather.
- E) Bob empties the trash if it is full or if it is trash day. Trash day is Monday. Bob emptied the trash on Sunday; therefore, he will empty the trash on Monday.

12. Dawn: The zoo has more cute animals than the aquarium. It has kangaroos, pandas, and boa constrictors! Seeing cute animals is exciting; therefore, let's go to the zoo tomorrow.

Devin: Some fish are cute. Penguins are cute. Snakes are not cute—they're scary! Hammerhead sharks are cool, and cool animals are more exciting than cute ones; therefore, we should go to the aquarium instead.

The claim that there are boa constrictors at the zoo is used in the argument to do which one of the following?
- A) provide evidence that zoo animals are scary
- B) support Dawn's claim that seeing cute animals is exciting
- C) provide evidence that some animals at the zoo are cute
- D) claim that more animals at the zoo are cute than the animals at the aquarium
- E) refute Dawn's claim that all zoo animals are cute

13. All animals that give birth to live young and produce milk are mammals. If an animal is a mammal, then it is also warm-blooded. Sheep give birth to live young and produce milk; therefore, sheep are also warm-blooded.

The argument conforms most closely to which one of the following generalizations?
- A) If a set has a property, then all members of that set also have that property.
- B) Properties possessed only by some members of a set cannot be ascribed to the entire set.
- C) A premise validly supports its conclusion if the consequences do not contradict the premise.
- D) In an argument, a definition is valid if and only if it does not contradict other definitions.
- E) Mammals are a biological class and therefore must all have the same properties.

14. Orange juice is sweet, and lemonade is sweet. Because orange juice and lemonade are made from citrus fruits, their sweetness must also come from citrus fruits; therefore, citrus fruits are sweet. However, oranges are sweet but lemons are not. Further, grapefruits are not sweet. Therefore, only *some* citrus fruits are sweet.

Which of the following is a technique of reasoning used in the argument?
- A) Demonstrate that the products of a process must participate in the qualities of the raw materials.
- B) Use an intermediary conclusion to come to a contradiction, and then invalidate the premise.
- C) Compare two objects to one another to draw an analogy about a similar conflict.
- D) Employ a conditional statement to demonstrate that its premise is not true, and therefore its conclusion cannot be true either.
- E) Draw an intermediary conclusion, and then use evidence to make the conclusion more precise.

15. Clinton: A new theater will have a lot of attendance; therefore, it should be built near a major road. Major roads are good at providing access to locations inside the city. Putting the theater nearby will help people from out of town to visit it.

Becky: The theater will hold an audience of 2,000 people. There is an empty lot in the traditional performing arts district, down by the university. Why not build it there?

Clinton and Becky disagree over whether
- A) the theater should be built near a university.
- B) the theater should be built near the center of the city.
- C) major roads provide good access to visitors.
- D) the theater will have a large attendance.
- E) to save money by using an empty lot.

16. Venus is a very bright star, usually the brightest star in the night sky. Depending on the weather, Arcturus or Sirius can shine more brightly; however, Polaris is the easiest star to find. Just find the Big Dipper constellation, and follow the edge of the "cup" in a straight line. Finding Venus is more satisfying, though, because it doesn't rotate in the same way that the stars move. This is because both Venus and the Earth are orbiting the Sun.

Which of the following can be properly inferred from the statements above?
- A) If I find the Big Dipper, then I can find the sky's brightest star.
- B) If I can use the Big Dipper to find Polaris, then it must currently be nighttime.
- C) The Earth's rotation causes Venus to wander instead of following a regular path.
- D) During the night, Venus is brighter than the Moon.
- E) The stars and Venus move through the night sky for the same reason.

17. The Battle of Verdun was fought between the French and the Germans during WWI. It was one of the most catastrophic battles of that war, with hundreds of thousands of casualties on both sides. The German general, Erich von Falkenhayn, claimed after the war that this battle's goal was to draw the French army into a protracted conflict at Verdun. Because Verdun is important to France's history and culture, he believed they would fight fiercely to defend it. Falkenhayn wrote that an attack at Verdun would allow the German army to inflict a defeat on the French, without as many casualties of their own.

Which of the following can most reasonably be concluded on the basis of the information above?
   A) Due to Falkenhayn's strategy, the German army won the Battle of Verdun.
   B) Neither the British nor the French lost as many men at Verdun as the Germans did.
   C) After WWI, Falkenhayn lied about the strategy he intended to use in this battle.
   D) The city of Verdun is important to the French people because they successfully defended it in WWI.
   E) The French valued Verdun as a strategic point but did not value it as a cultural landmark.

18. Max: Time is measured by the movement of objects. A certain amount of time has passed, for example, when the Earth has rotated once around its own axis. Thus, time is a construct. It is not "inherently" real because it is just something we perceive in connection with movement.

Miller: That's not an accurate understanding of the moving objects. Yes, movement is how we perceive time; however, there is still a *sequence* to their movement. If I break a vase, I can't "magic it" back together.

The conclusion drawn in Miller's argument is that
   A) time is subjective and a matter of an individual's perception within their own senses.
   B) time appears real because the order of events is consistent and can't be undone.
   C) we must demonstrate that sequential time is consistent if we want to prove time is "inherently" real.
   D) movement is the means by which we perceive the passage of time through our senses.
   E) time is "inherently" real because the order of movements is in a sequence that cannot be altered.

19. When starting a new school year, it isn't always clear how much information the students have retained from the previous year. Assessing the students' starting points should be a priority. If the teacher understands what the student already knows, then the teacher can appropriately explain new concepts that build upon that information. Without performing an assessment, the teacher does not have the tools needed to understand whether or not the new concepts will be comprehended.

This passage's argument begins by defining a premise, and then proceeds by doing which one of the following?
   A) assessing whether or not the reader understands the premise in order to then follow the conclusion
   B) establishing a claim and supporting it with an explanation and a counterfactual statement
   C) stating the conclusion before explaining how the conclusion is supported by evidence
   D) building point by point upon that premise until the conclusion is reached
   E) constructing an intermediary conclusion, and then using evidence along with it to draw a final conclusion

20. *Hamlet* is Shakespeare's best play because it most perfectly combines the necessary elements of a tragedy. The drama is centered on Hamlet's personal character, giving him opportunities to back away. Yet he never does, because that's not who he is—the tragic confrontation becomes not just possible, but inevitable.

Which of the following principles, if valid, most helps to justify the reasoning in the passage above?
   A) All drama should be about a character's inner nature and the decisions made by that character.
   B) The best stories are also predictable because their outcome is inevitable.
   C) Shakespeare's comedies are worse than his tragedies because they are not focused on personal character.
   D) Tragedies are the most artful form of drama because they combine many necessary elements together.
   E) If something is necessary, then it cannot be contradicted by specific events.

21. If apples are square, then Darwinism is nonsense. Apples are green. Pears are green. Both apples and pears are green; therefore, both apples and pears are square. Darwinism is, therefore, nonsense.

The conclusion drawn above follows logically if which of the following is assumed?
   A) Apples are square.
   B) Darwinism is not nonsense.
   C) Some green things are square.
   D) All green things are square.
   E) All square things are green.

22. If Mike wants to make it to the finals of his tennis tournament, then he must win a match during every single round. In the third round, Mike has a bye. During a bye, a player moves to the next round but does not play a match. Because he moved to the next round, Mike still has a chance to win the tournament.

Which of the following most accurately describes a flaw in the passage's reasoning?
   A) The definition of a bye is invalid because Mike did not move to the fourth round.
   B) The conclusion is invalid because Mike did not play a match during the third round.
   C) The conditional statement's premise is invalid because no evidence supports the claim that Mike wants to win the tournament.
   D) The argument is invalid because no evidence is provided that Mike moved to the next round.
   E) If Mike did not receive a bye, then he would still be able to win the tournament.

23. You have an oven that can bake a cake. If you want to bake a cake, then you must buy sugar, butter, eggs, flour, and baking powder. Mix together the sugar, butter, and eggs, and then add vanilla. Next, mix together flour and baking powder. If you have mixed the two sets of ingredients, then combine them together in a cake pan. Put the cake pan in the oven. If a cake comes out, then you followed the recipe. Either a cake comes out, or a mess comes out. If a mess comes out, then you did not follow the recipe.

The conclusion is drawn logically if which of the following is assumed?
   A) The person baking the cake owns an oven.
   B) If you follow a recipe, then the result will sometimes be a mess.
   C) The person baking the cake already owns vanilla.
   D) No one who follows a recipe fails to make a mess.
   E) Anything that comes out of an oven is not a mess.

24. Sherlock is a detective. Detectives solve crimes; therefore, Sherlock solves crimes. Sherlock lives on Baker Street. Crimes occur more often on Baker Street than on other streets in London. If a detective does not solve a crime, then they are not a good detective. Sherlock lives on a street with a lot of crime; therefore, Sherlock is not a good detective.

Which of the following, if true, most strengthens this argument's reasoning?
- A) Sherlock has solved more total crimes than any other detective.
- B) Sherlock is occasionally assigned crimes that occur on Baker Street.
- C) All detectives except Sherlock are assigned crimes to solve; Sherlock chooses which crimes he will solve.
- D) Some crimes cannot be solved by any detective.
- E) A detective ought to solve crimes in the area they live in.

25. The rainbow is made up of seven colors: red, orange, yellow, green, blue, indigo, and violet. Louis hypothesizes that, depending on the day of the week, one color in the rainbow is always brighter than the other six. Louis wants to test this hypothesis, so he takes a picture every time there is a rainbow, and then he records the date. On Wednesday, green was the brightest color. On Thursday, blue was the brightest color. On Saturday, violet was the brightest color; therefore, Louis concludes that the order of the rainbow's colors is correlated with the order of the days of the week.

The answer to which one of the following questions would be LEAST helpful in evaluating Louis's conclusion?
- A) How prominent is the brightest color on a given day?
- B) Which color is prominent in the rainbow on Mondays?
- C) How many total pictures did Louis take of rainbows?
- D) In which month did Louis collect his evidence to test the hypothesis?
- E) Was there any variation in color prominence in the pictures?

ANSWER KEY #1

Section I – Reading Comprehension

Passage 1

1. D: This passage's emphasis is split between describing the ancient and modern contexts of the Amarna letters and describing the contents of those letters. Because the first paragraph specifies that the letters provide an opportunity for psychological insight, we can reasonably conclude that the subsequent contextualizing information supports that purpose; option D is therefore correct. Option A is incorrect because Akhenaten's religious reforms are implicitly internal—causing conflict with Egypt's priests—not external with another major power. Option B is incorrect because the passage states that even in antiquity the use of familial vocabulary did not always indicate familial behavior. Option C is incorrect because the passage does not describe personal friendships between rulers. Option E is incorrect because while looting does reduce context, the passage does not assert that historians are "severely limited" in what they can learn from the Amarna letters.

2. A: We can infer that the term *lingua franca* is most similar to "common tongue" from the following sentence's description of Akkadian's use as an international written language by Bronze Age scribes; option A is therefore correct. Option B is incorrect because while "French language" is a literal translation of *lingua franca,* it does not capture the meaning of that phrase's use in the passage. Option C is incorrect because the context indicates a language actively in use, not one restricted to scholarly purposes. Option D is incorrect because "discourse" is a communicative act—like discussing with one's peers—rather than the language within which that discussion takes place. Option E is incorrect because "written in Akkadian" indicates that the answer must be describing a property of the Akkadian language, rather than a code of written or unwritten behavior.

3. B: Option B is correct because even though King Suppiluliuma is not mentioned in the passage, we can reasonably infer from the final passage that if Akhenaten called him "brother," then Suppiluliuma was also considered a "great king;" thus, we are able to answer this question from the information in the passage. Option A is incorrect because the passage does not describe the transmission of the Amarna letters from looters to historians. Option C is incorrect because the passage discusses the primary language but does not specify how many other languages are used. Option D is incorrect because the passage's claim "For Akhenaten, the sun disk Aten was the supreme deity" does not specify whether or not this "Aten" was a new deity or a traditional deity. Option E is incorrect because the passage does not discuss the translation or scholarship about the Amarna letters.

4. C: The general purpose of paragraphs 2 and 3 in this passage is to provide archaeological and social context for the Amarna letters. Option C is correct because "scribal annotations" describes the type of evidence in the letters by which historians have inferred the passage's context. Options *A* and *E* are incorrect because the passage is focused on the personalities of rulers, not scribes. Option *B* is incorrect because the passage is not presenting evidence to support an argument that ancient rulers were illiterate. Option D is incorrect because differences in wealth and status are not a significant element in this passage's description of ancient culture.

5. C: Option C is correct because, in the first paragraph, the author claims that the Amarna letters "[illuminate] how psychological factors . . . shaped the ancient world." In the second paragraph, the author goes on to tell the story of the letters' owner (Akhenaten) to explain how the letters survived to be discovered. Option A is incorrect because the first paragraph does not describe what the Amarna letters are. Option B is incorrect because the first paragraph does not argue that the Amarna letters contextualize history; further, the second paragraph's description is not stated to have come from the Amarna letters; therefore, Option E is also incorrect. Option D is incorrect because the first paragraph does not tell Akhenaten's story.

6. A: Option A is correct because the final paragraph of the passage describes how familial relationships were used in correspondence. It is reasonable to infer that this use of family terminology is evidence that larger political systems were viewed as essentially based upon family structure, such as the patriarchal authority of a father or pharaoh. Option B is incorrect because the passage notes that it is "unclear" whether the use of family terminology was rhetorical or sincere. Options C and E are incorrect because the passage's description of Akhenaten's religious reforms uses a neutral tone without further judgment of the reforms. Option D is incorrect because the background about Akhenaten is provided without reference to the Amarna letters; it is therefore likely that the letters are valuable but not essential to information about the period.

7. E: Option E is correct because correspondence between Hitler and Stalin is also political communication between heads of state. While not intentionally private, it is likely that such correspondence could provide psychological insight (like the Amarna letters). Option A is incorrect because a diary is a private record, not a form of communication. Option B is incorrect because this is a discovery in general, not a discovery that provides analogous insight into a historical person. Option C is incorrect because this information provides psychological insight but is not structurally similar to finding a document sent from one person to another. Option D is incorrect because discovering this biological cause of change is not analogous to discovering correspondence.

Passage 2

8. B: Option B is correct because we can infer from the context of flood dangers and erosion that the author views the primary reason to build a dam as reducing the risk caused by floods. Option A is incorrect because the passage does not specify what locations are most likely to have a flash flood—it just says dry riverbeds and lakebeds in general. Option C is incorrect because preserving water is a secondary benefit. We can determine this through the use of the connecting word *also* in the subsequent sentence. Option D is incorrect because the sentence in which this phrase is found specifies that dams should be constructed near settlements. Option E is incorrect because the author does not state that dams reduce the effects of erosion on the environment.

9. D: Option D is correct because the effects of water in the passage are described as part of the author's agenda to correct the "misconception" that water has no impact on the desert. Option A is incorrect because water erosion is an example that supports the author's overall motive. Option B is incorrect because the passage's tone lacks the urgency or the specificity necessary to indicate that the author is advocating immediate action. Option C is incorrect because the passage does not describe what to do if someone suspects there is a risk of a flash flood. Option E is incorrect because the passage describes one mechanism about how deserts are changed, but it does not describe the impact of changes from outside this environment on the role of water in the desert.

10. B: Option B is correct because capillary action supports the author's claim that groundwater is "moderately ... stable." Option A is incorrect because water does not remain on the surface due to evaporation (paragraph 1). Option C is incorrect because capillary action describes ordinary groundwater reservoirs, not fossil water. Option D is incorrect because the author suggests that fossil water ought to be preserved for "when no other sources are available." Option E is incorrect because, from the context in paragraph 3, we can infer that the description of capillary action is primarily to explain why groundwater is fragile, instead of describing it for the sake of a complete description of water's impact on the desert.

11. A: Option A is correct because the author's use of the word *remnant* in this context connotes that fossil water will run out, and that humans are lucky that it has survived for this period of time. Option B is incorrect because the word *scarcity* refers to the layperson's beliefs, rather than the scientific information the author will share later in the passage. Option C is incorrect because the word *protected* specifically refers to groundwater in the context of capillary action. This is also why Option E is incorrect. Option D is incorrect because the word *exceed* refers to the quantity of water required without making an evaluative judgment. Such a judgment might indicate the author's concern; however, without the use of rhetoric or emotional tone in that sentence, the answer is incorrect.

12. E: Option E is correct because the passage states that fossil water is "finite." Although the passage does not draw the analogy to oil and coal, the presence of this analogy strengthens this answer's identification of the passage's argument that fossil water is a finite resource. Options A and B are incorrect because the passage does not discuss the qualities of fossil water. Option C is incorrect because groundwater is *not* replenished easily since there is a "risk of not refilling naturally." Option D is incorrect because fossil water does not replenish at all.

13. C: One can infer from the first paragraph's discussion of water "misconceptions" and from the third paragraph's transition into "less thrilling" sources of water that the author chooses to describe flash floods first due to rhetorical purposes; therefore, option C is correct. Option A is incorrect because the author's focal point is water management, not safety for traveling in the desert. Option B is incorrect because the passage does not specify the frequency with which these three forms of water can be found. Option D is incorrect because the discussion of groundwater and fossil water does not require understanding the effects of flash flooding. Option E is incorrect because floodwaters are not described as "consistent."

14. B: Option B is correct because it is reasonable to infer that the velvet mesquite's deep roots are an adaptation that allows the plant to access the desert's "very deep" groundwater reservoirs. Option A is incorrect because the passage specifies that only humans can access fossil water. Option C is incorrect because the passage does not provide information from which we can reasonably infer the impact of a deep root system during a flash flood. Option D is incorrect because the passage does not describe the desert's soil composition or its impact on plant life. Option E is incorrect because it is more reasonable to conclude from the passage's information that the taproot is meant to "tap" into the deep groundwater rather than store water.

Passage 3

15. B: Option B is correct because the passage describes how a code of ethics might remain constant, but a person's actions while following that code will vary due to their internal values and character. Consequently, ethical theory is flawed because a code is not 100 percent consistent for all people.

Option A is incorrect because the passage does not claim that Bonhoeffer believed ethical theories ignore internal virtue. Options C and E are incorrect because the passage does not address whether or not Bonhoeffer believed faith was necessary for ethical action. Option D is incorrect because the answer describes a cause of failing to perform ethical actions, not a cause of failure in ethical theorizing.

16. D: The quote from Exodus is used by the author to describe Bonhoeffer's ethical quandary involving Operation Valkyrie as well as to demonstrate why he concluded that *all* ethical theorizing was insufficient; therefore, option D is correct. Option A is incorrect because Bonhoeffer's faith is indicated explicitly by "a Lutheran pastor," not the quote from Exodus. Option B is incorrect because the quoted rule, "Thou shalt not kill," is easy to follow in most situations—Operation Valkyrie was an exceptional situation. Option C is incorrect because Bonhoeffer's argument does not require the quote from Exodus; rather, the quote from Exodus helps *explain* the argument. Option E is incorrect because the passage does not discuss Bonhoeffer's relationship with the Bible as an ethical text.

17. A: Option A is correct because the final paragraph describes how Bonhoeffer's beliefs applied to his circumstances confronting the Third Reich. Option B is incorrect because the passage does not describe the composition of *Ethics*. Option C is incorrect because the passage does not begin by describing Bonhoeffer's beliefs about ethics. Option D is incorrect because Bonhoeffer did not synthesize the Bible with Mill. Option E is incorrect because the passage primarily focuses on describing Bonhoeffer's argument, not on how he did or did not impact history.

18. E: Option E is correct because the passage does not present a counterargument or attempt to point out flaws in Bonhoeffer's argument. This, plus the comparison to another philosopher's theory (Mill's utilitarianism), makes it reasonable to infer that the author wants to persuade the reader rather than educate. Thus, Options B, C, and D are also incorrect. Option A is incorrect because the passage focuses on Bonhoeffer's argument; his historical role is secondary.

19. D: Option D is correct because the explanation coheres with typically virtuous behavior ("compassionate") and relies upon consistency with the bystander's internal character rather than with an external code, making option E is incorrect. Options A and B are incorrect because the passage does not describe Bonhoeffer's ethics as reliant upon quantifying the "value" of a person's life in comparison to an external code. Option C is incorrect because the example of Operation Valkyrie makes it likely Bonhoeffer would say the opposite—that by abstaining from intervention, the bystander is also morally responsible for the consequences.

20. A: Option A is correct because Kant's ethics utilize an internal viewpoint—although with principle, rather than character—and emphasize avoiding contradiction. This is similar to Bonhoeffer's argument that principles often contradict value or character. Option B is incorrect because it provides an external "rule" without an internal component. Option C is incorrect because the "golden rule" is an external rule capable of contradiction (e.g., if a person wants to be treated poorly, then that person has the liberty to treat others poorly). Option D is incorrect because the statement justifies causing harm, whereas Bonhoeffer's argument is that, in some circumstances, actions that violate principles are not merely "justified"—they're morally *correct* (e.g., assassinating Hitler). Option E is incorrect because, although this ethical theory focuses on internal character, its focus on the "mean" is not as similar to Bonhoeffer as Kant's focus on avoiding contradiction.

21. E: The word *fulcrum* is used to describe the center of Bonhoeffer's argument, around which the rest of his argument revolves or moves; thus, option E is correct. Option A is incorrect because the word *heart* has an emotional connotation, whereas the word *fulcrum* has a mechanical connotation as a word used in engineering. The more emotionally neutral word *center* is a better option. Option B is incorrect because the word *context* does not adequately describe the relationship between "internal character"

and "Bonhoeffer's analysis." Option C is incorrect because the word *lever* retains the mechanical connotation but does not have the "central" sense that *fulcrum* or *center* preserves. Option D is incorrect because "Bonhoeffer's analysis" does not connect two separate ideas together.

Passage 4 (Parts A and B)

22. B: Option B is correct because the word *liberties* in passage A describes activities that the author asserts he and his heirs may take. This is analogous to passage B's assertion that the right to abolish the government is included in a people's "unalienable Rights." Option A is incorrect because the word *relief* is used in passage A to describe a type of payment owed to the Crown. Option C is incorrect because the word *reasonable* is used to modify the revenues that may be claimed by an heir's guardian. Options D and E are incorrect because the words *guardianship* and *entrusted* describe a particular person's relationship to an heir.

23. C: Option C is correct because passage A states that "ALL FREE MEN" are given certain "liberties," while passage B states that "all men . . . are endowed with certain unalienable Rights" of which "Liberty" is one. This is then the basis of the author's claim that people may abolish the government. Option A is incorrect because passage A does not assert that rights are given by God. Option B is incorrect because the concept of liberty is not the cause of passage A's claim that free people have the listed privileges. Option D is incorrect because passage A does not make this generalized assertion about authority and consent. Option E is incorrect because neither passage is concerned with a definition of citizenship.

24. A: Paragraph 6 of passage A specifically restricts an heir's right to marry. Consequently, we can infer that passage A is concerned in general about marriages and the transmission of property. Passage B's discussion of rights is more generalized, asserting only the specific right to abolish the government; therefore, it is unlikely that passage B would explicitly protect widows from forced remarriage, making option A correct. Option B is incorrect for similar reasons; it is unlikely that passage B's general assertion of "unalienable Rights" will lead to explicitly making this statement. Option C is incorrect because both passages are concerned with restricting the government's privileges involving property. Option D is incorrect because we can infer that passage A might assert this due to its concern with heritage, while passage B might assert this due to its general description of why free people have rights. Option E is incorrect because both passages are concerned with protecting freedoms, which would be abrogated by the opposite of this statement; in other words, both passages would disagree with the *opposite* of this statement, so we can infer that they both might explicitly state it.

25. D: Option D is correct because passage A shows a distinct focus on how heirs will receive their parents' property, and passage B presents an argument about why and for what causes a people might abolish their government. Option A is incorrect because passage B is *asserting* "unalienable Rights," not *negotiating* them. Option B is incorrect because "justifying secession" is not an audience. Option C is incorrect because passage A is not directed at the Church. Option E is incorrect because, logically, passage A is directed both at the king *and* at the people whose "liberties" it is describing.

26. B: Passage B refers to the king of Great Britain explicitly. We can infer that the "Crown" referenced in passage A is that of Great Britain because of the use of "pounds" and "shillings" as units of currency. Thus, Option B is correct. Option A is incorrect because passage B does not discuss legal guardianship. Option C is incorrect because only passage B states that the people's rights are being asserted due to "usurpations" of the government. Passage A merely lists privileges without describing complaints. Option D is incorrect because we cannot infer from the specific "liberties" listed in passage A that the text is creating a new social order. In contrast, passage B has a revolutionary tone due to its discussion of when a people may abolish the government. Option E is incorrect because passage B does not derive rights from being "governed"; rather, it states that rights are "unalienable" and given to all men by God.

27. A: Option A is correct because passage B uses the king's "usurpation" of rights to support its claim, while passage A does not. Options B and C are incorrect because neither passage specifically defines the terms *rights*, *freedoms*, etc. Option D is incorrect because passage B does not emphasize the king's "usurpations." The passage uses them as support for its argument, but passage B's focus remains on declaring a course of action. Option E is incorrect because passage B asserts that the "Creator" gave rights to the people, not that "freedom" gives rights.

Section II – Logical Reasoning

1. C: Option C is correct because in the third sentence it is specified that Rachel does not know whether or not the airbags work in her A250. Consequently, we can infer from the last sentence that she concluded "it's best to be safe." Options A and B are incorrect because it is not known whether or not the airbags function. Option D is incorrect because, while Rachel does lack information, her action in the last sentence demonstrates that she did choose to send in her A250. Option E is incorrect because we do not have enough information in the passage to infer that Rachel sent the car in because she drew this conclusion; it is more likely that her conclusion was similar to Option C.

2. A: Option A is correct because the passage's focus on scoring runs implies that it is more important to score points than to prevent the other team from scoring points. Option B is incorrect because this is a premise used by the passage to evaluate different strategies, such as trying to hit singles or home runs. Options C and D are incorrect because the passage's focus is not on the crowd's excitement, but on how to win games. Option E is incorrect because the passage does not define a team's goal—it only discusses strategy of how to win, not whether or not winning is important.

3. E: Option E is correct because we can infer from "nearly resulted" and "well-timed" that, had the counterattack come at a different time, Napoleon would have lost this battle. Option A is incorrect because, while the passage does support this inference, it is not as strongly supported as the correct answer. Options B and D are incorrect because "may be" in the first sentence does not sufficiently support these statements about other historical generals. Option C is incorrect because the attitude of the Coalition's generals is not discussed.

4. B: Option B is correct because we can tell from Linda's dialogue that she does not want to force Ralph to participate in activities. In contrast, we can infer from Nancy's dialogue that she feels Ralph ought to be encouraged to "hang out and have fun" even if he wants to decline. Option A is incorrect because the first sentence of Nancy's dialogue is not sufficient evidence to conclude that she believes Ralph is not supportive or caring. Option C is incorrect because the dialogue lacks sufficient evidence to determine how highly both Nancy and Linda value financial contribution in a partner. Option D is incorrect because it is reasonable to conclude that both women agree with this statement. The definition of "fun" is not contended in the dialogue; rather, the activities that *are* "fun" are in contention. Option E is incorrect because we can reasonably infer that both Nancy and Linda agree with this statement. Again, they disagree on which activities could be considered "fun."

5. A: Option A is correct because the argument's definition of "well-built" is used in both of the passage's conclusions. Option B is incorrect because the author's use of "or" is not to create an exclusive "either-or" situation in which the reader ought to pick between fabricated homes or trailers. Option C is incorrect because the argument does not attempt to refute any statements. Option D is incorrect because the author is dissuading the reader from purchasing a fabricated home or trailer; they are not advocating a specific course of action, such as "Therefore, you should buy a such-and-such home." Option E is incorrect because the argument does not provide evidence that supports the premise. For example, the argument does not demonstrate that its definition of "well-built" is true.

6. D: Option D is correct because the "long drive" is evidence that supports the argument that traveling to Yellowstone would waste vacation time. Option A is incorrect because Janessa's claim that the couple cannot afford the trip is not provided with support. Option B is incorrect because Janessa is arguing against visiting Yellowstone next year and is not in favor of it. Option C is incorrect because we can reasonably infer that the couple does not need to explain to one another why they took prior trips. Option E is incorrect because Janessa's statement in the dialogue is not about her bucket list activities.

7. C: Option C is correct because this principle coheres with Bob's reasoning that he ignored the government's rule in pursuit of a "higher" cause (telling the true story of the war). Options A and B are incorrect because Bob's reasoning does not rely upon special permissions for journalists as a professional class. Option D is incorrect because Bob does not argue that the temporary rule is illegitimate. Option E is incorrect because Bob's reasoning is not consistent with the claim that respecting authority is more important than telling the truth.

8. D: Option D's first sentence provides definitions that are similar to the first two sentences of the passage. This answer then uses a conditional statement to draw a conclusion; thus, Option D is correct. Option A is incorrect because the answer does not use a conditional statement. Option B is incorrect because the answer uses a comparison between trucks and cars rather than defining a property of trucks. Option C is incorrect because the answer's second sentence quantifies rats with "some" rather than making a claim about all rats. Option E is incorrect because the answer's argument is based on similarities between *some* gases rather than making a claim about all members of a category, such as all apples or all doctors.

9. B: Option B is correct because the answer is based upon the principle that if an action is unjust in a serious context (i.e., warfare), then it is unjust in related contexts (i.e., police actions). Option A is incorrect because this answer is based on setting an example, not avoiding exemptions. Option C is incorrect because the course of action has a qualifier, "if it's worth the expense." Option D is incorrect because the answer does not compare situations based upon a principle. Option E is incorrect because the answer does not use context, such as a Geneva Convention, as part of its argument about the injustice of prisoners of war.

10. B: Option B is correct because the author states that "many people suspect foul play." This fails to support the claim because "many people" does not logically constitute evidence. Option A is incorrect because the author does not assert that John Smith was murdered; for example, the passage is also logically consistent with implying that he was kidnapped. Option C is incorrect because the author does not imply that the police were involved. Option D is incorrect because the author does not make this claim about John Smith's third wife. Option E is incorrect because the author does have sufficient evidence based on the passage's quotation.

11. C: The passage's error is that the second sentence provides evidence that undermines the conditional statement. The lack of flowers does not logically indicate that there was not enough rain. This is most similar to option C because, according to the answer, it logically follows that if the speaker got a sunburn, then they did not bring an umbrella on vacation. If they did not bring an umbrella on vacation, then they did not go to the beach. The answer's second sentence contradicts its conclusion. Option A is incorrect because the answer is not flawed. Option B is incorrect because the conclusion is flawed by the use of the word *some* instead of *all*. Option D is incorrect because the argument's flaw is that the word *evergreen* is not defined as a property of pine trees. Option E is incorrect because the conclusion uses the second sentence's evidence to draw an unsupported conclusion.

12. E: Option E is correct because this assumption explains why the farmer chose to call the police rather than try to help the person in the field. Option A is incorrect because we have no reason to believe the farmer does not have this authority. Option B is incorrect because the passage's first sentence states that the bull chases people. Option C is incorrect because the first sentence does not state that the bull only chases strangers. Option D is incorrect because the answer's assumption, while valid, does not explain the cause of why the farmer called the police as well as option E does.

13. B: Option B is correct because, if Paul was low on oxygen, this assumption reasonably explains why Paul did not attempt to share oxygen. Option A is incorrect because this assumption contradicts the passage's first sentence. Option C is incorrect because this assumption does not cohere with the fact that Paul reached the surface alone. Option D is incorrect because dislike does not support Paul's option as strongly as having low oxygen. Option E is incorrect because this assumption does not support why Paul did "not attempt" to share oxygen.

14. D: Option D is correct because adding evidence that Julie travels frequently supports her decision to buy a more portable computer. Option A is incorrect because this assumption is relevant when comparing different laptops, not while comparing desktops and laptops. Options B and C are incorrect because the answers support Julie purchasing a desktop. Option E is incorrect because the durability of a computer is not relevant to the passage.

15. A: Option A is correct because if the local area does not receive heavy rainfall, then it is not likely that it will experience floods. Option B is incorrect because, without mention of other environments that *do* absorb water, this answer does not seriously weaken the argument. Option C is incorrect because the answer strengthens the argument by supporting the claim that floods are dangerous and should be mitigated. Option D is incorrect because, although this does weaken the argument, the existence of dams still indicates that dangerous floods can occur in this area. Option E is incorrect because the argument is centered on the danger of flooding, and failure to absorb rainfall does not substantially weaken the argument.

16. E: Option E is correct because this percentage would provide evidence that would substantially strengthen or weaken the passage's argument about people feeling "driven to fight against the enemy." Option A is incorrect because this answer is already implied by the passage's claim that Germany was "heavily bombed." Options B and C are incorrect because these raw numbers would not provide information about the populace's emotions following the bombing. Option D is incorrect because, while the impact of leadership is relevant, it is not as helpful in evaluating the argument as the population's overall opinion.

17. D: Option D is correct because this answer supports the passage's statement concerning adaptation and the ability to meet needs concerning water. Option A is incorrect because this answer contradicts the passage's statement that there is "very little water" in the desert. Option B is incorrect because this answer helps explain why harsh deserts *lack* life. Option C is incorrect because migration is not as helpful an explanation as adaptation; this is because the passage implies that plants and animals can be found in most deserts year-round through its counter-example of the Gobi Desert. Option E is incorrect because requiring "less water" does not explain how desert plants find water in the first place.

18. B: Option B is correct because it is reasonable to infer that lack of sweat on a hot day is consistent with a lack of water with which to sweat; therefore, this statement resolves the conflict by providing additional evidence of dehydration. Option A is incorrect because Dr. Condo's specialty does not provide evidence that he is correct; this is strengthened by the fact that his recommendation is to test for further evidence. Option C is incorrect because, with the listed symptoms, it is not reasonable to trust the patient's agreement as evidence. Option D is incorrect because Dr. Lem's specialty does not provide additional context to the passage. Option E is incorrect because this statement does not give more information about the patient.

19. C: Option C is correct because this answer best supports the owner's decision in the third year to advertise and hope for a larger crowd. Although the result was not what they expected, this answer still provides the best assumption that justifies their decision. Option A is incorrect because the festival's band quality is not discussed in the passage. Option B is incorrect because even if the owner assumes this statement, this answer does not help justify the owner's option to advertise. Option D is incorrect because this assumption does not cohere with the owner's actions. Option E is incorrect because the owner's action in the passage is not to decide whether or not to hold the festival.

20. A: This argument is flawed because the listed evidence for why ice fishing is best applies to winter activities in general, not ice fishing in particular; thus, option A is correct. Option B is incorrect because the first sentence is not a premise—it is the passage's conclusion, which is then supported by the rest of the passage. Option C is incorrect because the passage does not have a counterexample to refute. Option D is incorrect because the passage does not make this claim, and therefore is not required to provide evidence for the claim. Option E is incorrect because "fun" is sufficiently subjective that we reasonably cannot expect evidence to be provided that demonstrates whether or not an activity is objectively "fun."

21. B: Option B is correct because this statement's use of the word *expert* generalizes it to be about more than just the passage's situation and identifies it as in agreement with the sentence "the doctor is an expert." This general principle identifies the logic in the speaker's decision-making process. Option A is incorrect because this statement's use of the word *always* does not fit with the passage's implication that a painful procedure may be necessary for improving health. Option C is incorrect because the passage's third sentence directly contradicts this generalization. Option D is incorrect because this is not a generalization; this answer is a specific statement about anesthesia. Option E is incorrect because the speaker acted opposite to this generalization by consenting to the procedure.

22. E: Option E is correct because this answer is supported by the premise in the first sentence through the evidence of Darwin's observations. Option A is incorrect because the passage's premises do not support making the claim that a species is "in the process of diversifying." The passage's first sentence defines a "new species," not signs that an organism is *becoming* a new species. Option B is incorrect because the passage's premise contradicts this answer. It requires "substantial difference," not just variation. For example, a cat with spots is not necessarily a different species than a striped cat. Option C is incorrect because the passage does not logically support the claim that biodiversity is necessary for studying speciation. Additional information is required to infer that conclusion. Option D is incorrect because this answer's conclusion about the past is not supported by the passage; however, the correct conclusion, Option E, could be used as an intermediate step for reaching this conclusion.

23. D: Option D is correct because the idea of "intentionally choosing" is logically inferred from the dialogue's use of the word *self-mastery*. Option A is incorrect because this is the conclusion of Alexander, not Aristotle. Option B is incorrect because Aristotle's speech in the dialogue does not support this answer's second clause. Option C is incorrect because this statement is part of Aristotle's argument, not its conclusion. Option E is incorrect because Aristotle's argument does not address the idea of specific situations; rather, his argument describes ethical behavior in a generalized, non-specific manner.

24. A: Option A is correct because Cassie refutes Laura's argument by agreeing with Laura's evidence (that Front Street is the biggest road) but undermining its support (that it has too much traffic). Option B is incorrect because the dialogue does not draw a conclusion only from premises. Each conclusion also requires evidence, such as a street's access to the road. Option C is incorrect because neither speaker employs an analogy. Option D is incorrect because neither speaker employs a metaphor; in addition,

metaphor is not generally considered a technique of argument. Option E is incorrect because the dialogue's evidence is not provided by an authority.

25. C: Option C is correct because the answer provides evidence that supports the suggested action as well as evidence that weakens the opposite of the suggested action. Options A and D are incorrect because both answers use conditional statements with evidence to come to a conclusion. Option B is incorrect because this answer makes a claim and then supports it with evidence. Option E is incorrect because the answer uses evidence to contradict a premise.

Section III – Logical Reasoning

1. C: Option C is correct because the passage states that "most particles . . . constitute atoms." We know the particle's momentum, and so we cannot know its location; however, we can reasonably infer that it is probably in some atom—even if we cannot know which atom. Option A is incorrect because the last sentence of the passage indicates that momentum and position can be approximated simultaneously. Option B is incorrect because if the particle's position is known, then nothing about its momentum can be known. Option D is incorrect because "all particles" contradicts "most particles" in the passage's second sentence. Option E is incorrect because knowing the position means we cannot know the particle's momentum and can therefore not reasonably infer that the particle lacks momentum.

2. E: Option E is correct because we can infer from Ashlyn's counterargument that she does not agree with Stuart's claim that the oak is a danger. Options A and B are incorrect because Ashlyn does not contest either statement. Option C is incorrect because we can infer that Ashlyn believes Stuart's worries are unreasonable because of the oak's location, not the oak's age. Option D is incorrect because the passage is about whether or not the oak will damage a roof, not the danger posed by a thunderstorm.

3. A: Option A is correct because this claim in the passage's final sentence provides evidence that weakens the counterexample's conclusion. Option B is incorrect because this claim does not provide evidence about the existence of grilled cheese sandwiches; rather, that recipe's existence supports this claim. Option C is incorrect because, while this claim does support the passage's argument, that is not its role in the structure of the argument. Option D is incorrect because this answer reframes the claim rather than describes how the claim works in the argument. Option E is incorrect because the claim is in the premise of the conditional statement. The statement argues that if cheese is most often eaten as an ingredient, then its flavor in recipes is more important than its flavor on its own.

4. D: This passage's logical structure argues that if an action is both necessary and possible, then it should be performed. The tractor options fit Lanesha's needs, so she ought to buy the appropriate tractor. Option D fits best with the passage because its third sentence specifies that buying a new window is possible. Since it is both necessary and possible, John ought to buy the window; thus, Option D is correct. Option A is incorrect because this answer's argument uses premises to establish a flawed conclusion. Option B is incorrect because this argument does not include an element of necessity. Option C is incorrect because the answer's conclusion is conditional on a possibility being true, whereas the correct answer states that the possibility *is* true. Option E is incorrect because a second conditional sentence is introduced that restricts the speaker's options.

5. B: Option B is correct because this answer is supported by the beginning's sequential place in a story and by its role (grabbing attention). Option A is incorrect because the middle's role is to "keep [the reader] interested." Options C and D are incorrect because the "emotional reward" is associated with the ending, not the beginning. Even if it logically follows that the reader will not receive the emotional reward because they didn't start the story, option B is the most logical answer because it is more closely

associated with the passage's definition of a beginning. Option E is incorrect because we can reasonably infer that the concept of "not remembering" is more closely associated with retaining the reader's attention in the middle, rather than grabbing it during the beginning.

6. C: In this passage, the conclusion is the first sentence, which is then supported by the following sentences. Thus, option C is correct. Option A is incorrect because this answer is a claim used to support the conclusion. Options B and D are incorrect because both answers give a valid inference based on the available information, but neither inference is the passage's conclusion. Option E is incorrect because the passage's conclusion is not about the ease or difficulty of hiding in plain sight.

7. B: Option B is correct because this principle supports both of the speaker's attempts to create a model bridge as a valid experiment testing the safety of flexible bridges. Option A is incorrect because this statement is not a generalization—it is specifically about bridges. Option C is incorrect because this principle's justification of the test in the passage is not as strong as the more general analogy about examples in option B. Option C is weaker because it includes the qualifier "by any lay person." Option D is incorrect because this principle weakens the argument by supporting the inference that the passage's test was invalid since the flexibility of steel cable is not comparable to the flexibility of metal wire. Option E is incorrect because the principle's premise does not obviously support its conclusion; without the conclusion supported, this answer does not substantially support the passage's argument.

8. B: Option B is correct because the evidence available to the manager prior to emptying the customers' pockets did not allow the manager to reasonably infer that one of the men in the store was the thief. Option A is incorrect because this answer's inference is accurate, but it does not describe the manager's *flaw* in reasoning. Option C is incorrect because there is no evidence about the cash register in the passage. Option D is incorrect because the large amount of money could reasonably support suspicion in lack of other evidence. Option E is incorrect because we can reasonably infer from the passage that no one present noticed the robbery while it was occurring. Thus, the manager could not reasonably have called the police at the time that the culprit was performing the robbery.

9. D: Option D is correct because Gene's argument uses a conditional statement that implies this assumption. If this assumption is false, then the dialogue does not make sense. Option A is incorrect because this answer is a conclusion drawn from the correct assumption, based on Gene's conditional statement. Option B is incorrect, because if Janet cooked last night, then it could be Gene's turn to cook tonight. Option C is incorrect because we can reasonably infer from the passage's last sentence that this answer is not true; there must be at least one unstated option other than "Gene cooks," "Janet cooks," or "we get delivery." Option E is incorrect because this assumption does not provide information that allows Gene's argument to make sense. With this assumption, it is possible that it is Gene's turn to cook.

10. B: The passage's underlying principle focuses on maximizing the amount that the speaker "feels good" through combining mutually compatible goals. Option B is correct because this answer uses the conditional "*if* we help those households relocate . . ." Use of this conditional indicates that option B employs the same principle of maximizing positive outcomes. Option A is incorrect because the underlying principle tries to balance positive and negative outcomes. Option C is incorrect because the underlying principle employs positive outcomes to mitigate the negative outcomes. Option D is incorrect because the underlying principle focuses on protecting those who might harm themselves by accident (in this case, dogs). Option E is incorrect because the underlying principle focuses wholly on mitigating negative outcomes, without regard for positive outcomes.

11. C: The flaw in the passage is that the argument does not account for the option of "both" in the third sentence. Option C is correct because it creates the same flaw in concluding that Lawrence will not bring a flashlight. Option A is incorrect because this answer's flaw is that evidence that Jennifer likes apples does not necessarily exclude the possibility of her liking oranges; the answer is not framed with exclusive language using the word *or* and similar terms, such as *whether* or *either*. Option B is incorrect because this statement does not have a logical flaw. Option D is incorrect because the flaw is an unjustified leap in the argument from sentence three to sentence four. Option E is incorrect because this answer's flaw is assuming that if the opposite of the premise is true, then the opposite of the conclusion is true; however, it is logically possible that the speaker brings water bottle *always, some,* or *never* when it is not hot. We do not have information that uses the evidence provided, so we cannot logically draw a conclusion.

12. D: Option D is correct because the new evidence added (consistent radio waves) strengthens the passage by supporting the premise in its first sentence. Option A is incorrect because it contradicts the passage. Option B is incorrect because it agrees with the passage without providing additional evidence or strengthening the argument. Option C is incorrect because the passage does not allow us to conclude that planets with ice do not have any life. Option E is incorrect because movement is not a criterion in the passage for defining "similar life."

13. A: Asking how many colors of fuzzlewump exist does not help evaluate this argument because the passage's final sentence uses the qualifier "some"; therefore, the passage is only making a claim about blue and yellow fuzzlewumps, not *all* fuzzlewumps. In the latter case, querying about the number of fuzzlewump colors would be relevant; therefore, option A is correct. Options B, C, and E are incorrect because the answer to these questions could reveal more information about the connection between color and emotion, which would allow us to evaluate the passage's claim. Option D is incorrect because this question still concerns fuzzlewump emotions and may provide useful evidence in evaluating the argument.

14. D: Option D is correct because if this board game uses multiple pieces, it is reasonable to infer from the passage that Bridget may have moved a different piece on her most recent turn. This explains why the designated game piece has not moved, and it resolves the conflict. Option A is incorrect because we can infer the appropriate turn order from the passage, and it is not the point of conflict. Options B and C are incorrect because we can infer from Sam's account of the game's turns that whether play was paused or continued, Bridget's absence did not impact the taking of each player's turn. Option E is incorrect because this answer might explain why the conflict arose between Bridget and Sam, but it does not help resolve it.

15. C: Option C is correct because a teammate standing to Devon's left provides a reasonable explanation for why Devon felt someone touch his left arm—the teammate touched it, not an opponent. Options A and B are incorrect because these answers do not weaken Devon's argument as much as another answer that plausibly explains why Devon is mistaken. Option D is incorrect because, from the context, if Number 24 had touched Devon's arm, there would still have been a foul. The contention is not "Number 23 touched me," but rather "an opponent touched me." Option E is incorrect because Devon's argument is not about management of the clock.

16. B: Option B is correct because this answer provides an explanation that goes beyond the information in the passage but also agrees with the information in the passage. We can infer from the passage's description of the meal plan that calorie reduction is required to lose weight; therefore, options A and C are incorrect because, logically, the failure to lose weight is not due to "not following the plan" because calories are being reduced. Option D is incorrect because this answer logically coheres with the passage, but option B provides a specific explanation of why. Option E is incorrect since we can infer that losing weight requires eating less, which means that this answer's proposition that the meal plan is incorrect is a contradiction.

17. E: Option E is correct because assuming that the Church of England could persecute heterodox Christians entails that the Church was probably persecuting the pilgrims. Option A is incorrect because this answer's lack of specificity makes it weaker than Option E. Option B is incorrect because the passage's third sentence implies that this answer is false—that there was at least one nation in Europe that did not persecute the pilgrims. Option C is incorrect because this assumption does not alter our interpretation of the passage's information. Option D is incorrect because lack of membership in the Roman Catholic Church does not imply that the pilgrims had support or a relationship with King James I; in effect, this answer provides an absence of information, rather than constructive information from which we can draw an assumption.

18. A: Option A is correct because both this answer and the passage demonstrate the principle that an elected official should listen to the electorate, even if the official personally prefers a different course of action. Option B is incorrect because the hogs' food preference is not analogous to a community's consent to a new tax. Option C is incorrect because the captain follows the principle of acting against the community for their own good. Option D is incorrect because the answer's city council does not follow the option in the referendum. Option E is incorrect because this situation is not logically analogous to the passage; the painter does not seek the patron's opinion on her course of action.

19. B: Option B is correct because the passage's unstated premise, "if John is drunk, then I should not let him ride," is supported by the "sway in his step" as evidence. The third sentence refutes this, because John provides his fare. Option A is incorrect because this answer provides a conditional statement that is logically equivalent to the third sentence; however, this answer does not identify the third sentence's role in the passage. Option C is incorrect because John's fare is not a counterexample to the bus driver's belief that this passenger would cause trouble. Option D is incorrect because it is also not evidence that supports that claim. Option E is incorrect because the fourth sentence is not part of a conditional statement.

20. D: Option D is correct because Sally's argument against discipline is not "discipline is unimportant" but rather "it is not the *most* important." She weakens Harry's argument by claiming that he has not provided sufficient support for the conclusion in the first sentence. Option A is incorrect because Sally states that Ben "needs more" than discipline, but does not provide evidence. Option B is incorrect because Harry has not proposed a course of action to be weakened. Option C is incorrect because Sally argues that empathy is *more* important than discipline, not equal. Option E is incorrect because neither speaker makes a distinction between subjectivity and objectivity.

21. D: We can infer from the passage that if Nation A's defense is considered *casus belli,* then it is necessary that the reason given in the third sentence is recognized by the international community as a *casus belli*. Thus, Option D is correct. Because the information provided does not describe other causes of *casus belli*, there is little that we can infer about Nation B; therefore, we cannot logically conclude which nation is the aggressor or that Nation B lacks *casus belli*. For example, it is logically possible from this information that Nation B has *casus belli* due to some action of Nation A. Thus, Options A, B, C, and E are incorrect.

22. A: Option A is correct because it can be logically inferred from the passage's third sentence. That sentence's universal claim, if true, is not concerned with the facts of a particular situation. Option B is incorrect because we cannot logically infer the opposite from the passage's fifth sentence about wrong actions without assuming additional information. Option C is incorrect because the passage's conclusion about social structure does not necessarily entail that a person is more likely to tell serious lies. For example, it is logically possible that in a society structured around lies, only convenient lies are told. Option D is incorrect because this answer contradicts the passage's statement that lies are never permissible. Option E is incorrect because we cannot infer from the passage that lying to prevent a worse action is permissible.

23. D: Option D is correct because Larry implicitly agrees that they should advertise, and he disagrees with Moe's option because it is too expensive. Options A and C are incorrect because both men want to advertise the bakery. Option B is incorrect because we cannot logically infer from this passage that Moe believes that fliers are not effective since he does not respond to Larry. Option E is incorrect because we can infer that both Moe and Larry believe that increasing the bakery's profit will require some form of advertising.

24. C: Option C is correct because the passage states that "Money management is more important than running errands," but then it erroneously concludes that shopping is more important than going to the bank. Option A is incorrect because the passage does account for the closing time by making a decision about that potential consequence. Option B is incorrect because the passage's two conditional statements (sentences two and eight) have supported premises. Option D is incorrect because the passage does include the grocery store in the category of running errands. Option E is incorrect because we can reasonably infer from the passage that the grocery store closes much later than the bank, even if we do not know the specific time.

25. B: Option B is correct because we can infer that, if the speaker rented a car, the bus or a taxi was not available. Option A is incorrect because this assumption supports the speaker taking a taxi to work. Option C is incorrect because this answer supports the speaker taking the ferry to work. Option D is incorrect because this answer does not exclude the ferry; thus, this assumption also supports the speaker taking the ferry. Option E is incorrect because an assumption about tomorrow does not explain the passage's conclusion about today.

Section IV – Logical Reasoning (Unscored Section)

1. A: Option A is correct because the statement "Water is necessary for all life" does not logically entail that if there is water, then there is also life. For example, some other requirement may also be necessary, such as the existence of carbon. This answer identifies that water's necessity is not sufficient reason to assume that life exists on Mars. Option B is incorrect because Dr. Holstrand contests whether or not they have found water on Mars. Thus, adding that water must be liquid to allow for life will not resolve his conflict. Option C is incorrect because the location of liquid water does not resolve the conflict about whether or not ice is potential evidence of life. Option D is incorrect because Dr. Everson states that all life *as we know it* requires water. It is reasonable to infer that life on Mars would not be life "as we know it," and therefore the analogy between life on Earth and life on Mars is invalid. Option E is incorrect because, even if better evidence of ice on Mars is provided, we can reasonably infer that this would not resolve the conflict because such evidence does not explain why exploration has not already discovered Martian life.

2. C: Option C is correct because this statement, if true, suggests that teams with younger players have a consistent advantage over teams with older, more experienced players. Consequently, this statement does not support the passage's argument about how variance impacts football games. Option A is incorrect because split-second decisions are evidence that a good team can be weakened by a single player's misjudgment. Option B is incorrect because this answer adequately explains a cause of variance in football teams based on financial reasoning. Option D is incorrect because this answer provides an explanation for how even the best possible group of players could still lose a game due to poor coaching. Option E is incorrect because this answer describes how a quarterback's individual skill and preferences impact a team's ability to win games.

3. D: Option D is correct because this question's answer will allow us to directly test the passage's conclusion by identifying if the frequency of cheerleading injuries is gendered since males usually lift and females are usually lifted. Option A is incorrect because this question's answer will not allow us to compare injuries of male and female cheerleaders. Option B is incorrect because both genders participate in dance routines. Option C is incorrect because "during acrobatic routines" does not specify which behavior is dangerous during those routines. Option E is incorrect because comparison to another sport does not allow us to evaluate this argument about gendered injuries in *this* sport.

4. C: Option C is correct because this assumption supports the passage's sixth sentence and strengthens the passage's definition of bacteria. This supports the passage's conclusion because it supports the distinction between bacteria and viruses being about reproduction. Option A is incorrect because this assumption logically leaves open the possibility that viruses reproduce themselves by another means; thus, the conclusion would be correct that viruses are not bacteria but incorrect that they are not organisms. Option B is incorrect because this answer is self-contradictory. Option D is incorrect because information about the offspring's reproduction does not support the conclusion. Option E is incorrect because the passage requires an organism to be able to reproduce itself. We can reasonably infer from this that a virus's parasitic method of reproduction does not constitute performing the act on its own.

5. B: Option B is correct because this statement, if true, allows us to infer that the weather currently is cool; therefore, the argument ought to support Jeremy going hiking with Shana. Option A is incorrect because this answer does not specify whether Shana will go hiking alone or with Jeremy. Option C is incorrect: this answer supports the argument because, if true, it is evidence that Jeremy will go to the gym. Option D is incorrect because this answer is logically possible since we do not know Shana's conditions for going hiking. For example, if Shana only hikes when the weather is hot and sunny, then this answer's statement is true; therefore, this answer does not necessarily weaken the passage's argument. Option E is incorrect because if the weather was cool, then Jeremy would go hiking. The answer's relationship between weather and Jeremy is inaccurate, based on information in the passage.

6. D: Option D is correct because this assumption is required for the argument's connection between memory and wisdom to be coherent. Option A is incorrect because the eldest human is defined as someone currently living—if that person passes away, the next-oldest person will become the new oldest human. Option B is incorrect because the word *probably* reasonably suggests that the quantity of events is more significant than whether the events are in the past or more recent. Option C is incorrect because this statement is so generalized that it is meaningless—logically, all arguments involving time require the sequence of past into present to be valid. This answer is worse than option D because it does not directly address the argument presented in the passage. Option E is incorrect because we can reasonably infer from the passage that wisdom is an attribute possessed by anyone with long-ago memories, not just the oldest human.

7. E: Option E is correct because this answer supports the politician's argument in favor of road construction and weakens the journalist's question about infrastructure priorities. Option A is incorrect because the politician's argument does not engage with safety as a value; therefore, we do not logically know if safety makes roads more important than railways. Option B is incorrect because the politician's argument does not rely on comparing types of infrastructure, so this answer does not strengthen the argument as much as option E. Option C is incorrect because this answer contradicts the passage's statement that a new tax will be introduced. Option D is incorrect because this answer weakens the journalist's counterargument, but it does not strengthen the politician's argument in favor of road repair.

8. A: The passage's flawed reasoning is that excess weight slowing a backpacker down is not analogous to a sailboat sunk by a storm; this is due to the difference in severity of these consequences and the idea of "reduced movement" compared to "fatal result." Option A is correct because this answer's comparison retains the flawed idea that force that slows down is equivalent to a fatal result. Option B is incorrect because the answer is using a positive goal rather than avoiding a negative consequence. Option C is incorrect because the passage's reasoning does not compare the importance of different attributes—it just advises against overloading one's pack. Option D is incorrect because the answer does not provide a flawed example of the consequences of not making an itinerary. Option E is incorrect because the conditional sense of "if and only if" is not present in the passage's reasoning.

9. D: In the passage, we can infer that the speaker's principle is prioritizing the cheapest option, such as the discount rack, unless the price is very similar, like the $0.05 difference in bananas. Option D is correct because this answer expresses a similar principle by ignoring a small discount and waiting for a larger one. Option A is incorrect because this answer's principle is permitting an optional increase if it is small, rather than emphasizing cost reduction. Option B is incorrect because this answer's principle is about income, not expense. Option C is incorrect because this answer's principle is about frequency, not cost. Option E is incorrect because this answer's principle is egalitarian—buying each child their preferred muffin.

10. B: Option B is correct because this answer identifies that the passage's evidence does not support the conclusion that tomorrow is Sunday. We know that Timmy's bedtime on Saturday is later than on a weekday, but that does not allow us to conclude that today is a Saturday because, logically, it could be a Sunday; we require more information. Option A is incorrect because this argument uses Timmy's bedtime as evidence—it is not an argument about *what time* Timmy went to bed. Option C is incorrect because this is not a flaw in reasoning if the evidence and the reasoning support the prediction about the future. Option D is incorrect because the use of arithmetic is accurate. Option E is incorrect because this argument does not employ analogy.

11. C: Option C is correct because the answer uses an either-or decision in the same way while deciding about how to maximize a value (in the passage, "fun"; in the answer, "profit"). Option A is incorrect because the answer's argument concludes on picking both. Option B is incorrect because the answer does not provide a logical explanation for the conclusion. Options D and E are incorrect because both answers use the premise to logically define the conclusion rather than employing a principle or value to make a decision.

12. C: Option C is correct because Dawn includes boa constrictors in her list of cute animals; thus, this is used as evidence to support her argument. Option A is incorrect because Dawn is not arguing that zoo animals are scary. Option B is incorrect because this is not evidence that seeing cute animals is exciting—it is evidence that there are cute animals at the zoo. Option D is incorrect because Dawn is not using this evidence to demonstrate that a greater quantity of zoo animals are cuter than aquarium animals. Option E is incorrect because Dawn does not claim that all zoo animals are cute.

13. A: Option A is correct because the passage uses the definition of mammals to draw a conclusion about the properties of sheep. Option B is incorrect because the argument does not use a counterexample to demonstrate which properties are part of the "mammal" set and which are not. Option C is incorrect because this argument does not employ the contradiction of a premise to weaken another argument. Option D is incorrect because the argument also does not employ a contradiction between definitions to come to a logical conclusion about which is correct. Option E is incorrect because this answer is not a generalization—it is specifically about biology.

14. E: Option E is correct because the passage's intermediary conclusion ("citrus fruits are sweet") is supported by some evidence and refuted by other evidence. Thus, the passage refines their conclusion. Option A is incorrect because this is not a technique of reasoning, as is demonstrated by the definition

of citrus fruits in the passage. For an alternative example, the elements sodium (Na) and chlorine (Cl) are toxic, but table salt (NaCl) is not. Option B is incorrect because the passage does not conclude with a contradiction and refutation of the premise. Option C is incorrect because oranges and lemons are not used as part of an analogy about something else. Option D is incorrect because the passage's argument does not employ conditional statements (statements that use "if . . . then" to reason).

15. D: Option D is correct because we can reasonably infer that Becky's statement about the new theater's audience size is intended to refute Clinton's claim that the theater will have a large attendance. Thus, the issue in dispute is whether or not the theater will have sufficient attendance to merit placement near a major road for improved access. Option A is incorrect because the university is used in Becky's argument as a landmark, not as a reason to build the theater. Option B is incorrect because Clinton argues that the theater should be built by a major road, not necessarily in the center of the city. Option C is incorrect because Becky does not dispute that major roads provide good access. Option E is incorrect because neither arguer emphasizes saving money as a value when deciding upon which location to build the theater.

16. B: Option B is correct because the passage is about objects visible in the night sky. Consequently, it must be true that if someone can find Polaris, they must be doing so at night. Option A is incorrect because the passage does not state that Polaris is the brightest star. Options C and E are incorrect because the passage states that Venus "doesn't rotate in the same way that the stars move." Option D is incorrect because the passage specifies that Venus is the brightest *star* in the sky—the Moon is not conventionally considered a star, so it is reasonable to infer that the Moon is excluded from this definition, whereas Venus is defined in the passage's first sentence as a "star." (Remember: Answers should be based on the information contained in the argument and/or passage, even if the argument or passage states or implies something that is untrue in real life. In this case, the argument describes Venus as a star; in reality, it is a planet.)

17. C: Option C is correct because the passage emphasizes that Falkenhayn "claimed" the intended strategy would avoid a large number of German casualties; however, the passage's second sentence states that casualties on both sides were large and comparable in quantity. Option A is incorrect because the passage does not specify which army won the Battle of Verdun. Option B is incorrect because the passage's information does not allow us to conclude that the French lost fewer men at Verdun than the Germans. (Since the British are not mentioned, it is reasonable to conclude that they did not lose men in this battle; however, this answer's "neither . . . nor" language requires *both*). Options D and E are incorrect because the passage states that "Verdun is important to France's . . . culture"; therefore, it was important prior to WWI and neither answer can be a valid inference.

18. E: Option E is correct because we can infer that Miller is refuting Max's argument by refuting Max's understanding of motion. Consequently, Miller must be concluding that time is "inherently" real, whereas Max does not. Options A and C are incorrect because those conclusions do not refute Max's argument. Option B is incorrect because this answer uses the concept of *consistency* instead of *sequence* in its argument. Option D is incorrect because both Max and Miller agree with this statement, and do not present it as an argument.

19. B: Option B is correct because this passage's conclusion is that "assessing students should be a priority." It then justifies the conclusion by demonstrating what will happen if the conclusion is followed or is not followed. Option A is incorrect because the passage is not trying to assess its own reader. Options C and E are incorrect because the passage does not use evidence to support its argument. Option D is incorrect because the conclusion is not at the end of the passage.

20. A: Option A is correct because it provides general guidelines about the quality of drama that also support the specific argument made in the passage. Option B is incorrect because the passage specifies that a tragic confrontation is inevitable—not that "the best stories are inevitable." Option C is incorrect because this comparative statement is not a principle that could justify the argument. Option D is incorrect because only one necessary element is used as evidence in the passage. Option E is incorrect because this principle is so generalized that it does not substantially support the passage's argument about *Hamlet*'s quality.

21. D: Option D is correct because if we assume that all green things are square, then it follows from apples being green that they are also square and that Darwinism is nonsense. Option A is incorrect because this assumption does not demonstrate that both apples and pears are square. Option B is incorrect because assuming Darwinism is nonsense contradicts the passage's intended conclusion that Darwinism *is* nonsense. Option C is incorrect because if we only assume that *some* green things are square, we do not necessarily know that apples and pears are square due to their greenness. Option E is incorrect because this answer's assumption does not "flow" both ways—just because all square things are green, it does not mean that all green things are square.

22. B: Option B is correct because the passage's first sentence states that Mike must "win a match during every single round" to win the tournament. If Mike had a bye, then he did not play a match, and it logically follows that he cannot win the tournament. Option A is incorrect because the passage states that Mike *did* move to the fourth round (the next round). Option C is incorrect because evidence of this premise is not necessary for making this argument. Option D is incorrect because we can reasonably infer from the passage's final sentence that Mike did move to the next round—further evidence is not required. Option E is incorrect because this statement is logically accurate, but it does not describe the argument's flaw.

23. C: Option C is correct because the passage's argument in the second sentence does not indicate that the person must buy vanilla; thus, the passage's logic succeeds if and only if someone already has vanilla. Option A is incorrect because the first sentence states this explicitly—it does not need to be assumed. Option B is incorrect because this assumption contradicts the passage's conclusion in the final sentence. Option D is incorrect because this statement is equivalent to "everyone who follows a recipe makes a mess," which contradicts the passage's conclusion. Option E is incorrect because this contradicts the passage's statement that either a cake or a mess comes out of the oven.

24. E: Option E is correct because this answer strengthens the passage's conclusion by providing a logical connection between Baker Street having a lot of crime and Sherlock not being a good detective. Options A and D are incorrect because these answers support the opposite of the passage's argument—they provide reasoning that Sherlock *is* a good detective. Option B is incorrect because this answer does support the passage but not as strongly as option E due to the latter's imperative element. Option C is incorrect because this answer makes it logically possible that Sherlock chooses to solve other crimes, and does not have an obligation to solve crimes on Baker Street.

25. D: Option D is correct because there is no information provided in the passage from which we can reasonably infer that the time of year has an impact on the prominent color in a rainbow. Consequently, the answer to this question will provide the least information. Option A is incorrect because its answer could help us conclude the validity of Louis's data. For example, if the day's color is not very prominent, he could be mistaken. Option B is incorrect because this question's answer would give us a useful data point. Option C is incorrect because the quantity of evidence collected can help determine if the conclusion is sound. Option E is incorrect because variation would indicate that the hypothesis is probably incorrect—that variation would contradict the claim that one color is always brightest.

LSAT Practice Test #2

Section I – Reading Comprehension

Passage 1

The discussion of consciousness has been an important topic in philosophy throughout history, and divisive in more ways than one. Plato apportioned us into body and soul, setting the tone for the discussion for millennia to follow. Later, Descartes followed his lead, proposing a dualistic model for mind and brain. He postulated that each is comprised of a unique substance, one material, the other supernatural. These ideas continue to shape our understanding and inform our discussion of this essential subject matter.

Other than a few nods to the idea in ancient times, most notably by Aristotle, philosophers did not begin to consider materialist models of consciousness until the seventeenth century. Thomas Hobbes proposed that every mental state is the result of physical processes in the brain. He was critical of Cartesian dualism and rejected the idea that there was any immaterial or supernatural component to consciousness.

Although much has changed since the seventeenth century, dualism versus materialism is still hotly debated among contemporary philosophers engaged in understanding and explaining human consciousness. David Chalmers and Daniel Dennett are prominent philosophers primarily known for their work on consciousness and the mind, and who embrace markedly different approaches.

Chalmers proposes a new take on Cartesian dualism known as naturalistic dualism. It is important to note here that he does not believe in an immaterial substance as Descartes did. For Chalmers, dualism addresses what he refers to as the difference between the "easy" problems of consciousness, including explaining cognitive functions and behaviors, and the "hard" problem, which is explaining why and how we have subjective experiences. He argues that physical processes alone cannot fully explain consciousness, and that it must arise from these processes in some yet-to-be-understood way.

Dennett, a cognitive scientist as well as a philosopher, follows the example of Hobbes. He is critical of the distinction between the hard problem and the easy problem, arguing that the hard problem is merely a result of our misunderstanding of the nature of consciousness and our insistence that it be explained in terms of anything other than physical processes. It is his belief that what we perceive as consciousness is not a single, unified phenomenon, but rather a collection of brain processes and functions that have evolved as a set of adaptive functions that enhance an organism's ability to survive and reproduce. Dennett relies on this evolutionary perspective to explain why consciousness exists and how it operates.

He proposes what is known as the "multiple drafts" model of consciousness, wherein the brain produces various drafts of our experiences and narratives simultaneously, and the one that most draws our attention becomes the one we perceive as our conscious experience. In this model, there is no single principal place in the brain where consciousness happens.

Chalmers disagrees with this materialist take, and advocates for a non-reductive explanation of consciousness that accounts for not only the physical processes associated with our mental states, but

also our phenomenological experiences. He believes that we may need to seek out new fundamental laws of nature to fully understand consciousness, much like the way physical laws explain other phenomena, to understand consciousness as a distinct and fundamental aspect of reality.

These views have clashed for millennia, and the debate remains unresolved. Given the nature of consciousness and individual experience, the question may be one that cannot have a definitive answer. Philosophers acknowledge this possibility and continue to grapple with the consciousness problem, in search of answers that may not exist, enticed by the notion that there may be something more.

1. Based on the passage, which of the following can be inferred about the author?
   A) They espouse a materialist viewpoint and disagree with Chalmer's assertion that there is something beyond the physical that must be explained in order to solve the problem of consciousness.
   B) They lean toward a dualist perspective and believe that consciousness is more than the physical processes from which it arises.
   C) They believe Dennett and Chalmers are too extreme in their views and need to meet in the middle.
   D) They are committed to neither dualism nor materialism and are more interested in what we can learn from the discussion.
   E) They agree with Dennett that the "hard" problem is due to a misunderstanding of the nature of consciousness.

2. Which of the following best explains how the passage is organized?
   A) The author begins by stating that the debate between dualism and materialism can never be resolved and then delves into the history of this divide and the contemporary discussion.
   B) The author presents a history of the topic, segues into how that has influenced current discussion, and then concludes by stating the debate may not ever be resolved.
   C) The author contrasts two different viewpoints and then expresses a clear preference for one and builds a case for its validity.
   D) The author analyzes the validity of each philosopher's arguments deeply, critiquing their ideas to promote a specific viewpoint.
   E) The author presents fallacious arguments from past philosophers and then goes on to defend the position that we should not be basing our current discussion in historical ideas.

3. Which of the following, if true, best supports a materialist view of consciousness?
   A) Data from fMRI machines show that specific brain activity is correlated to specific sensory and emotional experiences.
   B) We can never truly understand the subjective experiences of another individual.
   C) The "easy" problem and the "hard" problem are arbitrary designations for which there is no justification.
   D) Descartes is right about the existence of an immaterial substance that comprises the mind.
   E) Dennett's "multiple drafts" theory is heavily flawed.

4. What was the author's purpose in writing this passage?
    A) to argue that we will never be able to answer certain questions in philosophy
    B) to establish a set framework for the discussion of consciousness, laying to rest the dispute between dualism and materialism
    C) to discuss the philosophy of consciousness, relating ideas from its history to the present conversation among contemporary philosophers
    D) to discuss the merits of the ideas of the "hard" problems and the "easy" problems of consciousness
    E) to discuss the work of contemporary philosophers in the field of consciousness

5. Which of the following factors is NOT mentioned in the author's analysis of the philosophy of consciousness?
    A) a discussion of Hume's theories concerning dualism
    B) a brief explanation of Cartesian dualism
    C) Thomas Hobbes's ideas concerning a materialist model of consciousness
    D) a discussion of Dennett's "multiple drafts" model of consciousness
    E) a definition of Chalmer's "hard" problem

6. Which of the following best describes the purpose of the third paragraph?
    A) to state that dualism and materialism are still debated among contemporary philosophers
    B) to introduce David Chalmers and Daniel Dennett to the discussion
    C) to discuss the manner in which history has influenced current philosophical discussion
    D) to argue that we should let go of the conventions established by past philosophers
    E) to segue from a discussion of the history of the philosophy of consciousness to the present day

Passage 2

In the early twentieth century, attitudes around visual art shifted and began to take on a new form. Western art moved away from realistic, representational work to something a little looser and freer as it entered an era of abstraction. Wassily Kandinsky, Russian painter and art theorist, is typically credited with leading the charge and opening new avenues for artistic expression with his ideas surrounding art, spirituality, and music.

Because Kandinsky was trained in cello and piano from an early age, musical expression strongly influenced his understanding of visual art. He notes in his text "Concerning the Spiritual in Art" that music evokes emotion and spiritual reaction in listeners with non-representational sounds. The musician is free to arrange these sounds however he chooses, unfettered by the limitations of adherence to a tradition of mimicking real-world phenomena.

Kandinsky argues that color and form should likewise be free, and the visual artist should make it his mission to evoke similar feelings and spiritual responses using these tools, rather than becoming mired in futile attempts to copy nature. He gave his paintings titles such as "Composition," "Improvisation," and "Impressions," emphasizing the synesthetic relationship between art and music, and set about treating colors and forms like a musician would sounds. These ideas became steadily more apparent in the evolution of his work. One of his later pieces, "Composition VII," is a flurry of color and motion, infused with an indefinable rhythm, and is considered a seminal work in the abstract art movement.

He espoused the position that artists are akin to prophets, and that their mission is to promote the refinement of the human soul through their work. In his mind, humans have a deep inner need to express themselves creatively, and to be moved by the creative works of others. It is therefore the duty of the artist to create transcendent works to satisfy this need and better his fellow humans. Kandinsky further believed that allowing artists free use of color and form, and encouraging the abstract expression of their inner worlds, is the best way to achieve this end.

Although it is not currently the fashion for artists to openly discuss spirituality and striving to better themselves and humanity through their art, Kandinsky's ideas continue to resonate and have influenced the development of many art styles through the twentieth century. His philosophy set the foundation for abstract expressionism, and later the neo-expressionist resurgence, and inspired artists like Jackson Pollack and Mark Rothko.

Through his unique, complex art and his philosophical writings, Kandinsky established a place for abstraction in modern art. His ideas redefined the boundaries of artistic expression, and changed the way we as a society understand and view art. His ability to infuse visual art with freedom and rhythm changed the landscape of modern art, and his legacy continues to inspire artists to push boundaries and create unique and meaningful work.

7. Which of the following statements most likely represents the author's views concerning abstract art?
    A) The worth and significance of an abstract art piece can be judged by its complexity.
    B) The best abstract art is the result of incorporating other art forms into one's process, just as Kandinsky integrated elements of music into his visual art.
    C) Abstract art must be executed with technical proficiency in order to have value.
    D) Abstract art can be judged on its ability to express the complexity of the human condition and move the viewer.
    E) Abstract art is far superior to representational art.

8. What is the significance of the titles of Kandinsky's paintings?
    A) to obscure Kandinsky's subject matter
    B) to emphasize the relationship between music and visual art
    C) to highlight Kandinsky's history as a musician
    D) to conform to the aesthetic norms of the time
    E) to align his work with traditional art forms

9. What is the purpose of paragraph four?
    A) to encourage visual artists to treat color and form the way musicians do sound
    B) to discuss Kandinsky's influence on later artists
    C) to state the author's beliefs about the role of artists
    D) to draw a parallel between artists and prophets
    E) to discuss the philosophical ideals behind Kandinsky's art

10. What is the purpose of the discussion of "Composition VII" in the third paragraph?
    A) to provide an example of how music influenced Kandinsky's art
    B) to give the reader an idea of what Kandinsky's art looked like
    C) to establish that Kandinsky's later works were quite different from his earlier works
    D) to provide an example of a seminal artwork in the abstract art movement
    E) to offer a visual representation of Kandinsky's philosophical ideals

11. The passage suggests which one of the following concerning attitudes toward art before the early twentieth century?
    A) that artists were not as interested in the spiritual aspects of their craft
    B) that art collectors were not interested in representational artwork
    C) that abstract art and representational art shared equal favor
    D) that visual artists felt they should not take inspiration from music
    E) that abstract art was not nearly as respected as representational artwork

Passage 3

Although many of the Founding Fathers were wary of political parties and envisioned a non-partisan government, politics in the United States is currently dominated by a deeply entrenched two-party system. Although independent parties exist, Americans tend to believe that a vote for a party other than Republican or Democrat is wasted, as no others truly stand a chance of winning. In recent years, these limited options have led to an increasingly staunch polarization in politics, rendering productive discussion virtually impossible.

The Founding Fathers may not have consciously chosen this path for us, but it is in part a result of the first-preference plurality (FPP) voting system they established. This method allows citizens to vote for one candidate and decides the winner based on a simple majority rule. Although it may seem like an intuitive way to choose our leaders, this simplistic system has a few glaring issues.

FPP voting systems only reflect the preference of the majority of citizens, ignoring the proportion of votes and the voices of those who find themselves in the minority. A candidate who wins an election by a single vote becomes the representative for one hundred percent of the people, when almost half of voters did not support them. This issue is exacerbated by the fact that each party chooses one candidate, and people must vote for their proposed candidate to support their party.

Alternative voting systems include ranked choice voting (RCV) or proportional representation. With RCV, each citizen chooses multiple candidates and ranks them by preference. The winner is chosen based on a preestablished formula that varies among the entities that use this system. We need not look too far for examples either; a number of jurisdictions across the US, including Maine, Alaska, and New York City, already use RCV in certain local elections.

With proportional representation, parties propose a list of candidates, and voters choose their party. Parties then receive seats in proportion to their share of the overall vote, lessening the distortion of popular opinion as it translates to representation. Majority still rules, but those in the minority get some say in governmental policy.

Either of these systems would help to ease the stranglehold the two-party system has on politics in the US. The first would allow voters who prefer less likely candidates to cast their primary vote for their first choice without fear of wasting it, as they would still have a say in the election with their secondary and tertiary votes. The second gives the voter much more direct power in choosing their representation. Their vote will count toward their party's total share of the overall vote and increase the proportion of power they receive.

Considering the current political climate in the U.S., it is imperative that we take steps to reduce polarization and ensure fair representation for all. With a practice as important as voting, perhaps the simplest option is not the most suitable one. Revising our methods in pursuit of a healthier democracy that is capable of cooperation and compromise may be worthwhile.

12. Which of the following principles is in line with the argument in the above passage?
    A) It is of paramount importance to respect tradition and preserve the intentions of those who came before.
    B) Governments are living, breathing entities, and must be allowed to evolve in a manner that suits them.
    C) The US should take its example from other countries and institute a new voting system.
    D) If a given system is not working effectively, it is important to explore other options until one finds a more suitable alternative.
    E) Excessive polarization in politics causes productive discussion to become virtually impossible.

13. According to the passage, how does proportional representation differ from ranked choice voting (RCV)?
    A) In proportional representation, citizens vote for their political party, and seats are awarded to that party in proportion to the percentage of the population that voted for them. In RCV, citizens may choose multiple candidates and order them in terms of preference.
    B) In proportional representation, citizens may choose only one candidate, and the candidate with the most votes wins the election. In RCV, citizens may choose multiple candidates and order them in terms of preference.
    C) In proportional representation, citizens may choose multiple candidates and order them in terms of preference. In RCV, citizens vote for their political party, and seats are awarded to that party in proportion to the percentage of the population that voted for them.
    D) In proportional representation, citizens vote for multiple political parties and order them in terms of preference, and seats are awarded to that part in proportion to the percentage of the population that votes for them. In RCV, citizens may choose multiple candidates and order them in terms of preference.
    E) In proportional representation, citizens vote for their political party, and seats are awarded to that party in proportion to the percentage of the population that voted for them. In RCV, citizens may choose only one candidate, and the candidate with the most votes wins the election.

14. What problem is the author trying to resolve in this passage?
    A) a lack of representation for minority voters
    B) stagnation due to excessive polarization
    C) the dominance of parties in the political structure of the US
    D) our overreliance on the visions of the Founding Fathers
    E) a lack of public interest in voting

15. Which of the following, if true, most strengthens the author's argument?
    A) Polarization can lead to healthy dialogue because each side has to work harder to understand the other.
    B) Proportional representation and RCV systems are more complex than FPP.
    C) Proportional representation and RCV systems have been instituted in most other westernized countries.
    D) FPP voting is the voting system of choice for corrupt, tyrannical governments because it is the easiest system to manipulate.
    E) The implementation of proportional representation or RCV systems has been shown to reduce polarization in other countries.

16. What is the primary purpose of the second-to-last paragraph?
    A) to discuss the differences between RCV and proportional representation
    B) to introduce alternative options for voting systems
    C) to discuss how the alternate voting systems proposed by the author would work to decrease polarization
    D) to defend the author's position that we should institute a new voting system
    E) to discuss the ways polarization is affecting our voting system

17. Which one of the following statements is the author of the passage LEAST likely to agree with?
    A) It is important that government structures evolve to meet the needs of the people.
    B) Traditional values are particularly important when deciding how to run our government.
    C) Governments should reflect the values of all its citizens, not just the majority.
    D) We should implement systems intended to reduce polarization in politics.
    E) Polarization is the biggest problem in US politics today.

18. Why did the author discuss the Founding Fathers in the introduction to the passage?
    A) to appeal to the reader's patriotic leanings and gain support for their position
    B) to discuss the preferences of the Founding Fathers and argue for their implementation
    C) to argue that we should let go of the past and implement modern systems that are suited to the country's current needs
    D) to contrast their vision of a nonpartisan government to the current reality of the government that resulted from the system they implemented
    E) to illustrate to the reader that they have a deep respect for history and would not propose changing the system unless it were necessary

19. Which of the following most accurately describes the author's likely attitude toward the belief outlined in the following sentence?

"Although independent parties exist, Americans tend to believe that a vote for a party other than Republican or Democrat is wasted, as no others truly stand a chance of winning."
    A) This belief increases the polarization and resultant stagnation in the US political system.
    B) This belief reflects the reality of the situation; an independent candidate can never win a US election.
    C) This belief helps to ensure that only the most qualified candidates are voted into public office.
    D) This belief allows citizens to focus on learning more about the candidates from major parties so that they can make a more informed decision.
    E) This belief precludes our ability to enact real change.

Passage 4 (Parts A and B)

Part A

Exoplanet research has exploded since the confirmation of the first planet known to exist outside of our solar system in 1992. The first exoplanets discovered were under constant bombardment of radiation from the dead neutron star they orbited and deemed uninhabitable; however, their discovery has led to renewed vigor in NASA scientists dedicated to the search for life on other planets.

Scientists estimate at least one exoplanet exists for every star, and more than five thousand have been confirmed so far. Their focus is primarily on planets that exist in the "habitable zone," a term for the distance from their star that would allow for the existence of liquid water on a planet's surface. Other factors that increase the likelihood of life are that the planet is of a suitable size, has an atmosphere that is conducive to life, and orbits a stable star that is not prone to outbursts of sterilizing radiation.

Using telescopes such as the Transiting Exoplanet Survey Satellite (TESS) and the James Webb Space Telescope (JWST), NASA scientists are identifying new exoplanets around nearby stars and detecting biosignatures that could indicate the presence of life. The development of a new telescope, the Large Ultraviolet Optical Infrared Surveyor (LUVOIR), could potentially take images of Earth-like exoplanets and analyze their atmospheres with greater accuracy, further narrowing down our search.

Although we have not yet found evidence of life on exoplanets, our increasing ability to study them has led many prominent scientists to believe that it is only a matter of time. NASA is collaborating with the European Space Agency and several other international entities involved in space exploration, working hard to resolve the age-old question once and for all: Are we alone in the universe?

Part B

Mankind has long dreamt of the ability to search for life on other planets, and to finally determine whether we are alone in the universe. The recent explosion in exoplanet research has NASA scientists excited as we finally have the technology and resources to perform a real search. Armed with telescopes such as TESS and JWST and the ability to send robotic vehicles to explore distant planets, these scientists desperately hunt newly discovered exoplanets for any signs of life.

Unfortunately, exoplanets defy all expectations as far as planetary behavior and can vary in unexpected and diverse ways. Typical barriers to life on exoplanets stem from the fact that most exist outside of the "habitable zone"—the distance from their star that is necessary to allow liquid water to exist on the planet's surface. Additionally, these planets often orbit unstable stars that spew radiation and would not allow for the survival of even the simplest forms of life. A suitable size and atmosphere are also necessary for an exoplanet to be habitable.

As we explore more and more distant exoplanets, we are discovering unexpected planetary traits that would be further barriers to life. Planets have been discovered that do not rotate but remain tidally locked, irradiated continuously on only one side while the other side remains a frozen, barren wasteland. Scientists have discovered gas giants as large as Jupiter, but close enough in proximity to their star that their atmospheres have become infernos, capable of vaporizing rock and dissociating water molecules by ripping their hydrogen atoms from their oxygen. This latter process was previously only thought possible in the atmospheres of stars.

These extreme variations suggest a panoply of scenarios for exoplanet structures that would not be conducive to life. The factors that had to convene for life to be possible on Earth are far too rare to be replicated often. Although it is technically possible that alien life could exist elsewhere in our universe, the search for life on exoplanets so near to ourselves is, statistically speaking, a fool's errand.

20. Each of the passages contains information sufficient to answer which one of the following questions?
    A) What are some unexpected characteristics of exoplanets that have surprised scientists?
    B) What are the basic factors scientists check for when searching for life on exoplanets?
    C) What is the likelihood that we will find life on exoplanets in the next decade?
    D) What are the specific capabilities of the TESS and JWST telescopes?
    E) What atmospheric components are necessary to support life on other planets?

21. Which of the following would the authors be most likely to agree on?
    A) If we do find life on other planets, it is unlikely to have reached the same degree of intelligence as we have.
    B) Life on other planets would necessarily have to be vastly different from us as far as its nature and the trajectory of its evolution.
    C) The exploration of exoplanets is an extremely exciting development in the field of astrophysics, and we have much to learn in this area.
    D) We should only study exoplanets that are candidates to support life, since resources are scarce, and these are likely to yield the most interesting discoveries.
    E) We should focus on learning about exoplanets and their solar systems broadly, rather than emphasizing the search for alien life.

22. Which of the following best describes the attitude the author of passage B has toward the arguments made by the author of passage A?
    A) They agree that their arguments are sound and that their conclusions are logical.
    B) They disagree with the premises of their arguments, and therefore disagree with the conclusion that we are likely to find life on other planets.
    C) They agree that the exploration of exoplanets is exciting but believe that the author is drawing unfounded conclusions.
    D) They cautiously agree with the content in passage A and tentatively support its conclusion.
    E) They agree that the exploration of exoplanets is exciting but believe the author's desire to find alien life is clouding their judgment and expectations.

23. According to the author of passage B, what is the purpose of the discussion of planets that do not rotate?
    A) to show that exoplanet research is confronting us with circumstances we would have thought impossible
    B) to discuss the geological implications of such unexpected planetary behavior
    C) to argue that life could not possibly be supported by such a planet
    D) to illustrate that there are barriers to life on other planets that we have not even considered
    E) to segue into a discussion of the unique characteristics of certain exoplanets

24. If the author of passage A were to read passage B, which one of the following would they most likely choose as their main critique of its arguments?
    A) The author makes an argument from ignorance.
    B) The author makes a hasty generalization.
    C) The author makes an unjustified assumption.
    D) The author makes an error of composition.
    E) The author creates a false dilemma.

25. Which of the following was NOT discussed in both passages?
    A) factors scientists are using to identify planets that are likely to support life
    B) the telescopes TESS and JWST, and the development of LUVOIR
    C) a definition of the habitable zone
    D) NASA scientists' interests in finding life on other planets
    E) unstable stars that emit radiation

26. Which of the following best describes the relationship of passage B to passage A?
    A) Passage B disproves the conclusions presented in passage A.
    B) Passage B provides additional context to the content of passage A.
    C) Passage B is a critical response to passage A.
    D) Passage B identifies factual inaccuracies in passage A.
    E) Passage B questions the motives of the author of passage A.

27. Given the information in both passages, which of the following statements must be true?
    A) The capabilities of TESS and JWST have streamlined our ability to evaluate exoplanets as candidates for hosting life.
    B) Exoplanets are unpredictable, and we will most likely find life somewhere unexpected.
    C) Without TESS and JWST, we would have no chance of finding life on other planets.
    D) Most exoplanets orbit unstable stars, making life on other planets an impossibility.
    E) All forms of life have the same basic requirements, and we can therefore safely rule out any exoplanets that are not in the habitable zone.

Section II – Logical Reasoning

Tina calls the city about a dangerous crack in the sidewalk in front of her house and is assured it will be repaired. The next evening, Jan trips over the crack while wearing sunglasses on the darkened street, breaking her ankle. She sues Tina, arguing that Tina has a legal responsibility to maintain a safe sidewalk. Tina claims Jan only got hurt because she was silly enough to wear sunglasses at night and could not see where she was going.

1. What is the primary flaw in Tina's argument?
    A) Tina fails to acknowledge that her report to the city might not absolve her of responsibility.
    B) Tina neglects to mention the steps she took in attempting to repair the sidewalk.
    C) Tina assumes Jan's injuries were solely due to her choice to wear sunglasses.
    D) Tina focuses on trying to make Jan look foolish, rather than presenting a defense of her own actions.
    E) Tina's argument assumes that no reasonable explanation exists for Jan's behavior.

Cindy can run an eight-minute mile, swim one hundred meters in under a minute, and ride a bike one hundred miles in seven hours. Some casual runners can run an eight-minute mile, and all elite runners can. Only elite swimmers can swim one hundred meters in under a minute. Most casual cyclists can ride a bike one hundred miles in seven hours, and all elite cyclists can.

2. Which of the following statement can be deduced from the passage?
   A) Cindy is an elite swimmer.
   B) Cindy is a casual runner.
   C) Cindy is an elite runner.
   D) Cindy is a casual cyclist.
   E) Cindy is an elite cyclist.

Educational experts claim that standardized tests do not accurately determine a student's intelligence or ability to retain knowledge. The structure of these tests can provide students from certain backgrounds an undue advantage over their peers, exacerbating the disadvantages faced by marginalized students. Therefore, experts typically recommend using a variety of methods for evaluating student talent.

3. What is the primary role of the second sentence in the above argument?
   A) to provide evidence for the experts' claim that standardized tests do not accurately measure student abilities
   B) to use the plight of marginalized students to appeal to the emotion of the reader and gain support for the experts' position
   C) to suggest that alternative methods may be superior in evaluating student intelligence
   D) to criticize the structure of standardized tests
   E) to point out an issue with the educational system

Over the past fifty years, college tuition costs have risen significantly, far outpacing the rate of inflation. As a result, those pursuing higher education often graduate with massive debt. Consequently, a generation of students has had to delay important milestones, such as establishing independent households and raising families. Proponents of student debt relief contend that removing this burden would not only improve the economy but also promote more equitable access to higher education.

4. Which of the following, if true, would most strengthen the arguments of the proponents of student debt relief?
   A) A generation of students has had to delay milestones such as moving out of their parental homes and starting families of their own.
   B) Student debt forgiveness programs in other countries have led to better outcomes for those who pursue a college education.
   C) Student debt forgiveness would encourage financial irresponsibility among those interested in pursuing higher education.
   D) It is expected that tuition rates will continue to rise at a rate that outpaces standard inflation rates.
   E) Student debt forgiveness would disproportionately benefit low-income students.

Trainer: I have developed a program designed to help people lose weight through a combination of strength training and cardiovascular exercise. I exclusively train college athletes, and all of my clients have lost weight using my program.

5. Which of the following correctly identifies the primary flaw in the trainer's argument?
    A) It confuses correlation with causation.
    B) It employs mistaken negation.
    C) It makes a hasty generalization.
    D) It commits the fallacy of composition.
    E) It uses a straw man argument.

Environmentalist: Factory farming contributes significantly to climate change, primarily through the excessive production of greenhouse gasses. Deforestation due to the increasing need for lands to grow feed for livestock exacerbates this issue immensely. Given these environmental concerns, adopting a vegan lifestyle is the only ethical avenue.

6. Which of the following correctly describes the error the environmentalist makes in their reasoning?
    A) They ignore the fact that not everyone can be healthy on a vegan diet.
    B) They rely on anecdotal evidence to support their claims.
    C) They assume that ethics are universally prioritized.
    D) They presuppose that supporting factory farms and veganism are the only options available.
    E) Their conclusion is not supported by their premises.

In a study on a phenomenon known as decision fatigue, a worker at a grocery store set up a sample table in the jam aisle. On one day, she served three flavors of jam from a popular brand. On the next, she served all of the flavors offered by the brand. The first day, the grocery store reported higher sales than normal of the brand's jam, while on the second day, the grocery store reported lower than normal sales.

7. Which of the following is most supported by the above passage?
    A) People prefer to have their minds made up for them.
    B) Having an excess of options led people to choose to buy nothing at all due to overwhelm.
    C) Samples cause people to buy items they otherwise would not have.
    D) Impulse buying can be a problem when people are faced with too many options.
    E) Decision fatigue can be used to inform marketing decisions for new businesses.

Dr. Smith, a world-renowned neurologist, recommends a whole-foods, plant-based diet to all his patients, stating that meat does irreparable damage to the human body whereas plant foods are healing due to their anti-inflammatory properties. He bases these beliefs on his own experiences and the teachings of his favorite online nutritionists.

8. Which of the following most closely describes the primary flaw in the above argument?
    A) The argument presumes that every individual human has the same dietary needs.
    B) Dr. Smith is making a hasty generalization.
    C) The conclusion of the argument does not follow from Dr. Smith's premises.
    D) Dr. Smith creates a false dilemma between strict vegetarianism and a meat-heavy diet.
    E) People would trust Dr. Smith due to his medical degree, but his nutritional knowledge is not taken from a similarly reputable source.

Although everyone has their own individual needs and preferences when it comes to diet, there is certain advice that is sound for everyone to follow. Natural, single-ingredient foods are always the healthiest options.

9. Which of the following most closely parallels the principle and structure of the above passage?
   A) Although everyone has unique needs and preferences when it comes to skin care, there are certain general rules everyone should follow. It is always wise to wear sunscreen.
   B) Although everyone has different tastes in literature, some books are considered classics and should be read by everyone. Shakespeare is an important part of any serious reader's diet.
   C) Although everyone has their own preferences in exercise routines, certain activities are recommended for everyone. Walking is an exercise that is accessible to most people and beneficial to health.
   D) Although people have different preferences for vacation destinations, some places offer experiences that everyone can enjoy. Natural beauty and cultural richness make them universally appealing.
   E) Although people have different learning styles, certain study techniques, such as active recall and spaced repetition, are effective for everyone. These methods have been proven to enhance memory retention and understanding.

To practice law, one must become an attorney. To become an attorney, one must attend law school and pass the bar exam. Since Jacob has attended law school and passed the bar exam, he must practice law.

10. Which one of the following arguments mirrors the logical fallacy in the above argument?
    A) To become licensed to perform surgery, one must become a doctor. To become a doctor, one must complete medical school and a residency. Since Michelle has completed medical school and a residency, she must be a doctor.
    B) To become a doctor, one must become licensed to perform surgery. To become licensed to perform surgery, one must complete medical school and a residency. Since Michelle has completed medical school and a residency, she must be a doctor.
    C) To become a doctor, one must become licensed to perform surgery. To become licensed to perform surgery, one must complete medical school and a residency. Since Michelle has become licensed to perform surgery, she must be a doctor.
    D) To become licensed to perform surgery, one must become a doctor. To become a doctor, one must complete medical school and a residency. Since Michelle has completed medical school and a residency, she must be licensed to perform surgery.
    E) To become licensed to perform surgery, one must complete medical school and a residency. Since Michelle did not complete medical school and a residency, she is not licensed to perform surgery.

Jane: It is morally reprehensible to consume meat knowing the cruelty inflicted on those poor animals and the damage one is doing to the environment. Anyone can be healthy on a vegetarian diet if they are careful about their food choices.

Linda: Many people suffer from autoimmune conditions, allergies, and food intolerances and are severely restricted in the foods they can eat. For some people, eating meat is vital to maintaining health.

11. Based on the above passages, Jane and Linda disagree on which one of the following statements?
    A) whether a vegetarian diet is more ethical than an omnivorous diet
    B) whether a vegetarian diet is better for the planet than an omnivorous diet
    C) whether it is possible for everyone to maintain good health on a vegetarian diet
    D) whether animal cruelty is an issue we should consider when making our food choices
    E) whether it is possible for anyone to maintain good health on a vegetarian diet

A manufacturing plant is accused of violating environmental regulations and will therefore be shut down. Evidence shows that cancer rates in a nearby town have tripled due to their negligence. A representative of the company claims the plant should be forgiven and allowed to remain open, as they donate a generous portion of their profits to cancer research and their contributions are responsible for the development of treatments that have saved countless lives.

12. Which of the following best describes the main flaw in the representative's argument?
    A) It does not consider that the new treatments would likely have been developed even without the plant's contributions.
    B) It fails to address how the company's actions directly contributed to increased cancer rates.
    C) It argues that the plant is not responsible for the consequences of its actions.
    D) It overlooks that its competitors successfully operate without violating environmental regulations.
    E) It asserts an irrelevant factor as the sole basis for its conclusion.

Public libraries provide important resources to their communities, offering free access to books and educational materials, social and creative programs, and—very often—services to help individuals prepare for employment. These services help youths and adults alike, and make a disproportionately significant impact on the lives of low-income citizens. It is imperative that we fund our libraries because a well-functioning library is vital to the health of any community.

13. For the argument to be logically correct, the author must make which one of the following assumptions?
    A) The services provided by libraries are actively used by the community members they aim to help.
    B) The impacts of libraries on low-income individuals is significant compared to other social services.
    C) Libraries are more effective than other public services in contributing to the health of the community.
    D) Libraries provide a range of services that are uniformly available across all locations.
    E) Libraries benefit all members of the community equally, regardless of income level.

A medication is not covered by a patient's insurance policy. The representative from the insurance company states that the doctor is not allowed to prescribe the medication without trialing three less expensive options first. The patient argues that the doctor stated that the other medications could cause adverse health effects. The representative counters by stating that if one of those options is sufficient to address the illness, it would save the insurance company a lot of money.

14. What is the main flaw in the representative's argument in the last sentence?
    A) It disregards the doctor's medical expertise and judgment.
    B) It misses the point of the argument it is intended to address.
    C) It suggests saving money takes precedence over patient health.
    D) It assumes that the cost savings to the insurance company is the most important factor.
    E) It fails to consider the patient's needs.

Representatives of an e-tobacco company argue that e-tobacco products should not be subject to the same taxes as traditional tobacco products. They argue that e-tobacco products are useful for those attempting to quit smoking cigarettes and should therefore be treated as quitting aids rather than tobacco products. Sales of e-tobacco products to those who have not smoked traditional tobacco products makes up a substantial portion of their income, and being forced to collect these taxes would place an undue burden on the company.

15. Which of the following best describes the primary flaw in the representative's argument?
    A) The representative fails to consider that e-tobacco products might not be as effective as other quitting aids.
    B) The representative creates a false analogy between e-tobacco products and quitting aids.
    C) The representative argues that e-tobacco products are not as addictive as traditional tobacco products.
    D) The representative's argument contradicts itself by claiming that e-tobacco products should be treated as quitting aids while also stating that their primary market is not former tobacco users.
    E) The representative incorrectly assumes that imposing taxes on e-tobacco products would undermine their effectiveness as quitting aids.

A supplementary summer education program for students with poor academic performance has proven effective in raising the students' grades the following school year. Students are typically enrolled in the program after having received an average letter grade of F for the previous school year, and generally receive an average letter grade of C the following school year. Therefore, a C-student who enrolls in the program would likely receive an average letter grade of A the following semester.

16. Which of the following most clearly identifies an error in the author's reasoning?
    A) It generalizes information about a specific group of students to create a universal principle.
    B) It fails to consider that the students enrolled in the program may have used additional methods to improve their grades.
    C) It assumes that the program will increase a student's average letter grade by the same amount, no matter what their grades were upon starting the program.
    D) It presupposes that C-students are as motivated to initiate change as those who are failing their classes.
    E) It draws a conclusion about individual students based on information about the group.

Perfect Paper has always prided itself on producing high-quality products from one-hundred-percent recycled materials. Our products are always high-quality because we are committed to purchasing materials from recycling plants that are committed to selling materials to companies creating high-quality products.

17. What of the following best describes the primary flaw in the above argument?
    A) It relies on circular reasoning to support its conclusion.
    B) It relies on anecdotal evidence to support its conclusions.
    C) It relies on the judgment of experts on a matter in which their expertise is irrelevant.
    D) It ignores the existence of possible counterarguments.
    E) It fails to address the broader implications of using recycled materials.

Questions 18 - 19

Jones: Smith's new book on politics is an absolute waste of time. He did not fact-check a single one of his assertions, and he will be lucky if he does not find himself sued for libel. His rhetoric is nauseatingly partisan, as though he cannot even entertain that others might think differently from him.

18. How can Smith best weaken Jones's argument?
    A) Smith can expose Jones's own bias by highlighting his own heavily partisan beliefs.
    B) Smith can gain support from others in the political community and have them back up his assertions.
    C) Smith can point out that the success of his book has led to a greater interest in politics among the youth.
    D) Smith can provide evidence for his assertions to show that he did fact-check his arguments.
    E) Smith can compare Jones's critique of his book to the practice of banning books and accuse Jones of advocating for censorship.

19. How can Jones best strengthen his argument?
    A) Jones can provide evidence that Smith cannot be trusted by exposing past misdeeds.
    B) Jones can provide evidence that Smith has made false claims in his book.
    C) Jones can provide evidence that he is nonpartisan and unbiased.
    D) Jones can provide evidence that Smith is being sued for libel.
    E) Jones can provide evidence that most people disliked Smith's book.

Elephants are the largest land animals alive today, and whales are the largest sea animals. A smaller species of whale is the sperm dwarf whale. Whales tend to be much larger than elephants; therefore, elephants are smaller than sperm dwarf whales.

20. Which of the following unjustified assumptions does the author make to support his conclusion?
    A) The largest land animals are not as large as the largest sea animals.
    B) The sperm dwarf whale is an atypical whale species in terms of size.
    C) Although most sea animals are larger than most land animals, there are exceptions to this rule.
    D) Whales and elephants are the largest animals alive today.
    E) There is no overlap in size between elephants and whales.

Mayor: Before beginning the project, we had predicted that if half of our citizens volunteered to work for one Saturday afternoon, we could clean up Elm Park and refurbish the playground equipment to make our town a nicer place for its families. Three-quarters of the town's parents volunteered. With such fantastic turnout, I thought we would finish early, but somehow the project took two Saturday afternoons instead of one.

21. Which of the following statements would resolve the apparent paradox in the above passage?
    A) The mayor's original projections were based on an incorrect assumption about the number of volunteers needed.
    B) The parent volunteers were too busy watching their children to contribute effectively.
    C) The majority of the town's citizens do not have children.
    D) The mayor assumed that all the volunteers would work equally hard.
    E) The volunteers lacked experience in refurbishing playground equipment, slowing their progress.

Alice's greatest ambition is to become a published author. In pursuit of this goal, she has enrolled in an MFA program and has begun learning from published authors. Her teachers are helping her to improve her writing style and learn how to navigate the industry.

22. Which of the following best describes the principle illustrated by the above passage?
    A) To achieve one's ambitions, it is often necessary to pursue higher education.
    B) One should work hard and pursue various learning methods to achieve one's goals.
    C) Personal practice is the most important means by which to improve one's skill.
    D) Education and the advice of experts in one's chosen field can facilitate success in said field.
    E) Listening to the guidance of experts is crucial for becoming an expert oneself.

Questions 23 – 24

Education experts warn that the teacher shortage in the US is having debilitating effects on our students. It is estimated that forty percent of students cannot read at a basic level, with the proportion rising to seventy percent among low-income students. Experts project that if current trends continue, literacy will become a rare skill, as valuable as the steady hands of a brain surgeon. The only way to end the teacher shortage is to offer exorbitant wages; otherwise, the US will face severe consequences. Those who oppose this proposed remedy are anti-intellectual and anti-American.

23. Which one of the following flaws is NOT present in the above argument?
    A) inflating an argument to an extreme and unwarranted level
    B) presuming that there are only two options available
    C) attacking the character of detractors
    D) presupposing what it seeks to establish
    E) making an inappropriate analogy

24. Which of the following, if true, would weaken the above argument?
    A) There has been a sharp decline in literacy levels worldwide, even in countries that pay their teachers generously.
    B) Teachers frequently overestimate the difficulty of their work and its importance.
    C) Literacy is not an important skill, and students who focus on vocational training rather than traditional education have better outcomes.
    D) Low literacy rates among low-income students results from factors unrelated to teacher compensation.
    E) Increasing teacher pay rates in other countries has proven to be effective in improving student performance.

Small businesses face many challenges in their first few years of operation, such as finding customer bases, solving cashflow issues as they arise, and finding dependable employees. It is no wonder that twenty percent of small businesses fail by the end of their first year, fifty percent fail by the end of their fifth year, and a whopping eighty percent fail by the end of their tenth year. Although many business owners do their research and prepare thoroughly, this preparation is often insufficient. To foster healthy competition with established companies, the government should offer assistance to small businesses for their first ten years.

25. The above argument relies on which one of the following assumptions?
    A) Government assistance will directly lead to a higher success rate for small businesses.
    B) Healthy competition benefits the overall economy.
    C) Established companies do not face the same challenges as small businesses.
    D) Small businesses primarily fail due to a lack of preparation.
    E) It is more ethical to support small businesses than large ones.

Section III – Logical Reasoning

Consultant: You have a lot of great ideas, and your startup has so much potential. The only issue is execution. No one seems to be clear on the specific tasks they should be focused on, and the schedule is a mess. You could increase productivity exponentially with an onsite manager. You have so many talented employees, and you are not taking advantage of them.

Owner: If having a manager would lead to me taking advantage of my employees, I do not want one.

1. What error does the owner make in his reasoning?
    A) He assumes that any manager he hires would treat his employees unfairly.
    B) He relies on his own experience as owner of the company rather than the recommendations of the consultant.
    C) He overlooks the possibility of becoming more involved with managing the company himself.
    D) He assumes his judgment is superior to that of the consultant.
    E) He confuses the two possible meanings for the phrase "taking advantage".

Runner's knee is a common affliction among runners who overtrain. It arises from repetitive stress on the knee due to excessive mileage and inadequate recovery time. Runner's knee is also common in cyclists; therefore, cyclists must also be overtraining.

2. Which of the following, if true, most weakens the conclusion of the above passage?
    A) The proportion of runners who overtrain is higher than the proportion of cyclists who do.
    B) Runner's knee also commonly affects swimmers who overtrain.
    C) In cyclists, runner's knee usually occurs due to poor form rather than overuse.
    D) Cyclists are less prone to long-term injuries due to overtraining.
    E) Cyclists tend to cover many more miles per week than runners.

Purchasing local honey not only helps small business owners in one's community but has also been shown to have health benefits. Those who suffer from seasonal allergies have reported that their symptoms almost disappear when they regularly consume local honey. Beekeepers liken it to a panacea that cures all ills; therefore, everyone should buy local honey and enjoy the health benefits.

3. Which of the following flaws is NOT present in the above argument?
    A) The author makes an appeal to an inappropriate authority.
    B) The author makes an appeal to emotion to justify their conclusion.
    C) The author relies on anecdotal evidence for one or more claims.
    D) The author uses a false analogy when making his argument.
    E) The author generalizes information to everyone that is only relevant to some individuals.

John: It should be illegal for companies to sell supplements that are not third-party tested. We have no way of knowing what they are really putting in those pill capsules! I'm smart enough to know better than to blindly trust, but most people are not educated on supplement laws, so they do not know about the lack of regulation. A lot of people could get hurt if we do not reform the laws surrounding supplements.

Emma: As the consumer, you have the option to buy only from companies who do engage in third-party testing.

4. Which one of the following best describes the primary flaw in Emma's response to John's argument?
    A) She dismisses the importance of transparency in the supplement industry.
    B) She places the entirety of the responsibility for health on the consumer.
    C) Her argument implies that companies should not be held responsible for immoral business practices.
    D) She misses the point of his argument and offers advice that does not address the core issue.
    E) Her argument confuses falling victim to deceitful practices to irresponsibility on the part of the consumer.

The damage one large corporation does to the planet is greater than the damage inflicted by the total population of individual consumers on any given day. Yet large companies insist that consumers must take personal responsibility for the effects that their individual purchasing decisions have on the environment. It is time to recognize that individual consumers are not the problem. Corporations must be held to stricter environmental standards in order to ensure the continued health of our planet.

5. Which of the following, if true, most strengthens the above argument?
    A) Corporations will not take responsibility for their actions unless government regulations force them to.
    B) The efforts of individuals will not make a difference in fighting climate change if corporations do not do their part.
    C) Studies linking stricter regulations with reduced pollution relied on correlation rather than proving causation.
    D) Many corporations do adhere to stricter environmental standards than are required by law.
    E) Locations that have implemented stricter environmental regulations on large corporations have experienced a marked decrease in pollution levels.

Mayor: In the interest of public safety, we will be instituting a new law requiring that pedestrians cross only at crosswalks. Every accident in which a vehicle struck a pedestrian in the past year has occurred outside of designated crosswalks.

6. The mayor's argument relies on which one of the following assumptions?
    A) Pedestrians are more likely to use crosswalks if the law requires it.
    B) The new law will be effectively enforced by authorities.
    C) The pedestrians are at fault for the accidents, not the drivers.
    D) Drivers should not have to watch for pedestrians unless they are in the properly designated area.
    E) Pedestrians will comply with the law and cross only at crosswalks.

Paul: It is a commonly held belief that touching a baby bird will cause its mother to reject it due to the change in its scent, but it turns out this is not true. Most birds have a limited sense of smell and would not be bothered by the scent of a human

Tom: One time my little brother found a baby bird. He touched it, and the mother never came back for it.

7. Which of the following does NOT describe an element of the flaw in Tom's argument?
    A) It ignores a major premise in Paul's argument and misses its central point.
    B) It draws an analogy that is not suitable for the argument.
    C) It treats a personal anecdote as evidence.
    D) It applies information from one situation to create a universal principle.
    E) It assumes a causal relationship without sufficient evidence.

Office manager: The new associates put in countless hours of overtime, and they are on salary, so they do not earn extra money for their extra work. The paralegals are also on salary, but they rarely work overtime. This means that our paralegals are earning a higher hourly rate than our associates!

8. Which of the following best describes the primary flaw in the office manager's argument?
    A) It ignores the fact that associates tend to be more ambitious than paralegals.
    B) It overlooks potential differences in the job responsibilities of associates and paralegals.
    C) It equates senior paralegals with new associates.
    D) It fails to consider that paralegals and associates are not paid the same salary.
    E) It relies on the accuracy of reported work hours.

Environmentalist: The hawksbill turtle is critically endangered. We must do everything we can to preserve this species. Major threats include loss of nesting sites due to climate change, accidental capture in fishing gear, and a black-market demand for their shells, which are used to make jewelry and ornaments. The best thing we can do to resolve this issue is to focus our energy on ending poaching activity once and for all.

9. Which of the following, if true, would cast the most doubt on the environmentalist's conclusion?
   A) The loss of nesting sites due to climate change is a far more immediate existential threat than poachers.
   B) Poachers who are discouraged from hunting the hawksbill turtle will poach other vulnerable species instead.
   C) Poachers are notoriously skilled at skirting environmental rules and regulations.
   D) Accidental capture in fishing gear is not as large of a threat to the hawksbill turtle as poachers.
   E) Ornaments and jewelry made from the shell of the hawksbill turtle have strong cultural significance.

Baker: Our cakes are not selling as well since we changed the recipe to cut costs. To increase profits to their previous level, we are going to have to increase the price we charge per cake.

10. Which of the following arguments most closely parallels the flaw in the baker's reasoning?
    A) People do not read as much as they used to since the advent of smartphones and social media. To increase the amount people read, we should make reading materials more accessible.
    B) People do not exercise as much as they should, and public health is suffering as a result. The government should offer initiatives to motivate individuals to work out.
    C) Students are not as interested in football since they learned about the potential for lifelong brain injury. To increase student engagement, we need to create exciting social events to promote our football team.
    D) People are not interested in working at fast-food restaurants due to poor working conditions. To increase employment rates, we are going to have to increase employee pay.
    E) Students' study habits have declined in overall quality in recent years. To improve their educational experiences, schools should offer classes that teach proper study habits.

Jack knew he wanted to pursue a career as a lawyer from an early age, and his ambition never wavered. As a result, he took his schooling seriously and graduated high school as valedictorian. He attended the most prestigious university and law school, and tomorrow, he starts his first job. Jack is sure to have an illustrious career, full of accomplishments.

11. Which of the following best describes the principle underlying the passage?
    A) It is important to establish one's career goals early in order to achieve success.
    B) Success is largely determined by the quality and level of one's education.
    C) Unwavering dedication to one's ambition will lead to success.
    D) Hard work and focus are key ingredients to success.
    E) Success depends on personal qualities rather than external circumstances.

Questions 12 - 13

Amy: Medical bias is a real problem. Studies show that doctors are less likely to believe female and minority patients, and the care of these patients suffers as a result, leading to worse health outcomes. It is important that everyone be a strong advocate for themselves, but we must also address this as the systemic issue that it is. Doctors should not be able to get away with dismissing patient concerns because the consequences to patient health and quality of life can be dire. There should be decisive and final consequences for this type of negligence.

Peter: It is true that medical bias is an issue; however, it is an issue of communication and not one of malice or incompetence. Although it can result in negative consequences for patients, doctors need to feel comfortable and confident treating their patients to achieve the best outcomes. If the consequences for dismissing the concerns of certain patients become too dire, then doctors will not want to take the risk of treating them.

12. Which of the following describes the point on which Amy and Peter most strongly disagree?
    A) whether medical bias is an issue of malice, incompetence, or communication
    B) how severe the penalty for patient loss due to medical bias should be
    C) how patients typically affected by medical bias should be treated by doctors
    D) whether medical bias constitutes negligence
    E) whether patients have a responsibility to advocate for themselves

13. Which of the following best parallels the principle behind the last sentence of Peter's argument?
    A) If police officers work in precincts that discipline officers for excessive use of force, they are less likely to use excessive force.
    B) If dentists were penalized for unnecessary extractions, they would go to greater lengths to preserve patients' teeth.
    C) If lawyers faced consequences for representing guilty individuals, individuals who appear to be guilty would not be able to secure representation.
    D) If judges were penalized for sentencing innocent people, many criminals would avoid consequences.
    E) If there are consequences to teachers when too many of their students fail, teachers will pass students they should not pass in order to avoid punishment.

In an effort to reduce her weight, Rachel started eating a low-calorie dessert recommended by her friend Rebecca. Rebecca lost ten pounds by simply switching to the dessert and making no other changes. Rachel, however, has gained weight since introducing the new food to her diet.

14. Which of the following, if true, would resolve the paradox in the above passage?
    A) Rebecca is more fit and active than Rachel and spends much of her time engaged in physical activity.
    B) Rachel works as an administrative assistant and leads a sedentary life outside of work as well.
    C) Rebecca replaced a high-calorie dessert with the lower calorie one, while Rachel ate the dessert in addition to her normal daily intake.
    D) Rachel has not changed any other habits that may be affecting her weight.
    E) Rebecca eats the low-calorie dessert more often than Rachel does.

Wealthy people are charged a high tax rate. To reduce the amount they owe, they often cheat on their taxes. A common way of cheating on taxes is to establish a charitable organization and use it for personal gain. Michael is a wealthy person who has established a charitable organization.

15. According to the information provided, which of the following must be true?
    A) Michael is charged a high tax rate.
    B) Michael cheats on his taxes.
    C) Michael's charitable organization is illegitimate.
    D) Wealthy people only establish charitable organizations for fraudulent purposes.
    E) Tax fraud is a common issue.

Questions 16 - 18

Activist: The consumption of animal products is unethical due to the heinous living conditions farm animals must endure. All farm animals live their lives indoors in crowded conditions, where they fight amongst themselves and often suffer injury and infection. Their food is poor quality and laced with harmful hormones, and animals that get sick are left to rot and infect the others.

Farmer: On our small family farm, we treat all our animals in accordance with the highest ethical standards. Every cow, pig, and chicken spends the majority of their time in our large, sunny pastures, grazing and socializing. We give them only the highest-quality feed, and our farm receives regular visits from a veterinarian to ensure that our animals remain healthy.

16. The farmer's argument points out which logical fallacy in the activist's argument?
    A) The farmer's argument points out that the activist has appealed to emotion rather than making arguments based on facts and logic.
    B) The farmer's argument demonstrates that the activist has exaggerated her claims to gain support for her position.
    C) The farmer's argument highlights the false analogy created by the activist in her argument.
    D) The farmer's argument points out that the activist has made an error of mistaken reversal in her reasoning.
    E) The farmer's argument demonstrates that the activist has made an error of composition in her argument.

17. Which of the following, if true, would strengthen the argument of the activist?
    A) Ethical standards are the most important consideration when one is making dietary choices.
    B) Veganism is better for the environment as farm animals are a major contributor to climate change.
    C) Small, family-owned farms tend to adhere to ethical standards for the treatment of animals.
    D) Factory farms that follow the practices described by the activist are responsible for ninety-nine percent of the meat consumed in the US.
    E) Government regulations prohibit farmers from keeping sickly animals in the same space as healthy ones.

18. Which of the following would the farmer and activist most likely agree on?
    A) The current ethical standards for the treatment of animals are woefully inadequate.
    B) Family farms are more ethical in their treatment of animals than factory farms.
    C) The government should institute regulations requiring farmers to adhere to ethical standards in their treatment of animals.
    D) Ethical standards in the care and treatment of farm animals are very important.
    E) It is a moral imperative to reduce the suffering we inflict on other sentient creatures.

Philosopher: An action can be considered morally sound if and only if it is performed with the correct motivation in mind. Consequences are irrelevant.

19. Which one of the following most closely adheres to the above principle?
    A) Mary adopted a neglected child because she wanted people to see her as altruistic and giving; Mary's action was moral.
    B) Wesley tried to take an injured dog to the vet and wound up making the dog's injuries worse in the process; Wesley's actions were immoral.
    C) Jaclyn offered a homeless man food, and he wound up getting food poisoning; Jaclyn's actions were immoral.
    D) Sandy reunited a lost child with his mother, hoping for a reward; Sally's action was moral.
    E) Paul injured his elderly neighbor while helping her with chores because she was unable to perform them on her own; Paul's actions were moral.

Politician: Terrorists will stop at nothing to achieve their aims. They are even willing to die for their beliefs. In order to deter acts of terrorism, I propose that the punishment for terrorist acts be the death penalty in all instances.

20. Which of the following best describes the primary flaw in the politician's argument?
    A) It fails to consider the moral implications of invoking the death penalty.
    B) It draws a conclusion that contradicts its premises.
    C) It relies on exaggerated claims to gain support for the politician's position.
    D) It appeals to the listener's emotions to gain support for its conclusion.
    E) It introduces an irrelevant premise to substantiate its conclusion.

Doctor: Individuals diagnosed with anxiety disorders are often later diagnosed as having immune disorders as well. It follows that patients diagnosed with anxiety disorders should be screened for markers that indicate the presence of immune disorders, and that patients with immune disorders should be screened for anxiety.

21. Which one of the following best describes the primary flaw in the above argument?
    A) It assumes that the correlation between anxiety disorders and immune disorders goes both ways without justification.
    B) It presents the correlation between anxiety disorders and immune disorders as a causal relationship.
    C) It assumes, without justification, that anxiety is a symptom of immune disorders.
    D) It generalizes information about one group of people to another group without justification.
    E) It fails to consider that anxiety may be the cause of the later-diagnosed immune disorders.

Children are reaching puberty markedly earlier than they did one hundred years ago. There are some who blame this on growth hormones in milk, some who blame it on vaccines, and some who believe it is due to microplastics interrupting normal hormonal activity. However, there is no evidence to back up any of these theories; therefore, there must be another explanation for this increased incidence of precocious puberty.

22. Which of the following best describes the error in the author's reasoning in the above argument?
    A) The author fails to consider that a combination of the three factors could be causing this issue, even if no one factor is singly responsible.
    B) The author rejects the theories of others but does not propose any of his own.
    C) The author fails to provide evidence that children are reaching puberty markedly earlier than they did one hundred years ago.
    D) The author intentionally misrepresents the data so that it appears to support his conclusions when it does not.
    E) The author confuses an absence of proof that these factors impact puberty with proof that they do not.

Teacher: Poor grades can severely damage a student's self-esteem and can instill a feeling of learned helplessness that destroys their motivation. This can lead to significantly poorer outcomes for these individuals; therefore, I inflate the grades of students who score below a C on their assignments.

23. Which of the following best describes the primary flaw in the teacher's argument?
    A) The teacher's tactic of inflating grades ensures that the students' grades do not reflect their understanding of the material.
    B) The teacher ignores the possibility of offering extra help to students who do not perform well on exams.
    C) The teacher's tactic of inflating grades does not help struggling students to learn the material.
    D) The teacher assumes, without justification, that the poor outcomes faced by students with low grades are due solely to the impact on self-esteem.
    E) The teacher's tactic of inflating the grades of students who perform poorly is not fair to the students who perform well.

Questions 24-25

Nicholas: It is immoral to keep exotic birds as pets. They find living in human environments stressful due to lack of social stimulation and an inability to engage in natural behaviors, such as flying and foraging, which can lead to behavioral problems such as feather-plucking, self-mutilation, and aggression. Additionally, exotic birds sold as pets have often been captured from the wild, which is traumatic for the individual bird and harmful to its ecosystem and population. Many species are threatened or endangered due to illegal trade and habitat loss. On top of this, most people who keep exotic birds do not know how to properly care for them, and malnutrition and neglect are common issues.

24. Which one of the following sentences contains the conclusion of the above passage?
    A) It is immoral to keep exotic birds as pets.
    B) They find living in human environments stressful due to lack of social stimulation and inability to engage in natural behaviors, such as flying and foraging, which can lead to behavioral problems such as feather-plucking, self-mutilation, and aggression.
    C) Additionally, exotic birds sold as pets have often been captured from the wild, which is traumatic for the individual bird and harmful to its ecosystem and population.
    D) Many species are threatened or endangered due to illegal trade and habitat loss.
    E) On top of this, most people who keep exotic birds do not know how to properly care for them, and malnutrition and neglect are common.

25. Which of the following, if true, would most weaken Nicholas's argument?
    A) Exotic birds are often bred in captivity to reduce the need for wild capture and reduce the stress on the animals.
    B) Most pet owners do extensive research before acquiring an exotic bird and are well equipped to care for them.
    C) Some species of exotic bird are bred in captivity and live long, healthy, happy lives in human environments.
    D) Not all exotic birds are procured through illegal trade, many are ethically sourced.
    E) Most owners of exotic birds understand their need for socialization and therefore keep multiple birds.

Section IV – Reading Comprehension (Unscored Section)

As discussed earlier in this book, the revised LSAT exam will include one <u>unscored</u> section that consists of either logical reasoning questions OR reading comprehension questions. These questions will be used by the creators of the exam to determine their appropriateness for future LSAT exams. This sample test uses reading comprehension questions.

Passage 1

Nudge theory is a topic in behavioral economics made popular by the 2008 book *Nudge: Improving Decisions About Health, Wealth, and Happiness* by Richard Thaler and Cass Sunstein. In this work, the authors discuss how structure can lead to better decision-making, and how we can modify the environment to induce people to make decisions that better align with their own interests and those of the public. Proper use of this knowledge allows us to circumvent the problem of willpower by creating environments that gently guide us toward our desired actions by making them more convenient.

The power of nudge theory can be illustrated through a variety of scenarios. Someone who is attempting to lose weight might nudge themselves into better eating habits by keeping only healthy

foods in the home, increasing the effort it takes to procure junk food. This increases the likelihood that an individual will make a healthy choice when hunger strikes because it exploits their cognitive bias toward convenience. A more complex scenario is shown by the difference in organ donor rates between countries that have opt-in versus opt-out organ donor programs. People are less likely to either opt in or out when they need to take action to do so, leading to a significantly higher rate of organ donation in countries that use the latter system.

There is, however, a nefarious side to nudging. The same methods that can be used to guide us toward decisions that align with our own and society's best interests can be exploited to induce behaviors that cause harm.

Corporate entities have capitalized on nudge theory and employ various techniques to increase the likelihood that customers will make purchasing decisions they otherwise would not. This practice, called dark nudging, intentionally induces mindless, automatic behavior by exploiting our cognitive biases and gently pushing us toward the behavior desired by the manipulator. Large businesses, such as fast-food and alcohol companies, generally encourage people to consume products that cause them harm, to engage in overconsumption, or as is often the case, a combination of the two. This practice substantially pads the bottom lines of these corporations but comes at a great cost to the consumer.

Examples of dark nudging are disturbingly familiar and easily found in everyday life. Drive-throughs at fast-food restaurants are a minefield of carefully placed nudges. Signage viewed before the menu presents images of the money-making items, exploiting the primacy effect and leading to higher sales of these items. The driveway then splits in two, giving customers the illusion of a much shorter line and hooking them with the implied speed and convenience. The menus are carefully designed to make the most expensive—and often least healthy—options more prominent so they are more likely to catch the eye. Obscuring these menus from view until a customer pulls directly in front of them also creates a feeling of haste and leads customers to more impulsive, less rationally considered decisions.

Even when applied with good intentions, nudge theory is manipulative and has been criticized as paternalistic by detractors. While it is inarguably beneficial to apply the theory to oneself to improve habits and ease cognitive blockages, practicing nudge theory on others in any context should be undertaken only with grave consideration of the ethical implications of influencing others without their knowledge or consent.

1. What is the author's primary purpose in writing the above passage?
    A) to discuss the ethical implications of the behavioral economics concept known as nudge theory
    B) to warn consumers about nudge theory so they are less susceptible to its manipulations
    C) to discuss the implications of nudge theory for the fast-food industry
    D) to use nudge theory to support an observation about the dual nature of behavioral economics theories
    E) to propose that corporations should not be allowed to employ dark nudges in their marketing

2. Which of the following best describes the parallel between paragraphs two and five?
    A) They each argue the ethical implications of nudging and dark nudges, respectively.
    B) They explain each type of nudging in a parallel style.
    C) Paragraph two defines nudging, and paragraph five defines dark nudging.
    D) They provide examples to familiarize the reader with nudging and dark nudging, respectively.
    E) Paragraph two discusses the issues inherent in nudging, and paragraph five discusses the issues inherent in dark nudging.

3. Which of the following nudges is not mentioned in the passage?
   A) creating a sense of urgency in the customer
   B) showcasing money-making options before the full menu
   C) putting colorful graphics on the menu
   D) splitting the drive-through line
   E) exploiting the primacy effect

4. Based on the reading, which one of the following options best describes the primacy effect?
   A) The first option seen is perceived to be the most popular.
   B) The first option seen is almost always chosen.
   C) The first option seen is perceived as the best value.
   D) The first option seen in perceived as the tastiest option.
   E) The first option seen is chosen disproportionately often.

5. Which of the following best describes the author's most likely attitude toward fast-food restaurants?
   A) grudging admiration for their ability to maximize profits
   B) disgust at their unethical marketing practices
   C) anger that they are harming the health of their customers
   D) irritation that their principles do not align with her own
   E) bafflement at their inability to empathize with their customers

6. Which of the following describes a belief likely held by the author?
   A) Nudge theory is not particularly different from other marketing strategies used by corporations.
   B) The work of Thaler and Sunstein did more harm than good in inspiring businesses to exploit nudge theory.
   C) The influence of dark nudging is a normal part of daily life that we should accept as an inevitability.
   D) If people are aware of cognitive biases and how they work, they can manage their responses and should not be susceptible to nudging.
   E) People should educate themselves on corporate education of cognitive bias to better protect themselves from its influence.

7. Which of the following most closely describes the principle underlying the author's argument in the final paragraph?
   A) Using cognitive biases to increase sales is an unethical practice.
   B) The ethical implications of an action cannot be determined solely the motivations of the actor.
   C) Nobody has the right to intentionally influence another person without their knowledge or consent.
   D) Questions of ethics are rarely straightforward and must be deeply considered.
   E) Behavioral economics theories should not be used for financial gain.

Passage 2

The brain is an enigma that has eluded scientific evaluation for most of human history. Until recently, we did not have the means to analyze its inner workings or a way to see anything other than the physical components of the organ after death. Mythology shrouded the science with such tenacity that many people still believe humans only use ten percent of our brains when the truth is that most of the brain is active most of the time, even when we are asleep.

In an effort to dispel these myths and learn the truth about the human brain and how it operates, scientists have spent decades working to understand precisely what goes on inside our heads. Two pioneers in this field, Rita Levi-Montalcini and Stanley Cohen, discovered a protein called nerve growth factor in 1951, sparking a revolution in a field of neuroscience. They received the 1986 Nobel Prize in Physiology and Medicine in honor of this groundbreaking discovery.

Nerve growth factor was the first of the subsequently named neurotrophic factors to be discovered and has paved the way for research of this vital class of chemicals and their roles in the survival, proliferation, and health of the neurons that compose our brains. They are required for the process of neuroplasticity, or the ability of the brain to adapt to new stimuli by creating new neurons and neuronal networks.

The discovery of these powerful proteins has disproven another myth that persists in our society: our brains do not stop developing when we reach adulthood, nor are we incapable of producing new neurons later in life. Neurotrophic factors and neuroplasticity make the brain malleable, and growth and change can continue through the length of one's life under the right conditions.

The discovery of Levi-Montalcini and Cohen has not only offered profound insights into the inner workings of our brains but also pointed toward techniques for understanding—and perhaps one day, even curing—the devastating neurological maladies that plague humanity. Scientists may be able to use nerve growth factor's neuroprotective and regenerative properties to treat afflictions like dementia, multiple sclerosis, and schizophrenia. Research indicates that this substance may be able to delay the onset of these neurodegenerative diseases, mitigate symptoms, and potentially even send them into remission. There is much work to be done in this area, but there is also a lot of reason to be optimistic.

The field of neuroscience is in a period of explosive growth, with a wealth of rapidly developing technologies giving us a better view into the brain every day. No longer a black box shrouded in mystery, the workings of the brain are now on display for all to see. We can map the electricity associated with emotional states and infer information from brain scans. The lessons we have learned from neuroscience in recent decades have been staggering, and progress in this field does not seem to be slowing down.

8. Which of the following best summarizes the primary purpose of the passage?
    A) to analyze the work of Rita Levi-Montalcini and Stanley Cohen
    B) to establish that the brain is no longer a black box, and we now understand its inner workings
    C) to explain how the discovery of nerve growth factor might be used to cure neurodegenerative diseases
    D) to discuss the development of the field of neuroscience from its infancy to the present day
    E) to assert that it is time to let go of the myths that cloud our understanding of the human brain

9. Which of the following neuroscience myths did the author mention in the passage?
    A) Most of the brain is active most of the time, even when sleeping.
    B) Right-brained people are more creative than left-brained people.
    C) Our brains stop developing when we reach adulthood.
    D) The brain is a black box of which we are unable to see inside.
    E) Brains continue to grow new neurons throughout life.

10. Which of the following best describes the author's reason for discussing 1986 Nobel Prize winners Rita Levi-Montalcini and Stanley Cohen?
    A) to highlight a breakthrough in neuroscience that sparked an explosion of subsequent research
    B) to criticize their methods and findings in the field of neuroscience
    C) to suggest that their discovery was the first significant breakthrough in the field of neuroscience
    D) to illustrate that gender diversity benefits the advancement of scientific research
    E) to compare their discovery with other major findings in the field of neuroscience

11. Which of the following statements is most strongly supported by the passage?
    A) Understanding the brain is the only way to understand human behavior.
    B) Advances in neuroscience will eventually allow us to precisely map physical brain states to emotional states.
    C) Neuroscientists have developed effective treatments for neurodegenerative diseases.
    D) Mythology provided a framework for understanding the brain before science could access it.
    E) It is never too late to improve the health of one's brain or to learn a new skill.

12. Based on the information provided in the passage, which of the following is NOT true concerning neurotrophic factors?
    A) They play a role in the growth of new neurons and neuronal connections.
    B) They are responsible for the brain's ability to adapt to new stimuli.
    C) They are vital to a healthy, well-functioning brain.
    D) They are active throughout the body and play a role in many different processes.
    E) They are composed of proteins.

13. Which of the following best describes the author's feelings about the persistence of neurological mythology despite scientific findings?
    A) She feels wary of people who prefer myths to scientific knowledge.
    B) She feels motivated to dispel ignorance by spreading knowledge.
    C) She feels disdainful toward those who cling to old beliefs in the face of new evidence.
    D) She feels pity for those who continue to believe in falsehoods.
    E) She feels critical of those who do not keep up with current scientific discoveries.

Passage 3

The lack of equity in access to higher education is one of the largest barriers to low-income students' pursuits of the American Dream. Yet in the US, this issue grows more severe with each passing year. Even after adjusting for inflation, college tuition costs have increased almost fourfold between 1970 and 2020. The rising costs of higher education have become prohibitive to many students, who instead opt for careers that do not come with the burden of significant debt.

Individuals who receive a lower-quality education face many difficulties as they enter the workforce. They are likely to be met with fewer career opportunities and to receive lower wages than those with more impressive academic credentials. The lack of a university degree can hinder career growth and reduce one's ability to secure promotions, locking those from low-income backgrounds into the same situation as their parents. This is the antithesis of the American Dream.

Education is key to social mobility, a core value for many US citizens. It is a common cultural ideal that hard work and tenacity are all that are required for success in life, and one does not need to be born wealthy to end up in the upper class. Unfortunately, our current reality stands in stark contrast to this ideal, with children from low-income families likely to end up in the same situations as their parents.

Lower educational accomplishment is also linked to poorer health outcomes. Social scientists theorize that this is due in part to reduced life satisfaction and mental well-being compared to individuals who have the opportunity to pursue higher education. Another factor is that low-income individuals tend to have limited access to health care and are therefore less likely to seek medical attention in a timely manner due to the expenses involved.

The negative effects this inequity in access to higher education has on individuals can be devastating, but they pale in comparison to the broader impact on society as a whole. Education is key to driving civic engagement and political participation. Individuals who pursue higher education tend to be informed about political processes and are more likely to vote and participate in community activities. Research also suggests a correlation between lower levels of education and criminal behavior. Social instability and a lack of access to the resources required to improve one's situation increase the likelihood that an individual will engage in criminal activity.

Communities with large disparities in access to higher education tend to experience reduced social harmony and slower economic growth. The divides created by this inequity beget social fragmentation, leading to isolation and a lack of desire to build a cohesive community. This can hamper the community's ability to attract new businesses and community members, hindering growth and fostering stagnation.

This systemic issue harms not only individual citizens by limiting their prospects and disallowing participation in the American Dream, but it also leads to weaker communities with higher crime rates and lower political and social participation. It is imperative that we reduce financial barriers to education, increase support for low-income students, and ensure equitable access to educational resources for all of our citizens. This is the first step in achieving a more just and prosperous society.

14. Which of the following best describes the author's primary purpose in writing the above passage?
    A) to discuss the negative impacts that a lack of access to higher education has on individuals and communities
    B) to argue that higher education is prohibitively expensive in the US
    C) to advocate for equitable access to higher education for all citizens
    D) to express dissatisfaction with the current educational system in place in the US
    E) to discuss the problematic nature of the educational system in the US

15. Which function is served by paragraph three?
    A) It discusses the root issue with inequity in access to education and how it impacts social mobility.
    B) It defines the American Dream, and states that it stands in stark contrast to our current reality.
    C) It outlines the challenges faced by individuals who cannot access higher education.
    D) It serves to transition from the author's discussion of the impacts of inequitable access to education on individuals to its impacts on society.
    E) It points out that the children of low-income individuals are likely to end up in the same situation, even though this is antithetical to the American Dream.

16. Given the information in the passage, which of the following must be true?
    A) Everyone deserves access to higher education.
    B) The current education system in the US hinders social mobility.
    C) A college education leads to better outcomes.
    D) Countries with affordable tuition have happier citizens.
    E) Social mobility is an important value in a healthy community.

17. Which of the following beliefs is most likely to be held by the author?
    A) Higher education is an important part of life and should be pursued by all.
    B) Social mobility would be improved if people would take responsibility for their choices and make better decisions.
    C) Programs that offer educational and career opportunities to criminal offenders would greatly reduce repeat offenses.
    D) Access to higher education should be a fundamental human right in a just society.
    E) The American Dream has never been anything more than a fantasy.

18. Why does the author discuss the concept of the American Dream?
    A) to inspire hope that change is possible
    B) to invoke outrage at its loss and a desire for action
    C) to aid in the discussion of social mobility
    D) to appeal to the emotion of the reader to gain support for her position
    E) to contrast the country's ideals from its current realities

19. Which of the following, if true, would most weaken the author's argument?
    A) Low-income students who attend college are no more likely to succeed than middle- or high-income students.
    B) Children who come from wealthy families often end up earning a lower income later in life.
    C) Countries that offer free education to their citizens experience the same outcomes as the US.
    D) The American Dream has always been a fantasy, regardless of college tuition costs.
    E) If college were less expensive, competition for admittance would bar lower performing students from accessing higher education.

20. Which of the following most closely mirrors the primary principle behind the passage?
    A) Equitable access to resources promotes social mobility and improves outcomes for individuals as well as communities.
    B) Access to education is crucial to securing health and success in life.
    C) It is the responsibility of the government to ensure that their citizens have access to higher education.
    D) Social mobility is a key factor to ensuring a just society.
    E) Inequity must be addressed in order for a society to be considered just.

Passage 4 (Parts A and B)

Passage A

Self-defense laws in the US vary from state to state, especially those concerning the use of deadly force. In New York, a law passed in 1968 states that individuals have a "duty to retreat" before the use of deadly force is permissible. To remain in compliance with this law, one must retreat if doing so does not compromise their safety or the safety of others, unless they are in their own home and not the initial aggressor.

There are very few exceptions to this law. Police officers and peace officers are not bound by this duty and may use deadly force without first attempting retreat. Additionally, an average citizen is exempt from the duty to retreat in cases where they reasonably believe that the aggressor is attempting to commit certain crimes, including but not limited to rape, kidnapping, and murder.

Only thirteen total US states employ this legal approach to self-defense and the use of deadly force. It stands in stark contrast to the "stand your ground" laws of states like Florida and Texas, which authorize citizens to use deadly force if they are in a place where they are legally allowed and they perceive an imminent threat.

Although proponents of "stand your ground" laws believe that they empower citizens to protect themselves and serve the interests of victims of crime, the issues with this doctrine outweigh its positives. This unfettered right to use lethal force leads to an increased incidence of escalation, especially in public areas where others may be harmed. It has also been shown that these laws are often applied in a manner that amplifies the already prevalent racial bias in the legal system.

"Duty to retreat" laws encourage de-escalation of violent situations and lead to a more civilized society. Citizens of states that enforce "stand your ground" laws should consider the impact these laws have on their communities and use their voices to call for change.

Passage B

"Stand your ground" laws, such as those in place in Florida and Texas, allow individuals to use deadly force if they perceive an imminent threat. They do not require an attempt to retreat before such force is permissible. These laws offer immunity from criminal prosecution for those who act in self-defense as long as the use of deadly force can be considered reasonable in the face of the threat.

Proponents of "stand your ground" laws believe that granting individuals the right to defend themselves empowers law-abiding citizens to ward off criminals without fear of legal consequences. They claim these laws also decrease the incidence of criminal activity and contribute to public safety by allowing citizens to respond to threats in an appropriate manner without obligating them to assess the potential for retreat first, a requirement that would take time that could potentially mean the difference between life and death for the victim of a crime.

Critics argue that "stand your ground" laws encourage the escalation of conflicts and lead to further violence, especially in public spaces where bystanders may be harmed. Many also point to the unfortunate reality that, in practice, "stand your ground" laws can exacerbate racial bias in the justice system.

Despite these issues, "stand your ground" is the most common approach to self-defense law in the US, adopted in at least twenty-eight states and Puerto Rico. Certain other states require a duty to attempt to retreat before the use of deadly force is permissible, whereas others decide on a case-by-case basis or defer to common law. The topic of self-defense law is hotly debated, and as discussion continues, the efficacy and consequences of these laws must be deeply considered as we work to ensure that they protect all members of society.

21. Which of the following best describes the relationship between the passages?
    A) Passage A presents a balanced overview of self-defense laws in general, whereas passage B argues for "stand your ground" laws.
    B) Passage A argues for "duty to retreat" laws, whereas passage B argues for "stand your ground" laws.
    C) Passage A offers a critical analysis of "duty to retreat" laws, whereas passage B presents a balanced overview of self-defense law in general.
    D) Passage A argues for "duty to retreat" laws, whereas passage B presents a more balanced overview of self-defense law in general.
    E) Both passages offer a balanced discussion of "duty to retreat" and "stand your ground" laws.

22. According to the passages, which of the following best describes the key difference between "stand your ground" and "duty to retreat" laws?
    A) "Stand your ground" laws require victims to engage with perpetrators of crimes, whereas "duty to retreat" laws require victims to attempt to retreat.
    B) "Stand your ground" laws require victims to attempt to retreat before the use of deadly force is permissible, whereas "duty to retreat" laws do not.
    C) "Stand your ground" laws do not require victims to engage with perpetrators of crimes, whereas "duty to retreat" laws do.
    D) "Duty to retreat" laws require victims to attempt to retreat before the use of deadly force is permissible, whereas "stand your ground" laws do not.
    E) "Duty to retreat" laws require victims to attempt to retreat even if they are in their own home and not the initial aggressor, whereas "stand your ground" laws do not.

23. According to the passages, which of the following is true about "duty to retreat" laws?
    A) Citizens are not required to attempt to retreat if they are in their own homes.
    B) Citizens are required to attempt to retreat if the perpetrator is attempting to kidnap someone.
    C) Citizens are not required to attempt to retreat if they are not the initial aggressors.
    D) Citizens are required to attempt to retreat even if doing so might jeopardize their safety.
    E) Citizens are required to attempt to retreat if a conflict occurs in a public place.

24. According to the passages, which of the following is NOT an argument employed by proponents of "stand your ground" laws?
    A) They empower citizens to ward off criminals without the fear of legal consequences.
    B) They increase the likelihood that conflicts will de-escalate, especially in public spaces.
    C) They lead to a reduction in the incidence of crime.
    D) They allow individuals to respond to threats naturally.
    E) They protect citizens from suffering consequences for defending themselves.

25. Which of the following questions can be answered using information from either passage?
    A) Which kind of self-defense laws are in effect in Florida?
    B) Which kind of self-defense laws are in effect in New York?
    C) How many states have "stand your ground" defense laws?
    D) What are the exceptions absolving the duty to retreat under "duty to retreat" laws?
    E) Are there any US states that use neither "stand your ground" nor "duty to retreat" approaches to self-defense law?

26. Which of the following points would the authors of the above essays most likely agree on?
    A) "Duty to retreat" laws reflect a higher moral standard than "stand your ground" laws.
    B) "Stand your ground" laws are a controversial approach that has sparked lively debate among proponents and detractors.
    C) "Stand your ground" laws are more in line with human nature than "duty to retreat" laws.
    D) "Stand your ground" laws contribute to a culture of violence and distrust.
    E) "Duty to retreat" laws lead to better outcomes for victims as most people get hurt trying to defend themselves against criminals.

27. Given the information in the above passages, which of the following statements must be true?
    A) "Stand your ground" laws are the most popular type of self-defense law in the US.
    B) "Duty to retreat" laws reflect a higher moral standard and a more civilized society.
    C) More states have "stand your ground" laws than any other type of self-defense law.
    D) "Stand your ground" laws exacerbate racial bias in the legal system.
    E) "Duty to retreat" laws do not allow lethal force under any circumstances unless a victim attempts retreat first.

ANSWER KEY #2

Section I – Reading Comprehension

Passage 1

1. D: The author does not seem to favor either dualism or materialism, and indeed the author ends the passage by wondering whether the questions posed in it could even be answered. From this, we can rule out options A and B. Option C is also incorrect. Although Chalmers and Dennett both have strong, opposing viewpoints, the author makes no mention of either or both being too extreme, nor does the author call for a compromise. Option E is incorrect; although the author presents Dennett's viewpoint on this matter, she does not make any indication of her own stance.

2. B: To answer this question, consider the structure of the passage. Strip the content down to its bones and consider the purpose of each paragraph. In this passage, the author uses the first two paragraphs to discuss the history of the philosophy of consciousness. Paragraphs three through seven discuss contemporary philosophers, highlighting the manner in which the historical figures influenced current ideas. In the final paragraph, the author states that the conflict may never be resolved. Option A is incorrect as it places the end of the passage at its beginning. Option C is incorrect because the author never expresses a clear preference for either position and ends with the claim that the issue may be unresolvable. Option D is incorrect; the author casually discusses the philosopher's arguments rather than deeply analyze them and offers a broad overview of the debate rather than arguing for a specific viewpoint. Option E is incorrect as the author does not make this argument.

3. A: Materialists believe that the mind can be reduced to the physical processes of the brain. Option A is the only selection that addresses the physical aspect of the mind, and evidence that emotions correlate to brain activity supports a materialist viewpoint. Option B is more of an argument for dualism, as it implies there is more to consciousness than physical processes. Option C is a criticism of natural dualism rather than support for materialism. For Option D, recall that the question asks you to consider that option as though it is true, whether or not it actually is. If Option D were true, this would be a compelling argument in favor of dualism and against materialism. Option E, if true, would also be an argument against materialism, as Dennett's "multiple drafts" theory is in support of materialism.

4. C: The author wrote the essay to discuss the philosophy of consciousness, beginning with a light overview of the history of the subject and relating that history to contemporary discussion. Option A is incorrect; although the author wonders whether we will ever be able to answer certain questions, she does not make an argument on this point. Option B is incorrect; the author merely discusses dualism and materialism and does not favor one over the other or propose a framework for resolving their differences. Options D and E are both discussed within the essay in support of the author's main purpose, but they are not the main purpose itself.

5. A: The author did not discuss Hume's contributions to this field; option A is therefore correct. Option B is incorrect as a brief explanation of Cartesian dualism appears in the first paragraph. Hobbes's ideas were discussed in paragraph two, rendering Option C incorrect. Option D is incorrect because Dennett's multiple drafts model is discussed in paragraph six. A brief definition of Chalmer's hard problem is included in paragraph four, which makes option E incorrect.

6. E: The third paragraph relates the historical information that preceded it to the discussion of contemporary philosophy that follows. Options A and B are incorrect. Although the information in these options appears in this paragraph, they do not describe its purpose. Option C is incorrect because this discussion spans multiple paragraphs. Option D is incorrect as the author does not make this assertion in the passage at all.

Passage 2

7. D: The author exhibits a deep respect for the work of Kandinsky and believes that the profusion of abstract art due to his influence is a positive outcome. She acknowledges that it is not in fashion to consider the spiritual aspect of art these days but goes on to discuss how such ideas continue to inspire artists. From this, we can infer that she finds merit in Kandinsky's philosophy. Options A and C discuss factors that may affect the value of abstract art, which is not a topic covered in the passage. Option B may seem correct at first glance since the author praises Kandinsky's synthesis of music and visual art, but there is nothing in the passage to indicate that the author believe this is the best method for elevating abstract art. Option E is incorrect. Although the author expresses a clear appreciation for abstract art, she does not comment on her feelings about representational art. It can be argued from the information presented in the passage that Kandinsky found representational art inferior, but the author's opinion is unknown.

8. B: Kandinsky's art relied heavily on the synthesis of music and art, and his art was an attempt to use color and form the way musicians use sound; for this reason, he named his works with musical terms.

9. E: The author uses this paragraph to introduce Kandinsky's philosophical ideals and discuss how they tie into his ideas about abstraction and music. Although his ideas concerning color and form as analogous to sound are mentioned in this paragraph, they are only a detail and not the focus. Option A is therefore incorrect. Option B describes the purpose of paragraph five and is therefore incorrect. Option C is incorrect as the author only discusses Kandinsky's beliefs and does not state her own. Option D is also incorrect. Although a parallel is drawn between artists and prophets, this is a detail of the subject matter rather than the purpose of the paragraph.

10. A: Leading up to the discussion of "Composition VII," the author explores Kandinsky's ideas concerning the synthesis of music and art. She then uses the example to illustrate specific instances of musical influence in the piece. Option B is incorrect because the author does not describe the painting with an intent to give the reader a clear mental picture; the aspects she describes would not be enough to create a coherent whole. Options C and D are incorrect. Although these ideas are mentioned in the discussion, they are details rather than the main purpose. Option E is incorrect as the author does not mention Kandinsky's philosophical ideals in the discussion of the painting.

11. E: The first paragraph of the passage states that attitudes began to shift toward abstract art and away from realism at the beginning of the twentieth century, implying that before this point, abstract art was not as highly respected as realism. Option A is incorrect because the author says nothing about the spiritual inclinations of previous artists. Option B is the opposite of what we should surmise from the passage, and is therefore incorrect. Option C is also contrary to claims made in the passage, and is therefore incorrect. Option D is incorrect: although the author discusses Kandinsky having taken influence from music, she does not contrast this with artists who came before him.

Passage 3

12. D: To figure out the principle outlined in the passage, try to restate the argument, removing the specific content. In this passage, the author argues that our voting system is not working and promotes exploring other options in an effort to resolve this problem. Option A contradicts the ideas in the passage because it recommends preserving tradition rather than implementing new systems. Option B is not in line with the passage: although the author expresses the need for the government to evolve,

nowhere does she suggest the metaphor that a government is a living, breathing entity. Option C is not a principle at all; it is a specific argument. Option E is a principle that is touched on in the passage, but it is not the principle underlying its central message.

13. A: This is the only option that defines both terms correctly. Option B confuses proportional representation with first-preference plurality (FPP) voting, the system currently in place in the US. Option C reverses the definitions and is therefore incorrect. Option D incorrectly states that citizens vote for multiple parties under proportional representation and is therefore incorrect. Option E confuses RCV with FPP voting.

14. B: The author addresses this problem in both the introduction and the conclusion, marking its place as the main point of the passage. Option A is incorrect: although lack of representation for minority voters is mentioned in the passage, it is only in support of changing the voting system for the primary purpose of addressing stagnation due to polarization. Option C is also incorrect; this is briefly mentioned as an issue in the introduction, but it is secondary to the issue of polarization. Option D is incorrect as the author makes no claims as to whether we are too reliant on the Founding Fathers. Option E is irrelevant to the arguments presented in the passage.

15. E: This option provides further support for the author's assertion that implementing one of these systems can help reduce polarization. Option A is incorrect as it contradicts the author's assertion that polarization is stifling healthy dialogue. Options B and C are irrelevant facts about the voting systems, and therefore are incorrect. Option D is a reason one might dislike FPP voting systems, but it does not necessarily support the author's position that we should consider RCV or proportional representation.

16. C: The differences between RCV and proportional representation are described before the second-to-last paragraph; therefore, option A is incorrect. Option B is incorrect for the same reason; the voting methods discussed in the second-to-last paragraph were already introduced earlier in the passage. Option D may be tempting, as this is a secondary purpose to the paragraph; however, the discussion of how the systems reduce polarization is more relevant to its primary purpose. Option E is incorrect; although the author discusses how changing our voting system can affect polarization, she does not discuss the ways in which polarization has affected the voting system.

17. B: In proposing that we alter the voting system to best suit our current needs, the author shows that she is more interested in effectiveness than traditional values. Although she uses the intentions of the Founding Fathers to introduce the topic in the passage, she does not make the claim that we need to adhere to their traditions. Option A is incorrect as the author specifically supports revising government structures to meet the needs of the people. Option C is incorrect as the author promotes a proportional representation model of voting, which would accomplish this end. Option D reflects the author's main purpose in writing the passage and is therefore incorrect. Option E, although potentially hyperbole, is more likely to reflect the views of the author than option B and is therefore incorrect.

18. D: The author follows the introduction of the Founding Fathers with a discussion of their vision versus the current political situation in the US. Option D is therefore the best answer. Option A is incorrect as the author does not engage in a bid for sentimentality in her discussion of the Founding Fathers. Option B is incorrect because the author does not argue for the implementation of the Founding Fathers' preferences. Option C is incorrect as the author does not advocate for letting go of the past, and instead seems to invite the reader to consider the past. Option E, while a potential motive, does not clearly align with the author's intent in the same manner as option D.

19. A: The author brings up this belief to support the argument that the US is essentially a two-party democracy and expands on how this leads to a polarized political atmosphere. Option B is a potential belief of the author, but there is no direct evidence in the passage that this is the case. It is therefore

incorrect. Options C and D imply that the author would have a positive sentiment toward this belief, but the author clearly does not. Option E could be true if *precludes* were not an absolute term. The author certainly believes enacting change is more difficult due to this belief but clearly does not think that it is impossible.

Passage 4 (Parts A and B)

20. B: In both passages, the authors outline the basic factors that scientists look for when evaluating the likelihood of exoplanets to support life, such as placement in the habitable zone, stable stars, and a suitable atmosphere and size. Only passage B addresses the unexpected characteristics of exoplanets; therefore, option A is incorrect. Although the authors of these passages disagree on the likelihood of finding life, neither passage discusses a timeline for finding life; therefore, option C is incorrect. Only passage A discusses the specific capabilities of the telescopes, whereas passage B mentions their names briefly without engaging in further elaboration. Option D is therefore incorrect. Although both passages discuss the components that are necessary to support life on other planets, as in option B, neither specifically discusses the atmospheric components. Option E is therefore incorrect.

21. C: Both authors are intrigued by exoplanets and what we can learn from them; they are just interested in different aspects. The author of passage A is more vested in the search for life on other planets, whereas the author of passage B is intrigued by the variety of conditions that can be found on these planets; however, both find this field of research to be exciting and feel we have much to learn. Options A and B are incorrect. Passage B makes no mention of the author's thoughts on hypothetical alien life, so we have no way of knowing that author's leanings on these topics. Option D is incorrect. This argument would most likely be supported by the author of passage A; however, the author of passage B is more interested in the variety of conditions on exoplanets. Option E is also incorrect, for a reversal of the same reason: although the author of passage B would support this argument, the author of passage A would disagree.

22. E: The author of passage B agrees with the premises proposed by the author in passage A; however, the author of passage B ends with a different conclusion due to a disparity in previously held beliefs and desires. Option A is incorrect because they do not agree with the conclusion that we will likely find alien life. Option B is incorrect because as stated above, they agree with the premises introduced in passage A. Option C, while tempting, is also incorrect. Although they disagree with the conclusions of passage A, they do not go as far as to claim these conclusions are unfounded. Rather, they suggest that these conclusions are inflated, making option E more applicable. Option D is incorrect: they agree with the premises in passage A and disagree with its conclusion.

23. D: The author mentions planets that do not rotate at the beginning of a paragraph that discusses unexpected and unique characteristics of exoplanets to illustrate that there are numerous barriers to life on other planets, many of which we had not even considered as possibilities. Option A is incorrect; this better describes an effect of this discussion rather than the purpose. Option B is incorrect as the author does not discuss the geological implications any further. Option C is incorrect as this argument is not necessary, nor is it explicitly made. Option E, while an accurate description of the structure of the paragraph where this information is presented, does not describe its purpose and is therefore incorrect.

24. A: The argument made in passage B relies almost entirely on the assumption that, because we have not yet found planets that are capable of supporting life, we are not going to. This is a classic example of an argument from ignorance, or confusing the absence of proof with proof of absence. Options B, C, D, and E do not describe logical flaws made by the author of passage B.

25. B: Although TESS and JWST are discussed in both passages, the development of LUVOIR is only discussed in passage A. Options A, C, D, and E are all discussed in both passages.

26. C: Passage B presents a skeptical view of the position presented in passage A, criticizing the conclusion that it is only a matter of time before we find life on other planets. Option A is incorrect: the author critiques the arguments in passage A but does not disprove them. Option B is true of the relationship between the two passages; however, it is not as accurate a description as option C and is therefore incorrect. Options D and E are incorrect as the author of passage B does neither of these things.

27. A: According to the articles, TESS and JWST have capabilities that allow us to identify exoplanets and detect biosignatures in their atmospheres that may indicate their potentials to support life. This streamlines the process of evaluating the potential of exoplanets as candidates for hosting life. Option B is incorrect; although the first clause must be true based on the reading, the second is conjecture. Option C is neither implied by the passage, nor is it necessarily true. Without these technologies, we would likely find other means to our end. Option D is similar to option B; although the first clause must be true, the second is not a necessary conclusion based on the reading. Option E is incorrect; nowhere in the passage is it claimed that all forms of life have the same basic requirements.

Section II Answer Key – Logical Reasoning

1. D: Tina's defense fits the definition of an ad hominem attack, a logical fallacy where one attacks one's opponent personally rather than addressing the relevant arguments. Options C and E are incorrect because they are secondary components of this ad hominem attack on Jan and therefore cannot be the primary flaws. Option A is incorrect as Tina had no reason to believe she had to take further action once assured that the city would address the problem. Option B is incorrect as it is a secondary flaw to Tina's ad hominem attack on Jan.

2. A: The key to answering this question is to look for the absolute in the passage. If Cindy can do something that only elite swimmers can do, then Cindy must be an elite swimmer. A number of both casual and elite runners and cyclists can accomplish the same feats as Cindy, but nowhere in the passage is it claimed that *only* they are capable of such feats.

3. A: The primary role of the second sentence is to provide evidence for the claim made in the first. Option B fits the definition of an appeal to emotion, a logical fallacy that is not employed here. The statement is made to provide evidence rather than tug at the heartstrings. Option C is suggested in the third sentence, not the second. Although the sentence does criticize the structure of standardized tests, Option D is incorrect as this is not the primary purpose of the sentence, but rather support for its primary purpose of providing evidence. Option E is incorrect for the same reason as Option D.

4. B: Option B states that the general outcomes predicted by the proponents have been shown to occur in other countries that institute student loan forgiveness, strengthening their arguments. Option A merely restates a premise of the passage and does nothing to strengthen it. Option C is an argument people typically use against student debt relief programs. Option D, while relevant, does not address the issue of student loans directly and is therefore incorrect. Option E adds a detail to the argument that could either strengthen or weaken the argument depending on the views of the reader, and is therefore incorrect.

5. C: The trainer takes information from a sample of clients comprised of student-athletes and applies this to the general population, committing the fallacy of making a hasty generalization. The trainer's argument does not confuse correlation with causation, and therefore option A is incorrect. There is no negation in the passage; therefore, option B is incorrect. The argument does not apply attributes of the whole to its parts, and therefore option D is incorrect. Option E is incorrect as the trainer does not inflate his claims in order to make a point.

6. D: The author creates a false dilemma in the passage by ignoring the fact that people may purchase meat from ethical sources or reduce consumption to mitigate the effects of factory farming on the environment, instead concluding that veganism is the only ethical route. Option A is incorrect: although this could be a consideration for some, the author makes no claims as to the healthfulness of a vegan diet. Option B is incorrect as we do not know the source of the author's evidence. Option C is incorrect: although this is a flaw, it is minor compared to the false dilemma. The author's conclusion would follow neatly from the premises if not for the false dilemma; option E is therefore incorrect.

7. B: Decision fatigue is the phenomenon where having too many options will lead people to choose nothing at all due to being overwhelmed by variety. The results of the study reflect this. Option A is incorrect as people were choosing their own jam on the first day as well, just from fewer options. Option C is incorrect; although this happened the first day, it is not supported by the second day's events. Option D runs contrary to the conclusion that can be drawn from the data. Option E, while potentially true, is irrelevant to the content of the passage.

8. E: The passage commits the fallacy of appealing to inappropriate authority. If Dr. Smith were giving advice relevant to his field as a neurologist and acquired from his extensive education, then we would be right to trust him. Considering his sources include his own experiences and the advice of online nutritionists, he has no more authority than anyone else to recommend a specific diet. Options A and B are secondary flaws in the argument, resulting from this primary flaw. Option C is not an error made in this argument. Option D is incorrect as Dr. Smith does not create a false dilemma; his beliefs would lead him to logically conclude that eliminating meat from one's diet is necessary.

9. A: The principle behind the passage is that although we are all unique, certain universal advice applies to us all. The argument then goes on to list an example of that advice just as option A does. Option B differs in that it lists a specific reading recommendation rather than general advice for the (literary) health of a reader, and is therefore incorrect. Option C offers a recommendation that applies to most but not all people and is therefore incorrect. Option D is incorrect because the second sentence elaborates on what makes certain experiences universally appealing rather than offering advice to the traveler. Option E is incorrect as the second sentence adds detail to the previous one rather than offers an example of the advice offered.

10. D: When answering this type of question, it is important not to get bogged down in the details of the argument, but rather to pay close attention to its logical structure. A strategy to overcome this difficulty is to map the passage as simple conditional statements:

- "In order to practice law, one must become an attorney" becomes L → A
- "To become an attorney, one must attend law school and pass the bar exam" becomes A → S
- "Since Jacob has attended law school and passed the bar exam (S), he must practice law (L)" becomes S → L

By the rules of logic, we can deduce L → S from the combination of L → A and A → S. S → L is therefore a mistaken reversal. Option D is structured in the same way:

- "In order to become licensed to perform surgery, one must become a doctor" becomes S → D
- "To become a doctor, one must complete medical school and a residency" becomes D → M
- "Since Michelle has completed medical school and her residency (M), she must be licensed to perform surgery (S)" becomes M → S

Once again, we can deduce S → M from S → D and D → M. M → S is a mistaken reversal, exactly mirroring the flaw in the passage.

11. C: Jane claims that everyone can be healthy on a vegetarian diet, but Linda brings up people with health conditions that severely restrict the foods they can eat, which directly contradicts Jane's claim that everyone can be healthy on a vegetarian diet. Linda makes no arguments about the ethics of eating meat, ruling out Options A, B, and D. Option E may be tempting, but Linda does not argue that a vegetarian diet is unhealthy for all; she instead argues that it just might not be healthy for some due to preexisting health conditions.

12. E: The representative argues that, since the plant has donated a lot of money to cancer research, it should not be held accountable for its actions. However, the plant's philanthropic activity does not negate the harm it caused. This factor is entirely irrelevant to the issue at hand and perfectly fits the definition of a red herring. Option A is not a flaw in the argument; whether the new treatments could have been developed without the plant's contributions does not matter to its central issue. Option B is also incorrect as this is a secondary flaw to the introduction of irrelevant factors. Option C is incorrect because the representative never argues that the plant is not responsible; he merely argues that the plant should not be *held* responsible. Option D is irrelevant to the argument at hand.

13. A: The argument hinges on the idea that library resources improve communities, and they can only do so if people use the resources that are available. Options B and C do not necessarily need to be true for the author's conclusions to be valid. Options D and E contradict statements made in the passage and are therefore incorrect.

14. B: The representative fails to address the information presented by the patient in her most recent argument, and the representative's rebuttal misses the point raised in the argument he is attempting to refute. Options A, C, D, and E are all secondary issues resulting from this primary flaw in the representative's reasoning.

15. D: The representative makes the argument that e-tobacco products should be treated as quitting aids, but then the representative contradicts that claim by stating that a substantial portion of her sales come from people who have never smoked tobacco products before. Option A is incorrect because the relative efficacy of quitting aids is irrelevant to the central argument. Option B is incorrect; the comparison to quitting aids is a contextually appropriate analogy. Option C is incorrect as the representative makes no claims as to the relative addictiveness of the two types of products. Option E is incorrect; the representative argues against the taxes because they would be a burden on the company, not because they would undermine their effectiveness as quitting aids.

16. C: The flaw in the argument fits the definition of a starting point fallacy. The argument does not acknowledge that it is far easier to increase one's grade from an F to a C than from a C to an A, even though both represent a two-letter-grade shift. Option A is incorrect as the argument does not attempt to create a universal principle. Option B is a flaw, though a lesser one. Option D can point toward a potential weakness in the argument; however, this presupposition does not constitute a flaw in the argument. Option E is the definition of a fallacy of composition, which is not employed here.

17. A: The argument claims the proof that Perfect Paper produces a high-quality product is that it purchases from a company that is committed to selling materials to companies that make high-quality products. The argument does not provide independent evidence for its conclusion; it merely relies on a circular set of assumptions, employing the circular reasoning fallacy. Option B is incorrect as the argument does not rely on anecdotal evidence. Option C is incorrect as the argument does not appeal to expert opinion. Option D is a potential flaw in the argument, but it is a far lesser flaw than the circular reasoning. Option E is not a flaw in the argument.

18. D: The best way to defuse Jones's argument is to provide evidence that his major assertion—that Smith did not fact-check his arguments and was excessively partisan—is incorrect. Option A is an example of an ad hominem attack. Option B is an example of an inappropriate appeal to authority. Option C is an example of a red herring; it is irrelevant to the argument that Smith's work is dishonest and biased. In option E, Smith employs a combination of a straw man argument and a false analogy.

19. B: The best way for Jones to prove his case is to provide evidence that the claims he made were correct. The only verifiable claim Jones made is that Smith did not fact-check his book properly. If this were true, it would strongly support Jones's arguments that the book was a waste of time and partisan to a fault. Option A would be an ad hominem attack on Smith, and is therefore incorrect. Option C would not strengthen Jones's position and is therefore incorrect. Whether Smith is being sued for libel is irrelevant to Jones's critique, rendering Option D incorrect. Option E would be tantamount to gathering anecdotal evidence and is therefore incorrect.

20. E: The author assumes that since most whales are larger than elephants, all species of whale are larger than elephants, implying that they believe there is no overlap in the sizes each animal type can achieve. Option A is incorrect as the conclusion concerns the largest land animal and the smallest whale species. Option B is incorrect because this assumption would lead the author to the opposite conclusion. Option C is incorrect as this assumption is unnecessary to the author's conclusion. Option D is incorrect because the author does not make this assertion, and it is not necessary to her conclusion.

21. C: The mayor is making an error of proportion in his reasoning. He originally projected that if half of the town's citizens volunteered, the work would only take a day. Three-quarters of the town's parents did volunteer, but he fails to realize that three-quarters of the town's parents could easily be less than half of its total citizens. If seventy-five percent of the town's parents only accounts for twenty-five percent of the town's total population, this resolves the paradox in the passage. Options A, B, D, and E do not reflect any obvious flaws in the mayor's reasoning.

22. D: Stripping away the content, the principle is that education and advice from experts can help a person achieve their goals. Option E is tempting because it is similar to option D; however, option D mentions education explicitly, increasing its parallel with the passage. Option E also implies that Alice's goal is to become an expert in writing rather than a published author, whereas option D only alludes to success in general. For these reasons, option D parallels the principle in the passage more closely. Option A is incorrect because it is not implied that education is necessary, merely that it is helpful. Option B is incorrect as the passage only lists one method Alice is using to pursue her goal. Option C is incorrect as the passage makes no mention of personal practice.

23. D: The best way to approach this problem is to identify examples of the flaws that are present and work through a process of elimination. Option A is exemplified in the claim that it is not long before we end up with a population where literacy is as rare a skill as the precision of a brain surgeon. Option B is presented in the second-to-last sentence, where the author says we must either raise salaries exorbitantly or suffer the consequences, ignoring other potential avenues. Option C can be ruled out since the last sentence attacks opponents of the argument on a personal level. The analogy between literacy and a surgeon's steady hands is inappropriate, ruling out option E. There is no example of circular reasoning that can be drawn from the text; therefore, option D is correct.

24. A: If option A is true, then the declining literacy levels must be due to a universal factor rather than one that would only affect the US, substantially weakening the author's conclusion that the only way to solve the literacy crisis is to resolve the teacher shortage by increasing teacher pay. Option B, while a common argument of those who oppose raising teacher salaries, is an ad hominem attack on teachers, and therefore logically flawed. Option C is irrelevant to the author's conclusion. Option D explains why

literacy rates would be lower among low-income students but does not address the declining literacy rates of the population as a whole. Option E would strengthen the author's argument rather than weaken it.

25. B: The argument states that we should help small businesses in their early years to increase competition, but it presents no reasons that we should encourage competition, instead assuming the reader agrees with this assumption. Option A is incorrect as the support offered by the government would not have to directly lead to a higher success rate for it to be valuable. Option C is incorrect as obstacles faced by large companies are not directly addressed by the argument. Option D contradicts the author's assertion that even prepared small business owners can fail. Option E is not at issue in the argument and is therefore incorrect.

Section III Answer Key – Logical Reasoning

1. E: The consultant uses the phrase "taking advantage" to mean that the owner of the company is not utilizing his employees properly. The owner, however, understands the alternate meaning of this phrase, and infers that the consultant is recommending that he *exploit* his employees. This is an error of equivocation. Option A nods toward this idea but misses the point. Options B and D are incorrect as his rejection of the consultant's advice is not in itself an error. Option C is irrelevant to the owner's argument.

2. C: The cause of the injury is different in each sport, weakening the conclusion that cyclists overtrain. Option A is incorrect as the conclusion makes no claim about the proportion of runners versus cyclists who overtrain. Option B is incorrect because the cause of runner's knee in swimming does not imply anything about the cause in cycling. Option D, while true, does not weaken the conclusion. The fact that overuse injuries are less common in cyclists than runners does not mean they do not occur. Option E points to an intrinsic difference between runners and cyclists but not one that explains the incidence of runner's knee in each population.

3. B: Although the author mentions supporting local business owners, he does not resort to using this information to appeal to emotion; he instead relies on the health benefits of honey to support the argument. The author does, however, appeal to the authority of beekeepers to make a health claim, making option A incorrect. Option C is incorrect as the author relies on self-reported information from allergy sufferers to support the argument that honey is good for the health. Option D is incorrect as the analogy comparing honey to a panacea is a false one. Option E is incorrect; the author only offers evidence that honey is healthy for allergy sufferers, but it then makes the claim that it is healthy for everyone.

4. D: John explicitly states that he is not worried for himself but for those who are less educated and vulnerable to the deceitful practices of the supplement industry. The response Emma offered in return failed to address the core of his argument, which centers on the need for regulatory reform. Options A, B, C, and E describe flaws in the argument, but they are all secondary to Emma's having missed the point of John's argument.

5. E: This option describes evidence of a direct causal relationship by showing that changing one factor leads to a change in the other factor, offering concrete evidence that regulations would reduce pollution. While options A and B describe reasons to argue for stricter government-imposed environmental standards, they do not strengthen the author's core argument. Option C, if true, would serve to weaken the author's argument. Option D is irrelevant to the author's argument.

6. A: The core of the mayor's argument relies on the assumption that the new law will induce pedestrians to use the crosswalks, thereby reducing accidents. While option E is similar, the efficacy of the law does not require perfect compliance, making this option weaker than option A. Option B is an assumption made every time a law is created, and therefore not particularly necessary for the mayor's argument. Option C is incorrect as the mayor's argument does not address fault or responsibility. Option D is incorrect as this assumption is not necessary for the mayor's argument to stand.

7. B: Tom does not make an analogy in his response to Paul; he simply recounts a personal anecdote, which renders option C incorrect. By employing this anecdote, Tom ignores Paul's assertion that birds do not rely on their sense of smell to identify their young, making option A incorrect. Option D is also a flaw, as Tom assumes his one anecdote can be applied to all similar situations. Option E points to a flaw in Tom's reasoning, as he has no proof that the mother did not abandon its baby for an entirely different reason.

8. D: If the paralegals and associates were paid the same salary, the office manager's conclusions would be correct; the paralegals would make more per hour than the associates. However, this is more than likely not the case. The office manager's argument therefore falls victim to the starting point fallacy. Options A and B are incorrect as the office manager makes no comments about ambition or job responsibilities. Option C is incorrect; nowhere does the manager mention seniority. Option E is also incorrect; although this is a potential flaw, it is a far lesser one.

9. A: The environmentalist's conclusion relies on the premise that poachers are the single most important and immediate threat to the survival of the hawksbill turtle. If this is not the case, then it would not make sense to focus all of our energy on this one threat when the environmentalist mentions three, any of which may be the most critical factor. Option B is irrelevant as the author's argument is only concerned with preserving the hawksbill turtle. Option C, while a valid concern about implementation, does not counter the environmentalist's conclusion. Option D, if true, establishes that poachers are a bigger threat than fishing accidents, which would strengthen the conclusion that we must address poaching. Option E, while culturally relevant, does not cast doubt on the author's conclusion that poaching, as well as the illegal trade of hawksbill turtle shells, should be stopped in an effort to save this critically endangered species.

10. C: The flaw in the given passage is that, although raising the price would address the issue of decreased profit, it would not address the issue causing the decreased profit, which is likely the decline in quality. Similarly, the school's efforts to increase student engagement with football would address the surface issue of lack of engagement while ignoring the core issue of safety. Options A, B, and E all propose solutions that would directly address the issue raised in their first sentences, and therefore do not mirror the flaw in the passage. In option D, the proposed solution does not address all of the concerns raised in its first sentence, but it does address one in the form of low pay. For this reason, it does not parallel the flaw in the passage as closely as option C.

11. D: This option best reflects the principle that Jack's hard work and focus were instrumental in his success so far and will lead to further successes in the future. Although options A, B, and C reflect factors that led to Jack's success, they are too narrow to accurately reflect the underlying principle of the passage. Option E is incorrect: although Jack's personal attributes are relevant, the passage specifically emphasizes his hard work and focus, making option D the better answer.

12. B: This is the only point that both Peter and Amy address on which they each take clearly opposing positions. Option A is incorrect: although they likely disagree on this point as well, Amy does not state a clear position on this claim. Option C is incorrect as neither author questions that patients should be

treated fairly by doctors. Options D and E are also incorrect: although Amy makes her position clear on these claims, Peter does not address them directly.

13. E: Peter's last sentence reflects the principle that imposing penalties on professionals can alter their behavior in ways that lead to worse outcomes for the people those consequences are meant to protect. Similarly, a rule that imposes consequences on teachers for the number of students who fail can lead to teachers passing students who do not comprehend the material, leading to worse outcomes for those students. Option A is incorrect because a reduction in the use of excessive force is a positive outcome. Option B is incorrect for the same reason; a reduction in unnecessary extractions would benefit patients rather than harm them. Options C and D, while tempting, discuss nonbehavioral outcomes of consequences to professionals, weakening the parallel.

14. C: Rebecca's weight loss indicates a calorie deficit, whereas Rachel's weight gain indicates a calorie surplus. Since the passage states that Rebecca changed nothing else, only option C explains how this might occur. Options A, B, and D would not resolve the paradox, as they do not indicate behavioral changes in either party, which would be required to induce the changes in weight. Option E is incorrect as eating the dessert more often would be more likely to lead to an increase in weight.

15. A: The passage makes the statements, "Wealthy people are charged a high tax rate," and "Michael is a wealthy person." Since both statements are absolutes, it follows that Michael, as a wealthy person, must be charged a high tax rate. Option B is incorrect; the passage says wealthy people often cheat on their taxes, not that they all do. Option C is incorrect for a similar reason: the fact that most wealthy people establish charities for fraudulent reasons does not mean that they all do. Option D is incorrect due to the presence of the word *only*. Option E is incorrect: although the passage states that tax fraud is common among the wealthy, it makes no claims about the prevalence of tax fraud among the general population.

16. B: The activist exaggerates her claims by making the statement that all farm animals are treated the way they describe, when the truth is that only certain types of farms operate in this manner. The farmer's argument points out this flaw by stating that farms that treat animals ethically do exist. The activist is engaging in the straw man fallacy, where one exaggerates an argument to gain support for their position. Options A, C, D, and E are incorrect as the farmer's argument does not suggest the presence of these fallacies.

17. D: If factory farms are responsible for the production of the overwhelming majority of animal products consumed in the US, then the activist's argument is no longer marred by the straw man fallacy, strengthening it significantly. Option A could arguably strengthen the activist's argument but in a far more indirect manner, as it would not address the central fallacy. Option B is irrelevant to the activist's discussion of animal cruelty. Option C would actually serve to weaken the environmentalist's argument, as it draws attention to its fallacious assumption that all farms operate in the same manner. Option E discusses regulations as opposed to reality and is therefore irrelevant.

18. D: The activist bases her argument that no one should consume animal products on an assumption that farm animals cannot be treated ethically. The farmer bases his argument on the standards that his farm adheres to in caring for their animals, which highlight the farmer's ethical treatment of the animals. Therefore, both parties clearly believe that ethical standards in the care and treatment of farm animals are very important. Option A would draw no argument from the activist, but the farmer makes no statement that would allow us to infer his position on current ethical standards. The farmer would agree with option B; however, we can infer from the activist's argument that she believe it is impossible to treat farm animals ethically, making this option incorrect. Neither side discusses government intervention, rendering option C incorrect. Option E is clearly a value of the activist, and likely a value of the farmer; however, there is no direct evidence for the latter.

19. E: According to the philosopher's principle, only motivations—not consequences—matter in evaluating the morality of an action. Because of this, we can ignore the consequences stated in each answer option. The correct option will either state that someone with a selfless motivation is moral, or someone with a selfish motivation is immoral, making option E the best answer. Options A and D state that people with selfish motives behaved morally, and options B and C state that people with selfless motives behaved immorally; therefore, none of these options follows the philosopher's principle.

20. B: One of the premises introduced by the politician is that terrorists are willing to die for their beliefs. This premise contradicts the conclusion that the death penalty would be an effective deterrent. Option A is incorrect as the morality of the death penalty is outside of the scope of this argument. Option C is incorrect as the politician does not exaggerate his claims. Option D is incorrect because the politician's premises are based in fact rather than emotion. Option E is incorrect as the premises are relevant to the conclusion; the issue is that the conclusion does not logically follow from them.

21. A: The premise only states that patients diagnosed with anxiety are later diagnosed with immune disorders and says nothing about the opposite relationship. The first clause of the doctor's conclusion therefore holds; however, the doctor only arrives at the conclusion in the second clause by employing the logical fallacy of mistaken reversal. Options B and E are incorrect as the doctor says nothing about a causal relationship between anxiety and immune disorders. Option C is incorrect because the doctor's conclusion does not rely on this assumption, nor is it stated in the passage. Option D is incorrect because, although the doctor does mistakenly apply information about patients with anxiety to patients with immune disorders, this issue is secondary to the fallacy of mistaken reversal.

22. E: The author does not provide proof that these factors do not impact the onset of puberty; the conclusion is based on the assertion that there is no proof. This is a classic example of the logical fallacy of making an argument from ignorance, or confusing absence of proof with proof of absence. Option A is incorrect as this is secondary to the argument from ignorance. Option B is incorrect; the author's failure to propose her own theory does not constitute an error in reasoning. Option C is incorrect as the author introduced this point as a premise, not a conclusion. Option D is incorrect as there is no reason to believe that the author misrepresented the data.

23. D: The teacher's argument puts the entirety of the blame for poor outcomes on self-esteem issues and learned helplessness. It is possible, however, that the poor outcomes could be caused by the same factors that are causing the poor grades, or they could be due to the students' difficulties with learning. The teacher assumes a causal relationship from mere correlation. Options A and C describe potential issues with the argument in that students will not actually learn the material, but these issues are not central to the teacher's reasoning and are therefore incorrect. Option B is incorrect as it points out an alternative strategy the teacher might employ but does not address the flaw in reasoning. Option E is incorrect: while it describes an issue of fairness, this flaw is secondary to the assumed causal relationship.

24. A: Although this is the first sentence of Nicholas's argument, it contains the conclusion of the passage. Every statement that follows is a premise that supports this conclusion.

25. C: Nicholas lists the following reasons for his conclusion that it is immoral to keep exotic birds as pets:

- Exotic birds experience stress and behavioral issues when kept in human environments.
- Capturing exotic birds is harmful to their ecosystems and populations.

- Many species are threatened by illegal trade and habitat loss.
- Many pet owners do not know how to properly care for their pets, leading to neglect.

Option C is the only answer option that adequately addresses all of these claims. By stating that there are species that live long, healthy, happy lives in human environments, it addresses the first and last points, and by stating that these birds are successfully bred in captivity, it addresses the second and third reasons for Nicholas's conclusions. This weakens Nicholas's argument, as it demonstrates that there are exotic bird species one can keep as pets without engaging in ethically questionable behavior. Options A, B, D, and E each address one or more of Nicholas's reasons, but none address all four.

Section IV Answer Key – Reading Comprehension (Unscored)

Passage 1

1. A: The author concludes the essay by stating that even nudges made with good intentions are ethically suspect, and we should carefully consider the implications of employing such methods. Option B is incorrect as the author makes no statement as to whether knowledge can mitigate the impact of nudges. Option C is incorrect: although the author discussed the fast-food industry in the passage, it was introduced to illustrate an example of dark nudging. The author could have accomplished this end with another example without compromising the integrity of the passage. Option D is incorrect. The author only mentions the duality of behavioral economics theories in passing. Option E is incorrect; although the author clearly believes that the use of dark nudges is unethical, he does not make a call for any kind of regulation.

2. D: Both paragraphs provide examples, clarifying the concepts of nudging (in paragraph two) and dark nudges (in paragraph five). Neither paragraph addresses the ethical implications; option A is therefore incorrect. Each paragraph does explain each type of nudging in a parallel style; however, this is secondary to the explanation of what that style actually is; option B is therefore incorrect. The terms are defined before paragraphs two and five, so option C is incorrect. While paragraph five engages in some discussion of the issues inherent in dark nudges, paragraph two does not do the same. Option E is therefore incorrect.

3. C: Although it is a common nudge that we encounter in everyday life, the passage does not explicitly mention this tactic. The others are all listed in paragraph five.

4. E: According to the passage, fast-food companies exploit the primacy effect to boost the sales of particular items. This implies that that the first option seen is chosen disproportionately often. Option B is incorrect as higher sales do not equate to "almost always." Options A, C, and D are not supported by the information provided in the passage.

5. B: The author discusses the unethical nature of the use of dark nudges in a tone that betrays disgust. Option A is incorrect as the author expresses no admiration for these companies. Options C, D, and E are secondary to the author's issues with the ethics of fast-food restaurants that exploit cognitive biases to upsell their products.

6. E: The author values autonomy, as is evident in her assertion that, while it is ethically sound for individuals to use nudge theory to change themselves, there are severe implications to consider when using nudge theory to influence the behavior of others. Based on this, we can infer that the author would be a proponent of self-education and awareness. Option A is incorrect as the author finds dark nudges a particularly manipulative form of marketing. Option B is incorrect: although the author discusses the harms done by Thaler and Sunstein's work, she does not make the claim that it has done more harm than good. Option C is incorrect and seems to be a sentiment the author would likely disagree with. Option D is not supported by the text, and is therefore incorrect.

7. B: In the final paragraph of the passage, the author argues that dark nudges are not the only morally dubious nudges and brings up the critical argument that nudging is paternalistic, implying her agreement. Option A could be considered the principle underlying paragraph four, but not the final paragraph. Option C is not suggested by the paragraph, as the author does not prohibit nudging; she merely argues that it should be employed with great attention to any ethical implications. Option D, while true, is no more relevant to this argument than any other ethical argument. Option E is likely a belief held by the author, but it does not align with the principle underlying the specific argument made in the final paragraph.

Passage 2

8. D: The passage discusses the field of neuroscience by beginning with myths, exploring the impact of an early discovery, and segueing into current research. Option A is incorrect as the author introduces the scientists to bolster her discussion and does not actually analyze their work. Option B is incorrect because the author does not claim that we now understand the inner workings of the brain. Option C is incorrect: although this is discussed in the passage, it does not describe its main point. Option E is asserted by the passage; however, this assertion does not constitute its purpose.

9. C: This myth is mentioned in paragraph four, when the author discusses lessons learned from the discovery of nerve growth factor and neuroplasticity. Options A, D, and E also appear in the text; however, options A and E are factually correct, not myths, and option D is neither a fact nor a myth, but a description. Option B, while a common myth about the brain, is not mentioned in the passage.

10. A: The purpose of the author's discussion of the scientists can be discerned by its placement in the passage. The author introduces them at the end of a discussion of the history of neuroscience, and immediately preceding a section that discusses subsequent and potential findings based on their research, making option A the best answer. Option B is incorrect as the author does not criticize their findings or methods. Option C is also incorrect. The author makes no mention of this being the first significant breakthrough in the field of neuroscience and merely states that it was an early one that sparked a lot of subsequent research. Option D is incorrect as the author does not address gender diversity in the passage. Option E is incorrect because the author discusses their discovery as a prelude to other major findings rather than engages in comparison.

11. E: The passage focuses heavily on dispelling myths around brain health, specifically those that place limitations on brain development. The last sentence of paragraph four specifically supports this sentiment. Option A is neither asserted by the author nor implied in the writing. The author mentions that we can map brain electricity but does not claim we will be able to do so with any kind of precision; option B is therefore incorrect. Option C is incorrect: although research is being done in this area, the passage states that there is much work to be done before we have treatments. Option D is incorrect; although the author mentions myths around brain health, she does not engage in commentary about utility.

12. D: Neurotrophic factors are only active in the brain, and the passage does not assert otherwise. Options A, B, and C are mentioned in the third paragraph. Option E is briefly mentioned in the first line of the fourth paragraph.

13. B: The essay itself is an attempt to spread knowledge and dispel myth, making this option the best option. Options A, C, and E are incorrect as the author does not express judgment toward those who still

believe these myths. Option D, while plausible based on the tone of the text, does not necessarily follow from the passage.

Passage 3

14. C: The author discusses the issues described in options A, B, D, and E in service of her primary purpose, which is advocating for equitable access to higher education for all citizens. This purpose is apparent throughout the essay and confirmed solidly in the author's conclusion, which calls for a reform of the educational system in the US to make access more equitable.

15. A: While other options describe elements of the paragraph, this answer option best describes its function in the context of the essay. Option B, while true of the paragraph, does not describe its function. Option C is also incorrect; while this is true of the paragraph, it is in service of its discussion of the root issue of inequity regarding access to education. Option D is incorrect; the author continues to discuss the impact on individuals after this paragraph and transitions to discussing the impacts on society later in the essay. Option E is incorrect as this is pointed out in service of the primary purpose.

16. B: The author makes multiple arguments that support the conclusion that the current educational system in the US hinders social mobility, and explicitly states that this is the case in the third paragraph as well as the conclusion. Option A, although a likely belief of the author, does not necessarily follow from the passage. Option C is incorrect: although the passage states that a college education is correlated to better outcomes, it does not state that the latter is a necessary result of the former. Option D is incorrect as the author does not address tuition cost or happiness in other countries. Option E is certainly a value held by the author, but it is not a necessary conclusion based on the information in the passage.

17. D: The author highlights the severity of the consequences of inequity in access to education to both individuals and communities and calls for reducing barriers and increasing access to create a more just society. These arguments align with the idea that access to higher education should be a basic human right. Option A is incorrect; although the author emphasizes the importance of higher education for the general population, she does not make the claim that it is an important part of every individual's life. Option B is contradicted by the bulk of the author's opinions in the essay. Option C, while feasible, does not address the core of the author's argument. Option E is not supported by the text.

18. E: The second paragraph best illustrates the purpose of the author's invocation of the American Dream when she describes it as the antithesis of our current reality; however, it is clear throughout the essay that the author presents this concept for contrast. Options A, B, and D are not in line with the manner in which the author discusses this concept. Option C is a possibility; however, its assistance in discussing social mobility is secondary to its use as a means to illustrate contrast.

19. C: If countries that offer perfect financial equity in access to education experience the same outcomes as the US, then the factor causing these issues cannot be prohibitively expensive education; this would substantially weaken the author's argument. Option A is incorrect because it implies that low-income students who receive an education have a similar likelihood of success as higher-income students, which would serve to strengthen the author's argument. Option B is a reversal of the author's premise and is irrelevant to her conclusion. Option D is incorrect; the prior existence of the American Dream is irrelevant to the issues we currently face. Option E is incorrect as it focuses on academic barriers to education rather than financial ones.

20. A: This option best captures the essence of the passage, which argues for equitable access to a resource that is critical for social mobility while pointing out the negative impacts that inequitable access has had on individuals and the community. Options B, C, D, and E are all secondary to this primary principle.

Passage 4 (Parts A and B)

21. D: The author of passage A concludes by stating that "duty to retreat" laws are superior and those subject to "stand your ground" laws should call for change. The author of passage B presents a balanced discussion of "stand your ground" laws before discussing other approaches that states take to the issue of lethal force invoked in self-defense cases; therefore, option D is the best answer.

22. D: "Duty to retreat laws" require victims to attempt to retreat before the use of lethal force is permissible, whereas "stand your ground" laws do not. Options A and C are incorrect as neither type of self-defense law requires a victim to engage with the perpetrator of a crime. Option B is incorrect because it reverses the relationship between the two types of law. Option E is incorrect as neither type of law requires a duty to retreat if one is in one's own home and not the initial aggressor.

23. E: Options A and C are incorrect because each on its own is insufficient to remove the duty to retreat. Both of these factors must be present in the situation to exempt a victim from their duty to retreat. Option B is incorrect as certain crimes, such as kidnapping, create an exemption from the duty to retreat. Option D is incorrect because citizens are not required to attempt retreat if it would jeopardize their own safety or the safety of others.

24. B: The opposite argument—that "stand your ground" laws lead to higher incidence of conflict escalation—is often used by critics of "stand your ground" laws. Options A, C, D, and E are all presented as arguments of proponents of "stand your ground" laws in either paragraph four of passage A or paragraph two of passage B.

25. A: Both passages mention Florida as an example of a state that employs a "stand your ground" approach to self-defense cases involving lethal force. New York's law is only mentioned in passage A, making option B incorrect. Option C is incorrect because it can only be answered by information from passage B. Option D is incorrect because it can only be answered with information from passage A. Option E is incorrect because it can only be answered with information from passage B.

26. B: Both authors discuss the arguments of proponents and detractors of the "stand your ground" law, and their treatment of this topic indicates that they both believe it is a controversial approach that has sparked a lively debate. Option A would be supported by the author of passage A but not by the author of passage B, and is therefore incorrect. Option C is incorrect as neither author makes an argument for their personal position on this point. Option D would be supported by the author of passage A, but not necessarily by the author of passage B, and is therefore incorrect. Option E is not supported by information in either passage.

27. C: According to passage B, at least twenty-eight states have "stand your ground" laws; as this is more than half of the total number of US states, option C must be true. Option A is incorrect as commonness does not necessarily imply popularity. Option B is a moral judgment that is supported by passage A, but not passage B. Option D is tempting because this is a common criticism of "stand your ground" laws that is mentioned in both passages; however, both passages state that these laws *may* exacerbate racial bias, not that they necessarily *do* exacerbate racial bias in all instances. Option E is contradicted by information in passage A and is therefore incorrect.

SCORING WORKSHEETS AND RAW SCORE CONVERSION CHART

Note that on the actual exam, Section IV will be unscored; for this reason, it is not included in the scoring worksheets.

- Use the Answer Key that corresponds with each practice test to check your answers.
- Use the appropriate scoring worksheet to enter the number of questions you answered correctly in each section; the total number of questions you answer correctly is your **raw score**.
- Use the "Raw Score Conversion Chart" to convert your raw score into the 120 – 180 scale.

Scoring Worksheets

LSAT Practice Test 1 Scoring Worksheet
Section I:
Section II:
Section III:
Sum of all questions answered correctly:

LSAT Practice Test 2 Scoring Worksheet
Section I:
Section II:
Section III:
Sum of all questions answered correctly:

Raw Score Conversion Chart

Raw Score	Scaled Score	Raw Score	Scaled Score	Raw Score	Scaled Score	Raw Score	Scaled Score
78	180	58	160	38	144	18	128
77	180	57	159	37	144	17	127
76	179	56	158	36	143	16	126
75	178	55	157	35	142	15	125
74	176	54	156	34	141	14	124
73	175	53	156	33	141	13	123
72	173	52	155	32	140	12	122
71	172	51	154	31	139	11	120
70	171	50	153	30	138	10	120
69	170	49	153	29	138	9	120
68	169	48	152	28	137	8	120
67	168	47	151	27	136	7	120
66	167	46	150	26	135	6	120
65	166	45	150	25	134	5	120
64	165	44	149	24	134	4	120
63	164	43	148	23	133	3	120
62	163	42	147	22	132	2	120
61	162	41	147	21	131	1	120
60	161	40	146	20	130	0	120
59	161	39	145	19	129		

Dear LSAT test taker,

Great job completing this study guide. The hard work and effort you put into your test preparation will help you succeed on your upcoming LSAT exam. Thank you for letting us be a part of your education journey!

We have other study guides and products that you may find useful. Search for us on Amazon.com or let us know what you are looking for. We offer a wide variety of study guides that cover a multitude of subjects.

If you would like to share your success stories with us, or if you have a suggestion, comment, or concern, please send us an email at support@triviumtestprep.com.

Thanks again for choosing us!
Happy Testing
Trivium Test Prep Team